The Chief

A Memoir of Fathers and Sons

Lance Morrow

COLLIER BOOKS

MACMILLAN PUBLISHING COMPANY

New York

For James and Justin

Macmillan Publishing Company
866 Third Avenue, New York, N.Y. 10022
Collier Macmillan Canada, Inc.

Grateful acknowledgment is made to the following for permission to reprint previously published material.

Fall River Music Inc.: Lyrics from "Where Have All The Flowers Gone?" by Pete Seeger.
Copyright © 1961 by Fall River Music Inc. All rights reserved.
Harcourt Brace Jovanovich, Inc., and Faber and Faber Ltd.: Excerpt from "The Hollow
Men" in *Collected Poems 1909–1962* by T. S. Eliot. Copyright 1936 by Harcourt Brace
Jovanovich, Inc.; Copyright © 1963, 1964 by T. S. Eliot. Reprinted by permission of the
publishers.
Macmillan Publishing Co., Inc. and A. P. Watt Ltd.: Excerpt from "The Wild Swans at
Coole" by W. B. Yeats. Copyright 1919 by Macmillan Publishing Co., Inc., renewed 1947
by Bertha Georgie Yeats. Excerpt from "Under Ben Bulben" by W. B. Yeats. Copyright
1940 by Georgie Yeats, renewed 1968 by Bertha Georgie Yeats, Michael Butler Yeats and
Anne Yeats. Except from "Easter 1916" by W. B. Yeats. Copyright 1924 by Macmillan
Publishing Co., Inc., renewed 1952 by Bertha Georgie Yeats. Excerpt from "The Dedication
to a Book of Stories selected from the Irish Novelists." All selections reprinted with per-
mission of Macmillan Publishing Company from *The Poems of W. B. Yeats*, edited by Richard
Finneran, New York, 1983; and with permission of A. P. Watt Ltd. as agent for Michael
B. Yeats and Macmillan, London, Ltd. from *Collected Poems of W. B. Yeats*.
Jerry Vogel Music Co. and The Songwriters Guild: Lyrics from "Ballin' the Jack" by Jim
Burris and Chris Smith. Printed by permission of the copyright owners, Jerry Vogel Music
Co., Inc., and Christie-Max Music Co. (The Songwriters Guild).

First Collier Books edition 1986
Published by arrangement with Random House, Inc.
Macmillan books are available at special discounts for bulk purchases
for sales promotions, premiums, fund-raising, or educational use.
For details, contact:
Special Sales Director
Macmillan Publishing Company
866 Third Avenue
New York, N.Y. 10022

Library of Congress Cataloging-in-Publication Data
Morrow, Lance.
The chief : a memoir of fathers and sons.
1. Morrow, Lance. 2. Morrow, Hugh, 3. Journalists—
United States—Biography. 4. Rockefeller, Nelson A.
(Nelson Aldrich), 1908—1979. 5. Vice-Presidents—
United States—Biography. 6. New York (State)—
Governors—Biography. 7. United States—Politics and
government—1945– I. Title
[PN4874.M5865A33 1986]   070'.92'4 [B]   85-23715
ISBN: 0-02-005400-9

10 9 8 7 6 5 4 3 2 1
PRINTED IN THE UNITED STATES OF AMERICA

Contents

The Chief

1 · Rockefeller Center

My father and I sit at a table looking south from the sixty-fifth floor of the RCA Building in Rockefeller Center. At the noon hour, the Rainbow Room becomes the Rockefeller Center Luncheon Club. The enormous room, all terraces of Art Deco and Lucite, holds a thin December light. The perspective is imperial: New York lies below us. It is dark and bustling and faintly sinister down in the crevices of the lowest streets. Out of them the buildings abruptly rise—stone and steel and crystal bristling into the upper air.

We perch for lunch at the top of the civilization. It is winter in the late seventies. We look out at lower Manhattan, the cold channels out to the sea. The harbor is frozen. A low winter sun glares off the ice. I see the Statue of Liberty stranded there, inert, frigid.

Around us sit other men in dark blue suits, the sort of suits that never exactly fit, serious suits with no taint of unreliable elegance about them. The wing-tip shoes are shined but never shiny. The rep striped ties hang with a masculine abstraction about them, a sort of interchangeability.

It is New York midtown power at lunch—men, for the most part. They work quietly at their enterprises and cases, at their watchful bonhomie. Their faces are utterly American. I detect in them a certain Midwestern prominence of bone, a rawness that New York has not polished off: Is it wind or alcohol that has given some of them a rough, red nineteenth-century coarseness? Their eyes have an archaic American hardness—sharp, masculine, commercial eyes. They admit no light; they are as impenetrable as aggies.

My father's brown eyes, however, are as liquid as a deer's. They are intelligent eyes, but not calculating. Moods move across them like winds on pond water.

My father's head is more massive now than it was when he was younger. He has the Morrow nose (which I have not): a thin, handsome aquiline prow that is the strongest feature of his face. His black hair has gone to gray-white, thin on top. But, being sixty-three now, my father seems to me smaller than he was before. Is that a trick of generational perspective? Can a man shrink noticeably, by an entire suit size? The child grows, and imagines that his father is diminished. Nothing ever has the mythic proportions that memory gives it.

Even so, my father *is* shorter and smaller now. When we stand together, I am almost as tall as he.

Our lunches are a wary ballet. We deal with each other as formally as ambassadors. At best, father and son, we behave like colleagues of long mutual experience: intimates and strangers at the same time. The substructure of our conversations is a wondrously subtle system of protocols—of evasions, euphemisms, indirections. There are long silences, long abstracted gazes around the landscape. We are accustomed to it. I sometimes find it heartbreaking.

My father arranges the flatware at his place until the geometry pleases him. I do the same. He moves his fingers lightly over the flatware, making svelte, deft passes. We would both like a drink.

When the waitress arrives ("Hello, Agnes." "Good afternoon, Mr. Morrow") my father leaves it to me: Will I have white wine? he wonders. No, I will have iced tea. I see the spirit in his eyes collapse minutely; all right, then, he will have iced tea too. He will be virtuous with his diabetes. We will be virtuous together. Morrows should be virtuous with alcohol. Once, my great-grandfather, Colonel Albert Morrow of the U.S. Ninth Cavalry, was court-martialed for being drunk on duty. There was another family story. My grandfather, Hugh Morrow, Pennsylvania country doctor sometimes paid in those Depression days with bushels of apples and slabs of bacon, once had his patients complain that he was drunk when they came to his office for treatment. Dr. Morrow decided that afternoon that he would never drink again, and he did not.

The iced teas arrive. We begin a ritual roll call of my father's children, of my brothers and sisters. Who has heard from whom? Have I heard from Cathy? Have I heard from Patrick? Have I heard from Tina? Have I heard from Hughie? We pause at each, and exchange what news we have.

This day, we even pause at Mike.

"Do you get to the cemetery much?" I ask.

"Not too much," he answers.

We sit for a moment in silence. My father breaks off some bread and butters it with a crude, mashing motion that tells me he is upset. Punishing the bread.

"It drives me crazy," I say. "Every time I go up there it's on the anniversary, in January, and there's always five inches of snow on the ground, and I can't find the marker."

My father's eyes grow alarmed. I see in them a small explosion of outrage, the first bud: I have accused him (unjustly, unjustly) of being stingy with the headstone to mark my brother's grave. It is a simple rectangular stone that lies down flush with the grass, level with the earth.

I see what I have done. I leap to retrieve or deflect the accusation: I snatch it out of midair. I imagine for an instant that my father is going to burst into tears, partly for poor Mike, and partly at the injustice of being called a cheapskate—a cheapskate on such an occasion, giving Mike the no-frills burial. Poor Mike. He was only seventeen when he died of cancer. I do the sort of thing that Mike was good at.

"That fucking cemetery," I sigh, with a slight burlesquing tone, looking away, leading my father away as well. "I love those great palazzo mausoleums along there [meaning next to Mike's grave]. Those Italian contractors' visions. Mussolini grandeur. I guess it's a form of competition, to see who can get planted with the most style. The Mafia's Forest Lawn. We should all go out in that kind of magnificence."

Mike is buried in Gate of Heaven Cemetery in Valhalla, New

York, the Catholic cemetery closest to my father's house in Bronxville. Gate of Heaven goes in for somewhat grandiose effects: Renaissance condominiums for the dead.

I see that the outrage has left my father's eyes. A small gust of absolution has wafted across the white table linen. My father laughs gently, looking away, and his absolution wafts back across to me. We have forgiven each other.

But we move off now to the safer ground of politics.

"Poor Jimmy Carter hasn't got a clue, has he?" I ask, and my father gives his soft rueful hoot that means *Oh brother!* and we are on comfortable territory again.

It is the secret of our relationship, our modus vivendi. Our two gazes, when we get together, are fixed not upon each other, but upon some third object, some third reality, usually politics or journalism. It works. We can be together. We can take a certain warmth from each another—take it sidelong, almost—while outwardly fastening upon some harmless business between us. It is a form of emotional triangulation and distancing, very Japanese, I came to think, in its exquisite evasiveness. Or maybe merely clumsily masculine, a way of loving each another without ever saying so, or even directly feeling it. We can ride along side by side, horsebacking across some political territory, say—firing at jackrabbits, comradely.

We almost invent these pretexts. Among us, in our family, love tends to be handled covertly, surreptitiously, as if it did not exist at all, or as if it had been obscurely forbidden.

From time to time I have felt for my father a longing that was almost physical, something passionate, but prior to sex—something infantile, profound. It has bewildered me, even thrown me into depression. It is mysterious to me exactly what it is I wanted from my father. I have seen this longing in other men—and see it now in my own sons, their longing for me. I think that I have glimpsed it once or twice in my father's feelings about his father. Perhaps it is some urge of Telemachus, the residual infant in the man still wistful for the father's heroic protection. One seeks to return not to the womb, which is enclosing, a warm, passive oblivion, but to a different thing, a father's sponsorship in the world. A boy wants the aura and armament of his father. It is a deep yearning, but sometimes a little sad—a common enough masculine trait that is also vaguely unmanly. What surprises me is how angry a man becomes sometimes in the grip of what is, in essence, an unrequited passion.

The waitress arrives. My father loves the ceremonies of eating, of restaurants. Today, to reward himself and his diabetes for staying away from wine, he will have oysters (always specified as "blue-points," for as long as I can remember, just as spaghetti is always ordered *al dente* in an Italian restaurant). I will have oysters too, and then crab salad.

My father pats his stomach lightly with the fingertips of both hands, in a half-satirical gesture of well-being and anticipation. There is the lightest ghost of W. C. Fields in the motion, mixed with the true gourmand sensuality.

He asks, "What do you hear from Elise?"

In conversation between me and my father, my mother is never "your mother" or "mom" or somesuch, but always "Elise."

My father asks the question looking away, offhandedly. The long-divorced always ask the question like that, I think: the voice by long habit cooled down to a temperature just above irony.

"It's worse now," I answer. Old stories: my mother's brilliance and wreckage. My father takes it in with a look of attention and quiet wonder. I detect that in some emotional time warp, he is (after so many years, after two more marriages) still in love with her, for an instant. Or at least still capable of being amazed by her vitality and intelligence, her sheer passion for life, her embrace of it, and her defiant suffering and folly. He is even still capable of being obscurely wounded by them all. He admires her folly some-how, I think. He even worships it in secret, I tell myself. No, that is ridiculous. His face wears an expression of rapt detachment.

A woman once told me, after I had known her for years, about the night that she became the parent of her parents. The parents were both psychically incompetent, in different ways: the mother frantic, schizoid; the father a suicidal depressive. The daughter was ten years old. The night before her father was to enter a mental hospital, the child listened to her parents rage at each other in another part of the house. The child—dutiful, sane, eerily mature, terrified—quietly ironed name tapes onto her father's shirts and trousers and socks. As if she were sending him off to camp.

The child had become the only solid citizen in the house, a parent, while the older generation went past her, retrograde: tumbling backward, downward.

My parents were a gentler case. I came to act, now and then, as mediary between them, ambassador, a precocious little man with astonishing dignity and powers of tact and concealment, and a genius for the nuances of adult anger. But their world tore apart all the same.

The oysters: they arrive on a bed of crushed ice, fresh and wet and plump. My father takes an oyster fork and lifts one from its half shell and dunks it in cocktail sauce. It comes up coated red. I squeeze lemon on my half-dozen oysters and then grind pepper onto them and eat them like that: no cocktail sauce. My father watches the process, eyebrows arched slightly, as if amazed.

"Phony" has always been one of my father's choice words of dismissal (and of self-defense). He can utter the word with a lovely sneer, his upper lip actually curling around the first syllable in a little dramatization of disgust. He uses "phony" as a noun, a synonym for other favorites: "horse's ass" or "stuffed shirt." His sneer sometimes even has a guttural bottom to it, a kind of gangster snarl. He used to like to describe a favorite scene from *Appointment in Samarra*—the scene in which Al Greco stands on a hill above Gibbsville, Pennsylvania, on a Christmas Eve and snarls: "Merry Christmas, you stuck up bastards. Merry Christmas from Al Greco!"

My father loved that. I have never understood quite why. It seemed to have something to do with phonys, with my father's Pennsylvania boyhood, with (maybe) a sense of exclusion from places, privileges. There was the Depression in the scene: being cold and lonely and excluded and defiantly tough. Fuck you, you phony son of a bitch!

My father sometimes went in for the spasm of dismissal. It was a sort of pre-emptive eruption, a way (childish, almost) of seeing that he was losing the game and standing abruptly and overturning the table and stalking out. In any case, when *phony* comes, it is a tremblor of that.

I catch a vibration of the word while we sit in our privilege among the corporate sea lions, eating oysters—mine peppered.

I grow self-conscious. I am always aware of my father's psychological Gibbsville, his contexts of judgment and condemnation. I feel that he judges hard.

I glance at his hands: they have grown pudgy and liver-spotted. I see my own hands, thickening in the beam now, like his. I see a liver spot formed on the back of the left hand just under the third knuckle. *Mon semblable, mon père.*

I wear a gold signet ring from Tiffany that my wife gave me for my birthday, my initials in opulent illegible curlicues on the oval. A New York City clubman. I play squash at the Harvard Club. I have become much of what my father once almost subliminally instructed me to dislike, to resent: a John O'Hara character with a gold signet ring and a club on Forty-fourth Street and a locker at the squash courts and a $300 tweed jacket. I see it in his eye.

And he performs a perfectly typical deflection, a displacement. He swivels the barrel away from me and fires at an absent son: "I got a call from Patrick the other day. Sometimes that bird is such a phony . . ." These obscure family treacheries.

It is that little gangster snarl again. Why? He has aimed the blast this time at Patrick—Pat the genius mimic, the rock impresario, his third son. Every time his group won a gold or a platinum record for sales, Patrick had the record inscribed to my father and sent it to him. The records always bore Pat's affectionate, satiric title for my father: The Chief.

But the "phony" was meant for me. There must be better things to be than the man your father always vaguely envied and detested. I play squash.

I play the game with an almost self-destructive glee and fury. I ride to the sixth floor of the Harvard Club, to the squash courts. I dress in the locker room with a ceremonial pleasure. I like the smells of Bay Rum and witch hazel and talcum powder there. Lawyers and bankers walk around naked, making knowledgeable, boring conversation about their trades: intricate talk, expertise. Deals. The attendant calls me "Mr. M." I talk to the squash pro about the new racquet that Head has made, an indestructible graphite that the other manufacturers will imitate. We talk about the wonderful geometries of the game, about lob serves and the three-wall nick—that lovely shot in which one chops the ball, hard and close, into the side wall, and it fires from there to the front wall, then shoots fast down toward the floor, hitting the other side wall at the same instant it strikes the floor. The all-but-ungettable nick. The trouble is that if you miss the nick, it is not a very hard shot to return.

I go to the court. I enter the bright white room through the small door in the back wall. I walk to the front right-hand corner of the court and deposit there my extra sweatbands and my small bottle (half the size of a roll of Life Savers) of nitroglycerine. I am ready.

The hard black ball fires around the cubed whiteness. The game is so intense as to become almost abstract: all speed and angle and calculation and possibility. It is a spiritually pleasing game, three-cushion billiards run into a fourth dimension. I have never thought of anything on the court except the game at that instant. I did not know until I was well into my thirties about the transcendent possibilities of games.

I race my heart. I have never used the nitro, or not since I was in the hospital just after the attack. (Opponents regard the pills, if they recognize them, as a sinister form of gamesmanship.) I run my heart to see that the piping is clear, that the two coronary bypasses are working. I race it to make it work, daring it not to do so. It is a form of bravado.

The fifth dimension of the game is an exhilarated sense of death in the white room, but always outrun, outspeeded. When I had my heart attack, in Kansas City, it ran me down and stepped on my chest. Passive, I curled up, slow-motion, into a fetal ball of pain, contracting into myself, coalescing around the constricted fire below my solar plexus. It never occurred to me that I would die. I grew peaceful. I was dazed, almost bemused.

"Ah," says my father, looking up from his Crab Louis. "There's Nelson."

He says it in a curious, awkward way, as if the fact makes him uncomfortable. I look. Plowing across the Rainbow Room comes Nelson Rockefeller.

He is retired from public life: ex-Vice President, ex-Governor of New York four times over. He still moves with a politician's energy, with a headlong rolling motion, legs too short, torso inclined forward. The thick-lensed and thick-framed tortoise-shell glasses obscure his eyes in the winter lunchtime light. The men at their lunches do not look up.

Behind Rockefeller walks William Ronan, a former academic who has become one of Rockefeller's most durable cronies and operators. The two make their way to a table opposite us, by the windows on the north side of the room. They sit with their heads together, in profile to us, with Central Park and all of the city to the north behind them, looking up the Hudson to the Cloisters and the Palisades and the George Washington Bridge. I watch them surreptitiously for the rest of our lunch. They huddle with a gangster air—Renaissance Italian gangsters.

I see my father watching them too, out of the corner of his eye, feeling their presence. It is a complicated look: furtive, longing, aggrieved.

My father worked for Nelson Rockefeller for twenty-one years.

He had started as a journalist—a Washington correspondent for the Philadelphia *Inquirer*, then the *Saturday Evening Post*'s assistant Washington editor. In the mid-fifties he and my mother were divorced. It was an ugly and noisy parting. At about the same time, my father left the *Saturday Evening Post*.

He went to work in politics, first for Senator Irving Ives of New York, and then for Ives's successor, Kenneth Keating. Keating was a white-maned, pink-faced little man with the smallest hands and shortest fingers I have ever seen. He later became ambassador to Israel during the Nixon years. I did not think that Keating was particularly bright. But my father, writing speeches for him, earned him a reputation as the wittiest man in Washington. My father accomplished this with several burlesquing, frolicsome speeches. In one of them Keating (Morrow) surveyed various political figures as if they were bizarrely distinctive weapons systems, anthropomorphic ordnance. Bobby Kennedy, for example, was a guided missile whose engine made a relentless *hoffa-hoffa-hoffa* noise as it arced toward its target. The Washington of the late Eisenhower years was not a notably hilarious place, and Keating became a star.

Nelson Rockefeller took Keating's wit away from him. Rockefeller recruited my father to write speeches during his first campaign for governor of New York, in 1958. At first my father was supposed to be just a temporary loan. But after the campaign my father moved his family to New York and settled down to a long association with the Rockefellers.

Over the years, he advanced in the intimacy and influence of his service. I monitored my father's course, at a distance, by the terms that newspapers used to identify my father when they mentioned him now and then. In these references, he progressed from "speech writer" to "speech writer and press adviser" to "adviser," then to "Rockefeller friend and political adviser," and eventually to "long-time Rockefeller intimate and adviser." He became a crony.

I traced his progress by the Christmas gifts that Rockefeller sent. My father's house in Bronxville was strewn with these mementos, these tokens of grace and favor. I could walk through the house and reconstruct the relationship like an archaeologist on a dig.

Rockefeller usually engraved the dates on his gifts. The earliest items were office-desk equipment: a large bronze letter opener in a sheath, decorated with the Great Seal of New York State and engraved "NAR Christmas 1959." Then a more expensive office-desk clock, same seal, engraved "HM from NAR, Christmas 1960."

In the early sixties my father advanced from Rockefeller's mass office Christmas list to the next order of favor. Steuben glass paperweights and cigarette boxes began to arrive. At last, in the late sixties and the seventies, came personal items: pieces of African and pre-Columbian sculpture, large engraved silver cigarette boxes, pictures of Nelson with Happy and the children, warmly inscribed.

The pictures found their way onto a living-room shrine arranged on a table set against one wall. On the table beside the Rockefellers stood a framed photograph of a very young, very skinny Senator John Kennedy, inscribed *"To Hugh with affection and admiration."* Next to it was a photograph of my father shaking hands with

Richard Nixon at a reception, my father wearing a huge bland grin. Into the corner of this picture frame, my stepmother had tucked a small slip of paper that said COUNT YOUR FINGERS.

Nelson Rockefeller was generous. Over the years, he lent my father a handsome amount of money, something well over $100,000. It helped to pay Mike's hospital bills in the two years he was dying of cancer. The money may have helped to pay for Mike's headstone. It helped pay for my stepmother's illnesses—for her pulmonary embolisms, her other troubles—and for the period when my father had three of his ten children and stepchildren in college at the same time.

Having lent the money, Rockefeller forgave the debt. I knew nothing about the money. I learned about it from the newspapers. Rockefeller revealed these and other gifts to the Senate committee holding hearings on his confirmation as Vice President in 1974. My father never told me about the loans.

Rockefeller was capable of large gestures of decency. When at last my stepmother lay dying of cancer in her bed in Bronxville, I stopped by to visit one Sunday afternoon. She asked me to close the door, and then, with a wan, pleased look, she said, "Don't tell your father, but look what Nelson did."

She showed me his Christmas present—a sweet, handwritten note, and a check for $25,000. "To help with the fight," he wrote. She dispatched one of my stepbrothers with the check to buy my father a Mercedes-Benz. She thought it would cheer him up. He had always wanted a Mercedes.

For all of Rockefeller's generosity, I did not like him. In some ways I came to hate him. Someone said that Rockefeller had a "second-rate intellect but a first-rate intuition about people." But that, I thought, was elegantly wrong. Nelson Rockefeller did have a second-rate intellect. But he also had a faulty intuition about people, I thought. He had his shrewdnesses, his manipulative canniness. But he was almost never required to live on the same terms as the rest of the world, and so I thought that he did not comprehend it very well.

His feet seldom touched the ground. One night my wife Brooke and I hitched a ride to Washington on Rockefeller's plane. He was flying down to address a Republican dinner. We rode in limousines from Manhattan. At La Guardia the limousines pulled up to the foot of the ramp. We bounded three steps onto the plane.

The flight took an hour. A steward served drinks and snacks. The plane was arranged like a somewhat vulgar, tubular living room. Rockefeller and his wife sat aft on lounges. Nelson held his hands up with abject patience as Happy wound her wool around them. It was a scene of unlikely domesticity. Rockefeller reached down, now and then, his arms and hands still banded with the yarn, and took a sip of his Dubonnet.

My father and Brooke and I sat in the front of the plane, near the pilot's cabin. I perched on the front of my lounge. We did not speak to the Rockefellers during the flight. We had become part of the crew, part of the servant corps. Once Rockefeller needed to make a call from a pay telephone at an airport. He turned to my father and said, "Hey, Hughie, you got a nickel?"

Perhaps there is nothing wrong with that. In the lore, the worker comes up to the campaigning Kennedy and says, "I hear you've never worked a day in your life." Then he leans closer: "Let me tell you, you ain't missed a thing."

In Washington, limousines again came onto the tarmac to the foot of the ramp. There was never a line to stand in, never an inconvenience. The way was effortless. It seemed a perfect immunity from the mess and struggle of the world.

Rockefeller kept up a circus of democratic noise and gestures ("Hiya fella!"). But I came to think that he was something of a solipsist on a grand scale, one with a large sense of his own possibilities and what the world owed him. Or perhaps it was simply that he was an essentially feudal man, with a feudal lord's complacent expectations and a dismissive ease with his servants. It enraged me to think of my father as one of the servants. It especially enraged me because Rockefeller was a high-handed seigneur playing a democratic game. He wanted power by right of birth but had to acquire it a messier way, by right of votes, by popular consent. There was an element of fraud in the transaction, but I admired him even so—a little—for the gamble he took by exposing himself to rejection by his inferiors. Still, I found Rockefeller's world sinister. He had wrong affinities. I measured them once in a peculiar context.

I took my son Jamie to school at eight-fifteen every morning. He was in first grade in a private school on the East Side of Manhattan near Central Park.

It pleased me to see our shadows together, Jamie's and mine, the morning sun behind us as we went up Ninety-first Street. Jamie sat in the kiddie seat on the back of my bicycle. He was getting too big for it so I walked the bike to school instead of riding it.

Jamie loved dogs that year. The dogs of the Upper East Side would be out for their morning walks. I would see a dog and point: "Cute dog. Cocker spaniel." Jamie would see one and point, speaking like a connoisseur: "Cute dog. Dachshund."

The first bodyguard that I would see was the one in the cream-colored overcoat and the matching cream-colored big-brimmed hat. The overcoat was soft, like camel's hair, and cinched at the waist with a bathrobe tie. The overcoat bulged peculiarly at the chest and on the sides above the hips: gangster bulges, ordnance—an Uzi, I imagined, and a .45. The man's face was dark and heavy. He kept his hands in his pockets.

In a moment, as Jamie and I advanced toward the school, a brown Mercedes sedan would sweep around the corner from Madison Avenue. It would stop in front of the school. Four more men in overcoats with bulges—gorillas from the Savak academy, I thought—got out and stationed themselves between the car and the front door of the school. They, too, kept their hands in their pockets, and they frisked the street with their eyes.

Then the Shah's son stepped out of the Mercedes. He was twelve years old. He was a perfect miniature of his father. He was dressed in American prep school clothes—tweed jacket, button-down shirt, school tie, gray slacks—but he wore them like a uniform, or a disguise. They fit him too smoothly, too well, in a European way, as if they represented a part of a temporary impersonation. The head emerging from this outfit was held with a bearing (a mixture of Prussia and St. Moritz) that he had not learned at an American prep school. Unlike the other boys, he carried no school books.

The Shah's son would pause for an instant on the sidewalk as if he were amused by the scene he had created. Then he stepped briskly inside, and his guards closed like dark waves in his small, sharp wake.

All through the winter of the Iranian revolution, I pushed Jamie on my bicycle to school and watched the Shah's boy arrive in his Mercedes. There was violence in the air. The Shah's brother-in-law was assassinated in Paris. The Shi'ite masses in Teheran screamed for blood. *"Margh bar Carter! Margh bar Carter!"* they chanted. Death to Carter. The Shah moved from one resort-fortress to another in his exile. The boy's bodyguards outside the school grew grimmer, more alert.

My fears rose. I wondered if the Ayatollah Khomeini's death squads would go for the boy in the street, before he went inside, or would wait until he was in class. Would they try to take him alive, for ransom, for dramatic purposes (a kidnapping prolongs the media attention)? Or would they blow up the school?

Jamie's classroom was on the street level, in a direct line of fire from the front door. In my imagination now I saw a world of alien violence piling out of cars with machine guns and grenades, in ski masks, blowing up the first grade, tearing through the halls, exploding the children, sending them flying, firing everywhere, the terrorist blood gone blackly wild, pumping death.

It seemed to me that the Shah and the Ayatollah and Henry Kissinger and Nelson Rockefeller were all somehow spiritual collaborators.

The Shah's son seemed so like his father. He was all hauteur and vulnerability delicately balanced. That is unfair to the son, no doubt, who must have been a pampered, bewildered, stricken boy.

The Shah and his son, my father and I, Jamie and I: I thought about the tenderness and the capacity for violence in the configurations.

I read one day about an Iranian who said that Savak agents had cut off his young son's arm with a power saw. He was only a child.

And in the television scenes of those days, mobs like a black foam washed and surged through the streets of Teheran.

Finally, they arrived at the American embassy. The day after the American hostages were taken, my father called me at my office at *Time* magazine. His voice was agitated. "Lanny," he demanded, "what are you going to do about Iran?"

He meant, what was *Time* going to write about it, what was I going to write about it.

But I thought, *"What are you going to do about Iran?" Oh, Pop, I see that the torch has passed.*

2 · My Father's Trade

I went into my father's trade. It did not occur to me to enter any other, to be anything else. I think that I made the emulation a strategy of identity. It expressed a basic kind of longing.

My father started working for newspapers in State College, Pennsylvania. It was during the Depression. He had dropped out of Bucknell after one year and never finished college. My grandfather, Dr. Morrow, could not stretch a country doctor's income to support seven other children and at the same time send the eldest to college. My father at the age of nineteen took up provincial journalism.

I began working for newspapers in the same territory, a little to the east of State College. When I was sixteen, my father got me a summer job working as a reporter-photographer for a paper called the Danville *News*. The paper, eight pages published daily on a flat-bed press, was owned by an old friend of my father's from the State College days.

My father drove me up to Danville one Saturday in early June of 1956: a five-hour drive from Washington up through the Maryland countryside, past Gettysburg, past Harrisburg, and on up the Susquehanna River toward the coal region. Danville was not a coal town. It lay beside the river on the edge of farming country. It had a chemical plant and a state mental hospital. It was the Montour County seat: a plain American town of almost impenetrable moral neutrality, matter-of-fact and short on charm, but livable, in a disappointing way.

My father deposited me on Front Street, at the house of the

widow Evans. He looked over the situation, the town, Mrs. Evans, with an air of cheerful but enigmatic irony. He seemed to mean that, good Lord, he had left exactly this more than thirty years before, and here it was again, and thank God he could leave it again. He got in his car and waved and drove south.

Mrs. Evans was a small, shrewd white-haired woman whose arthritis gave her a brittly dignified, slightly incensed posture. She had worked for years as a nurse at the state mental hospital. Her husband, who also had worked there, was dead now. She took in boarders. She gave me the front bedroom in her white frame house and she made me breakfast every morning—one poached egg on toast, with orange juice and instant coffee. I paid her $10 a week. Her house was furnished with antimacassars everywhere and with Presbyterian magazines, which she kept in racks.

The editor of the *News* had answered an ad in his own paper to find me a room in Mrs. Evans' house. I think that she was bemused by me. She regarded the newspaper as a faintly disreputable place to work. She did not think highly of me for doing so. It was not, I guess, that the newspaper told lies, but that the version of truth available there was somehow sketchy and pointless and unworthy. I encountered the attitude everywhere in Danville. It confused me. My father's business, which I idealized, struck others as feckless and even vaguely parasitic.

Mrs. Evans' other boarder was a smooth pink man of indeterminate middle age. He wore white wash-and-wear short-sleeved shirts. I think he was somehow emotionally retarded: his life was an emotional blank. He was single. He had no family that I knew of, except, it seemed, a sort of ghostly mother in a home somewhere, whom he visited on Sundays.

The boarder gazed at the world with solemn, washed blue eyes that were permanently fixed in an expression of mild wonder. He moved slowly, imperturbably. When the temperature rose above 85 degrees, he would cross the street to ask me, "Hot enough for you, Lance?" Then he would patiently wait for me to reply.

One Sunday afternoon he asked me if I wanted to come for a ride with him. We got into his black two-door Chevrolet. It was the totally stripped-down model: no chrome anywhere, no radio, nothing extra. It had a three-speed gearshift, which he worked with a painstaking deliberation, whole seconds passing while he engaged the gear. We rode for an hour in virtual silence, up and down the main highway along the Susquehanna. We never went more than 30 miles per hour. Cars passed us going 65 or 70, the drivers flashing angry looks as they shot by. We went south as far as Sunbury. The boarder decided to turn around and go north to Bloomsburg. He missed the exit. He slowed to a stop and then calmly engaged the reverse gear and backed up into the oncoming traffic. Horns blared: near-misses. The boarder's expression never changed. I watched him in profile. He looked a little like my father, if someone had done a comic balloon in the shape of my father's head. There was the same curve of the nose, only puffier, and something of the same large brow. There was even, deep in his bovine placidity, something of my father's sweetness of character, a semi-saintly abstractedness that bordered sometimes on the trance of narcissism.

In the little white frame house the three of us, Mrs. Evans, the boarder and I, lived together virtually in silence. Neither the boarder nor Mrs. Evans ever expressed the slightest curiosity about me and my work. It never occurred to me to ask them about their lives. It was the first time I had lived on my own: my arrangement in Danville seemed a sort of satirical duplication of the emotional evasiveness that was my family's style and necessity.

But the work meant that I could at last apprentice myself to the idea of my father. The Danville *News* published from a one-story building just off Main Street. It was designed along the lines of a railroad car, or a diner. Half the building was the composing room— a garage-dark place with a couple of linotypes and much blackly ink-stained metal printing paraphernalia: fonts and chases and proof-presses and rollers covered with their almost ominously viscous ink. Behind the composing room reposed the ancient flat-bed press: it was a vaguely sinister, nineteenth-century device. It looked like the Industrial Revolution: a dark, satanic press. Every afternoon at two it labored into deafening motion to print the day's run of 8,000 copies.

I arrived at the *News* office at eight in the morning. My desk sat in the small grubby editorial office behind the lobby where the secretary took classified ads. I put on a telephone headset and sat in front of a typewriter. I called all the state police substations within forty miles of Danville.

"Hello, Danville *News*," I would tell the desk sergeant in a briskly casual front-page voice. "Got anything overnight?" The desk sergeant would read his accidents and fires and other mayhem (if there were any) in a monotone of constabulary prose: "At 3:05 the subject, driving a black Plymouth sedan proceeding south on Route 11, attempted a left turn and struck . . ." I would take down the information on the typewriter. Then I would write a little accident roundup story for the front page.

It was not a bad apprenticeship to my father's trade. I wrote headlines. Routine baseball stories for the sports page presented the most difficult headline problems. I had to compile a list of synonyms for "beats," as in BLOOMSBURG BEATS SHAMOKIN. Defeats, of course. "Edges," if the score is close. "Clobbers," if not. But the countryside was littered with semi-pro teams with busy schedules. The sports page would carry a paragraph on each of these games all through the summer. Having used up the obvious handful of synonyms, I struggled to find others. I could reverse the process. I could write: SHAMOKIN BOWS TO BLOOMSBURG. But that takes more picas. Writing headlines encourages compression and (maybe) verbal energy, as well as simplification. It is a maddening, trivial and curiously interesting exercise: fitting words (those unruly, flyaway, chaotic things) into small physical spaces, trying to negotiate compromises between meaning and the tiny niche available to express it. The meanings were not complex. The sports headline in the Danville *News* in 1956 was not a haiku. But the game was new to me, and I could play for hours, more time than we had until deadline, surely, trying to find the exact words with which to make an escape from the limitations imposed by the form.

Headlines for games had a binary simplicity: one team won, one team lost. Or else they tied. But when I started writing headlines for stories about other matters—highway accidents, county supervisors' meetings, national news from the AP ticker, or the local crime that occurred very rarely in Danville—then the task became more interesting and even morally complex. How could one use severely limited space to explain events that might have more than one dimension? One can become almost spiritually corrupt at the game. One learns to perform a kind of triage with the truth: since it is not possible to save all possible nuances when composing this headline, this billboard, then one must select the most important, the most essential point, and let the others go. On the other hand, writing headlines can train the mind to get at essences, to reach into a bewildering mess of words and isolate the basic truth of an event and seize it and proclaim it with four or five hard, clear words.

The bunkspace for the headline, the niche on the page, was determined by the layout, the design of the page. That layout was governed by the rudimentary and improvisational aesthetics of newspaper-making, by the editor's sense of appropriate symmetry and typeface, by the length of the story in question, by the amount of news that day and by the priorities of importance assigned to each individual item of news, by the photographs that might be available, by the quality of the photographs and their relationship, if any, to the news stories. All of these factors arranged themselves rather easily, almost automatically, in the judgment of the editor. He made his decisions by instinct. He saw the page in his mind. A good cook does not have to work from recipes. Since I had yet no such instinct, I found the problems arising from these questions fascinating: What news gets how much space and why?

I did not do layouts. They were the task of Jack Feeley, the editor. Jack was a talented, dyspeptic New Yorker who had some-how found his way into rural Pennsylvania. He wrote most of the paper himself, the local news items, the editorial page. His sports writer was a pugnacious-looking little man named Ted Jones. Ted looked as if Carmine Basilio had been crossed with Max Lerner. He worked the telephone all day, with the headset on, his head tilted sharply, his jaws grinding away at a wad of chewing gum even through his words. He talked out of the corner of his mouth. As he took information in through the telephone headset, he beat it out on an ancient and dirty Royal typewriter. He punished the machine as if it were a punching bag. His small body shook in the chair, like bouncing rubble, as he rattled out each burst of words.

The society editor, Lois Little, took care of the Social Notes

From All Over. I believe she was paid by the inch (of type that she got into the newspaper). The arrangement tended to make her wordy about the garden club and the visiting out-of-towners and the Women of the Moose—the news on her beat.

Lois was a dear, plain woman, rail-thin and gabby. She had thick red hair, of which she was proud. She wore those bizarrely feline eyeglasses that American women wore in the fifties: the dark plastic frames, sometimes flecked with rhinestone chips, swept to Oriental pussycat points on either side, exaggerating the corners of the eyes. The effect was to narrow the eyes of the wearer, and almost to hide them. They could make a girl-child look middle-aged.

Lois and I liked each other. When World War II started, Lois was a teen-ager just out of high school. The world had become exciting. She headed for Washington and became a secretary in the war effort. When she told me about those days, I saw—past those awful glasses—the little blaze of excitement, of avidity in her eyes. There were adventures then. She had lived with other girls in a tiny apartment. The town was full of men, full of the war, full of the gorgeous transient intensity that war gives to sex, to life. Cigarettes were scarce. Life was fun. A young woman out of small-town Pennsylvania would be independent for the first time: on the loose.

I saw this look in Lois's eye my first week in Danville. She invited me to come across the river for dinner. Lois's husband worked at the chemical plant. He was a short, thick man, about five feet four, with a crew cut and muscles. He looked like Mickey Spillane. He inspected me silently when I arrived at their house and then went to practice his archery in the backyard. He was a bow-and-arrow hunter. His bow required one hundred pounds or so of pull to draw the string. Taciturn, angry, he drew the string back until it creased his cheek. He held it a long moment, then let fly his arrows in the dusk.

Lois eyed him uneasily through the kitchen window and went on telling me about Washington during the war, about the days before she met this man and married him and came capitulating back to Pennsylvania.

I was lonely in Danville. I began to sense the journalist's peculiar noninvolvement. I stood off to the side of things. I was a stranger, staying only for the summer, and small towns tend to be tribal, exclusive. But there was more to it than that. My character was ideally suited, I suppose, to the role of standing aside and recording. So, I thought, was my father's. He was an instinctive observer. He possessed irony and urbane cynicism, detachment and a light, deflecting wit. He was a very funny and charming man. His gift of mockery would have been lethal if he had not as a rule used it with a fine internal kindness that implied the joke was also in some way upon himself—perhaps upon himself above all. His tone was gay and rueful and sometimes swellingly burlesque.

But beneath those, I thought, lay a kind of saintliness: an essential sweetness and even a passivity. It was the passivity that made him an excellent observer of the world.

A local undertaker's plump, complacent son invited me sometimes to join a party of teen-agers who climbed into the back of one of his father's Cadillac hearses and drove up to the drive-in movie in Bloomsburg. We drank beer in the back of that cave, that rolling crypt, and stared down the tunnel through the windshield at the movie. We would ride home bouncing in the back on the casket tracks and the undertaker's son would deposit me in front of Mrs. Evans' house in the middle of the night. I was sure that she watched this proceeding from an upstairs window, shaking her head, but she said nothing.

The gentry of Danville mostly lived across the river, in Riverside. It was John O'Hara country. The children of the local money were spoiled and woundingly supercilious. They were lazing through their summer before going back to the Hill School or Madeira, or starting Princeton. They had cars and a provincial country-club air. I went to some of their parties. The undertaker's son sponsored me. Once, a girl I did not know had a birthday party. Her parents invited at least a hundred and fifty people to come to the immense pond near their house for a swimming party. It was early evening. There were tables under the trees spread with picnic foods, and tubs of iced beer. The youth arrived in MGs and Austin Healeys. The girls were blond. The boys wore madras Bermuda shorts and loafers without socks, and blue Oxford cloth button-down shirts, sleeves rolled up to the elbows. They showed already, about their buttocks and stomachs, a rounded pudge of well-being. They had the tans of the handsomely summered, tans acquired in pools, on tennis courts. They were not tans gotten by working in the sun.

We had brought bathing suits. We swam out to the float in the middle of the pond. We hung from the edge of the float on arms crooked at the elbows, hair wet. The boys and girls flirted, and I listened. They talked about dates and going back to school, about fraternities and sororities.

These children outraged me in some obscure way. I was hurt by how much they were at home, and how comfortably. I dropped out of their circles. I had come to Danville to impersonate an adult in an adult world. The prep school adolescents had nothing to do with that. I preferred the company of the workers and farmers I met around Danville while I was doing stories for the paper. I preferred to go with some of them to the American Legion hall and drink beer there in the evenings. I felt more at home with them. I was a democrat. They seemed to me better people. They seemed more my father's kind of people. Or perhaps it was merely that I was at ease with them, that I even enjoyed a subtle authority over them. I would not have admitted that, of course.

I began going home to Washington, to my father's house, every weekend. I would tell him what I had learned about the newspaper business that week. He would recall his days on newspapers in the middle of Pennsylvania, dealing with the state cops just as I did, and the county coroner and the Elks Club meetings and the Rotary Club luncheons at the local hotel, with all the small-town characters and chicaneries. About these things he talked with a blend of irony and wistfulness. It was his youth and it was silly and mortal, and now I occupied the same territory, and it seemed not to have changed so much. I think he found it a somewhat surprising effect: to hear me describing things that also seemed to have happened to him in *his* youth. I was attempting to appropriate, to reconstruct almost, his earlier life, to lay my own upon the grid of his.

Years later I sat with my grandmother one afternoon, in her old age, and as we talked she began to confuse me with my father as he had been years before, her mind eliding events across great stretches of time. She asked me about the days when I used to swim at a quarry near Centre Hall, Pennsylvania; it was of course my father who had swum there as a boy. In her mind, I had become he.

Something of the same effect may have developed in my father's mind as we talked about newspapers and small-town Pennsylvania. We talked about these things while floating in a large round plastic pool my father had installed behind the house on Newark Street. We lay upon two rafts, on our backs, eyes serenely closed, taking the sun. We were floating in time as well, rocking lightly in the slosh of its dreamy liquid interchangeabilities: life for life, father for son.

On Sunday evenings I would go to the Greyhound station and find the bus (destination: Scranton, Wilkes-Barre) and begin the ride back to Danville. The bus was an almost interminable local. It stopped at every western Maryland waystation and hill town. The roads were narrow, black and steep: a dark rural run through small mountains. Every hour or two the bus would pull up to an all-night roadside café, a small, tacky island of light. We would all shamble off to go to the bathroom and buy orange Nehi soda or coffee. In fifteen minutes we started again.

The passengers tended toward the woebegone. There would always be a drained-looking country girl in late adolescence, with a baby or two. The babies would squall through the night. Some East Europeans were heading back toward the coal fields. They ate sandwiches that filled the bus with a dense onion smell. In the back of the bus in the twilight of weary forms, I would see a sailor or soldier or other young man in a slow-writhing sexual clutch with a girl. They would wait until the bus was about two hours into the countryside and almost everyone was dozing before they tried the actual connection. The air on the bus was thick and lubricous.

Usually I dreamed of Kate. I stared out the window into the darkness, though what I saw in the glass was mostly the glow of my own reflected half-profile, grieving for Kate. The Greyhound swaying and double-clutching through the rural hilly night seemed to me a capsule of utter loneliness. Kate was the first girl I loved, the daughter of a naval officer who lived in Georgetown.

One night I sat beside an unemployed coal miner who was going back home to Wilkes-Barre. He had a pint bottle of whiskey in a paper bag. We started talking in the dark, and he wiped his palm across the top of the bottle and companionably passed it over to me. I took a long pull. It burned handsomely going down my sixteen-year-old's throat. A man's drink. We passed it back and forth all the way to Danville, mingling our whiskey breaths and talking.

Times were hard in the coal fields now, he said. Some of his friends were working what they called bootleg mines, but it was dangerous. Bootleg mines were those that a company had already mined out to the limits of safety, honeycombing the underground with tunnels. When most of the coal was gone and the ratio of supporting pillars to empty underground space became dangerous, the mine would simply be abandoned. Then the bootleggers might move in to try to coax out more coal. Often the black space would give way. The earth would collapse. Bootleggers were always getting caught down there.

I said good night to the miner as we pulled into Danville. I shook his hand, which itself felt like a lump of coal. I was drunk. I got off the bus on the edge of town at midnight and walked unsteadily through the empty streets.

Danville State Mental Hospital lay just north of town, in farm countryside. When the wind was wrong, the heavy odor of a neighboring pig farm would drift across the vast hospital grounds. I often covered stories at the hospital. Once the governor came to present a state appropriations check to the hospital director in the lobby of the main building—a rather strange ceremony, I thought. Since visits of the governor to Danville were rare, I was assigned to tote my enormous Speed Graphic box camera over to the hospital and photograph the event.

The politicians and medical bureaucrats were all smiles there in the anteroom of their asylum. No patients were invited. The check was frozen in midair as it changed hands, and I took the picture. My exposure was wrong. The picture came out too dark. Jack Feeley muttered at me as he emerged from the little darkroom back at the office, but he printed the murky picture anyway, on the front page: shadow figures shaking hands in the penumbral mental institution.

The hospital had tennis courts, which I could use sometimes. They were mostly for the doctors and nurses. Occasionally, however, a comparatively well behaved patient would make his way onto the court and get himself a game. The patients played with ancient, fuzzless balls retrieved from the nearby woods and grass, and warped rackets that looked as if they had come out of an attic. I remember one tennis-playing patient. He was middle-aged and unshaven. He wore an Argyle sweater-vest on even the hottest days, and baggy gray flannel slacks. I saw in his country-club strut on the court a bright, lunatic playacting élan, a jauntiness. One afternoon, toward dusk, I was on the tennis court. I watched the patient playing another on the adjoining court, both men huffing through an incompetent pitty-pat game, but keeping coherent score nonetheless. When it came time for the court change, the patient in the Argyle sweater walked with a sporty briskness to the side of the net. As if it were the usual thing to do when changing courts, he opened his fly and, with an air of *comme-il-faut*, peed in a golden arc toward the center of the court.

Class B baseball teams from the neighboring countryside played games on the hospital's diamond. It had a wooden grandstand. The spectators for the games were usually the mental patients. That produced odd disjunctions between the action on the field and the reaction in the stands. The spectators would hoot and hooraw at the wrong times. They would become excited by irrelevancies on the field. A home run might elicit no fan reaction at all. It might be greeted only by vacant, depressed stares and silence. But the wooden stands would shake with stomping feet and howls and cheers and moans if, say, two outfielders collided while going for a fly ball, or if a dog trotted onto the field.

It was at these games, which I had to cover for the Danville *News*, that I first witnessed, up close, the magic imparted to a pitched ball by a man who knows what he is doing. There was a pitcher for the Bloomsburg team who threw a slow roundhouse curve. I used to place myself in the stands behind home plate, among the patients, and watch the ball come in. The physics of the thing astounded me. It was a preternatural event, telekinesis, a wonder something like ventriloquism. The ball would start on a sort of flyaway trajectory (as if it were heading for the trees beyond, out of control) and then in midflight some mysterious force like gravity or will would take hold and the ball would bore in rifling toward the strike zone and smack the catcher's mitt dead-center: the batter paralyzed in his crouch with a dumb, astonished look, as if still waiting.

When this happened, the patients would laugh, cackling and snorting. They were mostly older people, missing half their teeth. I wondered if they, too, thought it was magic, or just a good curve ball.

My father told me once about the way my grandfather could pitch a ball. Before he became a doctor, my grandfather played semi-pro ball down in Gainesville, Florida. My father would mime a pitcher's motion. He would go into a sort of tight, stylized windup, with his eye steadily fixed upon the hypothetical batsman, staring him down, taking his measure (*Try and hit this one, you son of a bitch!*), and he would swivel through the delivery and end the motion almost falling on his face. "Anyway, that was Dad's curve," he would say with a deprecating little laugh.

3·Centre Hall

One weekend my father drove with my stepmother up to Danville. They came to the *News* office just after noon on Saturday. I sat at my desk wearing my headset, taking information over the phone, banging it out on my typewriter. I nodded to my father and step-mother as they came in.

I was proud of myself. They had caught me at work. My father looked at me with a quizzical gaze mixing recognition and mild surprise.

That afternoon we drove west across Pennsylvania through farm country. My father was taking me and my stepmother to see the town where he grew up, Centre Hall.

It was late July. The summer trees were fat with their foliage. The countryside had the rich, heavy, slumbering look of rural midsummer.

My father and stepmother were newly enough married to be still almost gaily in love. I sat in the back seat of my father's station wagon. I joined them in a comfortable chatter. We saw Centre Hall, but quickly. My father pulled slowly alongside a white frame house where, he said, Dr. Morrow had practiced medicine and raised his eight children.

My father looked at the house with a sort of speculative remote-ness and surprise: the old memory, I think, became suddenly phys-ical and startled him. The house where he grew up had returned from the dead. He seemed to wander mentally around it for a few moments, remembering. Then he pulled away.

We drove back eastward again, and looped north. Toward evening we were rolling through the coal fields on a scruffy two-lane. I had bought a six-pack of beer (a local brand: Yuengling). My stepmother nipped out of a flask filled with sherry. My father did not drink. My stepmother and I began to glow a little with alcohol. We kept up a level of hooting hilarity. My father was driving aimlessly. We were, as he said, "stooging around." He liked to make that little satirical gangster noise in his conversation. He was acting as my stepmother's bartender with the sherry. Every so often he would rather tenderly ask, "You want a slug, baby?" She would burst out laughing. He would pour the amber sherry into the thimble-shaped flask cap as he drove, one eye on the road.

The coal towns were dingily gloomy in daylight; now the dusk and darkness swallowed them. We slid south in our small, bright capsule of well-being, down the western bank of the Susquehanna, toward Danville. I thought that my father seemed happier that night than I had ever known him to be. In the back seat, I drifted off to sleep.

I did not go back to Centre Hall for another quarter of a century. In that time, my father's family seemed to recede from me. His mother, his brothers and sisters were warm, reassuring presences when I was a child, especially my Aunt Sally, who lived with us for years and in some ways raised my brother Hughie and me. But they seemed now to belong to an order of prehistory. I saw my grandmother now and then. The summer after my heart attack, she died. She was eighty-eight years old. My Uncle Rowland tracked me down on the telephone one night on Martha's Vineyard, where my wife and I had taken a house. He told me, "Mother died yesterday, Lanny." He told me when the funeral services would be held, outside Baltimore.

The news made an intense but distant reverberation. Grandmother had grown shadowy to me. She had been fading off mentally, I gathered, for years, like a radio signal getting more and more remote as one drives deeper into the country.

I made arrangements to go to her funeral. I would fly to New

York from Martha's Vineyard, and then drive south to Baltimore with Hughie. But when the time came to get on the plane, I could not. My chest tightened with anxiety. There was too much past and death around that summer. I called Hughie and told him I was not coming. I went down to the beach and lay in the sun for hours, and listened to the sound of the waves.

Earlier that summer, my stepmother had died of cancer in her bed in Bronxville. So my father lost his wife, and then his mother, within the space of five weeks. His wife had been sick for months. They had found her cancer just after they had returned from the Republican National Convention in Kansas City. It was the usual story. They operated. They could not get it all—that phrase again. They treated her with chemicals and radiation through the winter. She went home to Bronxville to suffer through the last stages. She did it bravely. My father called me early one Sunday morning in June. He said, "Carol's gone."

Nelson Rockefeller came to the funeral. He actually made an entrance. He swept into the church after all the family had arrived. He came in a sort of subdued campaign flurry, and all heads turned, and I saw on my aunts' and uncles' faces that look of dazed surprise and involuntary wonder that people have when they see a celebrity: a burst of gladness and recognition. My father saw Nelson. For a moment my father looked younger; his face registered an unmistakable pleasure. The benison of Nelson's presence.

Several years later, after my father had remarried, I asked him if he would like to take a trip with me back to Centre Hall. We spent a couple of days, a weekend, wandering through the central Pennsylvania countryside, and through my father's past. I coaxed him to tell me about it. He seemed curiously eager to discuss it. I was surprised by that.

The family past had always seemed to me a vaguely disreputable prehistory . . . something hidden, something that needed to be hidden: there seemed to be secrets there—humiliations, failures, shadows.

My parents did not discuss the past. It was a door they did not open. But the past would overtake them sometimes. My mother's bouts with the past were painful. Her eyes would suddenly fill with an old terror, shot with tears. The past had taken possession of her again.

I did not understand. She would explain it afterward. She would say, half sobbing, "I had an unhappy childhood." That meant nothing to me or Hughie.

"I had an unhappy childhood." My mother's seizures, followed by the unvarying formula of explanation, left me with a sense that the past—the family past, her past, anyway—was a dark, palpable force, a predator that was loose in time. I saw it occupy her: saw it fill up her face and head like black poisoned gases, terrors, seeping in and contaminating her vitality and sanity and loveliness. The past transfigured her, transformed her toward a darkness. The process made me afraid. I was amazed and frightened to learn that the past could not be controlled, that memory could be so dangerous.

My mother could not hear Brahms' "Lullaby" without weeping. Her mother had sung it to her as a child. My mother could not approach Christmas without falling into turmoils of extravagant hope and despair. Christmas meant everything, all possibilities of security and love. Her family's emotions, some of them, had a nineteenth-century extravagance about them. There was a deep sentimentality, but beneath that layer of emotional marzipan, I sensed, lay a level of dark molten possibilities, not so nice. All unworldly expectations were pregnant with dangerous disappointment, with almost violent despair.

Years later, a friend whose father had been a Yugoslavian patriot dolefully described his father's funeral to me. The burial had to be held in a cemetery in the middle of the night. Even then, Serbs and Croats rioted in the dark over the man's casket, over the freshly dug hole in the ground. The casket had to be virtually tumbled in. They kicked the dirt in after it. They went on screaming obliviously in the dark.

The past in our family might have been something like that: an obscure midnight riot in a graveyard. The past was full of grievances. It lashed out sometimes in the dark. The past was insane.

Or it was like the lake where I go now in the summertime. Toward the end of one summer we came to the house and found that the lake had begun to drain. The dock stood up out of the water, as if it were on stilts. It was difficult to hoist ourselves up onto it after swimming, it was so high. The lake banks were like teeth when the gums begin to recede. The water drew away from the shoreline. As the water went down, it left drying mud and mud-caked rocks. An eerie sort of exposure began to occur, distantly alarming. The lake began to look ill, drought-stricken. It smelled: a strong, strange smell, deeply earthy, but rotting.

Jamie and I took the canoe out onto the water and paddled slowly around the lake. We wondered at everything: the familiar lake-side trees, whose roots we now saw reaching like mangroves toward the water. The docks whose timbers were exposed: brown and decaying. Some inlets where we always liked to paddle, looking for the turtles that sunned themselves on logs, were now too shallow to admit us. We heard the bottom of the canoe scrape the gravelly mud, and we back-paddled off and made for the center of the lake again. Now we slid noiselessly across the water. No one else was on the lake. The banks were still. There was no wind. The water seemed curiously dead.

At the head of the lake, at the place where the road crosses, we found a boy of twelve fishing without much conviction.

"Why is the lake so low?" I asked him as we drew near.

He shrugged without looking at me.

When we came in from the lake, I said to my wife, "The lake is spooky. They seem to be draining it."

She said, "They must be looking for that woman. They think she may have been killed."

"Who?"

"Her husband reported her missing weeks ago. There was a picture in the *News*. She's beautiful. They live at the head of the lake. There's something very fishy about it. They must be looking for the body."

I did not want to alarm Jamie, who was listening. I elbowed him in the ribs raucously and said, "Get it? Something fishy! Get it?"

"Very funny," he said.

After that, we stopped swimming. We did not take the canoe out on the lake as much. She might be down there.

I even began to look for her. I would study the water almost surreptitiously, trying to penetrate the murk, imagining the pale shape down there of a leg, a half-glow of flesh among the weeds, among the bass and sunfish.

My father himself rarely talked about the past, about his family. I never understood why. That silence filled me, over the years, with a vague, chronic sense of shame. The silence itself, the oblivion of personal history, seemed to me a sort of disgrace.

The past took a precise shape for me: our house on Mount Pleasant Street in Washington. We moved there when I was eight. It was a square white wooden Victorian house with two stories and an attic. It stood at the bottom of a steep hill. Our house was the dead end of the street. Beyond the house, for miles, lay Rock Creek Park.

An oak tree in the middle of the front yard kept the ground too darkly shaded for grass to grow. The yard was an expanse of dirt packed so hard it almost shone. On the other side of the house, the backyard had once been planted with boxwood in a formal English pattern. But it had fallen into neglect. It was now a squalor of weeds and bushes and unkempt boxwood. The longer we lived there, the more trash accumulated among the boxwood: cans and bottles. Mount Pleasant Street might as well have been the bottom of Tobacco Road. The vastness of the park, with its thick trees and bushes, seemed always to encroach upon our yard and house, as if to swallow them.

The house had been built on a hillside. The foundation was not strong. The house seemed to be sliding into the woods. The frame was skewed. The living room and dining room visibly tilted. The dining room was all but empty. It contained a green metal mangle, the kind that professional laundries use to press shirts, and a chrome-legged kitchen chair covered with mother-of-pearl vinyl that was torn to reveal its packed white padding. In a corner stood the huge console of a Zenith shortwave radio–phonograph that a friend had left with my parents while she journeyed abroad. Otherwise, the room was bare. The wood floor slanted almost steeply off. A marble let go on the uphill side of the dining room would immediately roll, gathering speed, noisily, and thwack the other side. Things in the house would always slide a little, as they do on a listing ship. Everything seemed on a downward drift. But the house did not right itself, or roll the other way, as a ship will. The house had that haunted tendency, a disposition toward collapse. The house felt as if it would crack with the strain of gravity and tumble down the hill into the woods.

I sometimes dream about the house. The house in my dreams also tends toward collapse. The frame of the house twists. The right angles will not stay right, but bend in their surreal way. My father stands at the head of the stairs, swaying. The only furniture in the house is a torn sofa with its springs exposed. From the ceiling of the dining room dangles an electric socket with a naked light bulb in it. Then my father is gone and the house is utterly empty, filled with that bright naked light. I look out. The yard is covered with fallen wet leaves, dark and matted. People come and look in at the windows, and talk about the slanting floor. I am filled with humiliation.

My father dispensed the past guardedly as we drove west, toward Centre Hall. He suggested that there, in the middle of Pennsylvania, he had enjoyed something like Penrod Schofield's childhood, an American idyll. He told me how happy he had been. For a change, the prehistory took on a bright and primitive American whiteness, like snow over a farm.

My father remembered how his father would gather the eight children in the parlor of the house in Centre Hall in the evening. One of the children would beg, "Tell us about out West, Dad." And Dr. Morrow would describe his childhood at the cavalry posts in Texas and New Mexico.

There was the story about the bear cub, for example. One day when Colonel Morrow was on cavalry patrol in the mountains, he encountered a mother bear with a cub. The cavalrymen were riding in a single file on a narrow mountain trail. The bears stood blocking the way. The soldiers had to shoot the mother. Colonel Morrow packed the cub into the game pouch of his tunic and rode back to the fort with the baby bear brawling in the small of his back. The tunic was tattered and shredded when the ride was over. But the future Dr. Morrow and his elder brother Albert had a bear cub for a pet. They kept him until he grew too large, and then they shipped him off to the Denver Zoo.

Dr. Morrow was born in 1873 in Fort Concho, in West Texas. He grew up on the frontier. His father was gone long stretches of time on his Indian business.

My father said that the doctor was a skinny man, about 150 pounds, a superb athlete. "He was an unbelievable shot," my father told me. "He had medals. He could break a hundred targets in a row when he was skeet shooting." Buffalo Bill.

I took from my father a sense of being utterly American. I thought of Morrows as extremely American people. I did not identify Morrows with a triumphant Americanism, but on the contrary, with the American side that is subdued and lonely and saddened by failure. It may have been the Scots-Irish vibration in our blood. Some of our eighteenth-century forebears came to America from the lowlands by way of Ireland; they were a twice-failed lot. We were good, decent, strong but obscurely saddened people, I thought sometimes. Competent. Perfectly American in our mistrust of grandiloquence and fraud and violence.

"Dad grew up with weapons, you know," my father said. "He carried a Colt .45 to shoot rattlesnakes from the saddle. He could put a Camel cigarette pack on a tree and walk way the hell away and drill it with his .45."

Dr. Morrow was ambidextrous. He liked to tell the story of something that happened during his internship at the Alexian Brothers Hospital in Elizabeth, New Jersey. A patient in the emergency room one night got wild and started flailing. Dr. Morrow squared off against the man: feinted with his right hand and then knocked him cold with his left. "That," my father said, "was a great event in Dad's medical career."

The doctor was not physically affectionate. He was not cold, exactly. "He was a little remote," my father said in a wistful tone. "He didn't go in for the laying on of hands with his children. I guess I inherited that from him." My mother, however, remembered Dr. Morrow as a remarkably tender and gentle man.

In any case, the doctor had a quizzical sweetness that he passed on to his son. The doctor may also have accounted for my father's sense of humor, his sense of satire, his relish for bombast. When the doctor told his children about life out West, he would often offer them his parody of a typical line of Ned Buntline dime-novel prose: "The swarthy crack of the Winchester rent the still prairie air. The redskin bounded thirty feet into the ozone, and bit the dust. Shoveltooth Saul, the exterminator, never missed his mark."

The doctor drifted around as a young man. Along the line, he got an education at the University of Colorado. He worked as a bank clerk. Eventually he came East to the College of Physicians and Surgeons in Baltimore and took his medical degree in 1912. But he had started late. He was thirty-nine years old. He married my grandmother, Marjorie Vickers, in Washington, D.C. He told her he wanted nine sons. A classmate steered him toward a practice in Williamsberg, Pennsylvania.

My father remembered his father driftingly, as one does. "Dad had very bad digestion," my father said as we drove toward Centre Hall. "I remember there was always a flake of white on his lips from the Maalox, or whatever it was that he took for his stomach. Mother always said it was the junk that he and Harry Wilson ate when they were medical students. Their stomachs never recovered from that." In the back seat of the car as we rode lay my father's open briefcase, with his jars of Maalox tablets in it.

"Dad had all his medicines right in the office. He hardly ever wrote a prescription for anything. He could simply dispense the medicine. I remember one time a guy named Howard Dunkel showed up at the door. I was the only one home. Dad was out on a case somewhere. A box of kitchen matches had gone up in this guy's hand. I was twelve or thirteen. I just made him lie down on the couch and treated him with Ichthyol, the standard burn reduction agent, some very thick stuff Dad had.

"His patients were mostly farmers. Most of his practice was treating emergencies. Tractors would roll over and crush a leg. Burns. Fractures. Childbirth. General internal medicine. He had to treat gunshot wounds from time to time. Hunting accidents. I can't recall any shots ever being fired in anger around Centre Hall.

"Once in a while we would cart one of the old ladies out to the funny farm. I drove one of them to the State Mental Hospital in Danville. She was very gentle and bewildered. We said we were going to visit friends. As we pulled up to the hospital, she said, 'Oh, yes, Cyrus, we've been here before, haven't we?' She was wrong, of course."

We were off the Pennsylvania Turnpike now, and approaching Centre Hall through the low mountains. They were dusted with a light snow.

My father remembered his father in terms of cars. He could locate a memory in time, could pin the event to the year, by recalling what kind of car his father had at the time.

"He got a new Ford every year until 1925," my father said. "Then he got a four-cylinder Dodge coupé. In 1928 a Chrysler. In '30, another Dodge. In '32, an Auburn. In '35, a Chevy. In '38, a Pontiac."

The cars were, in a sense, emotional vehicles for the doctor and his son. They seemed to make approaches possible, a masculine intimacy: the trip was a rite and adventure. The mechanics of the machine, the mystique of it, created the context for a partnership, the rides on which inexpressible closenesses might be felt.

"I learned to drive at the age of ten," my father said. "I was driving for Dad from the age of twelve on. I took him everywhere on his calls. My father indulged me. I just loved to drive. My most vivid memory is of the telephone ringing in the middle of the night. I would get up with Dad and drive him to his patients.

"Every winter, the roads drifted shut. We would have to cut the wire fences sometimes and drive out over the fields. One night I got pneumonia. We kept tearing up our chains. We broke open two miles of road that hadn't been used all winter. I hit snowbanks, trying to break through like an icebreaker. The windshield was completely covered with snow. I'd back up and hit it, and then back up and hit it again, breaking through. We were trying to get to a farm where a woman was in labor. We just made it. It was a bitter night. I helped Dad with the delivery. The farmer was dead drunk. It was a hard labor. I got the water and the towels for him."

Dr. Morrow's practice in Williamsberg began to fade after World

War I. "There was a great flu epidemic. Dad was working twenty hours a day taking care of flu patients. I was a baby. One very hot day he was riding with the top down on his Ford runabout, and he got pneumonia. Dad damn near died."

There was a shadow of incipient hard times always. Dr. Morrow was a middle-aged country doctor with (as the years passed) eight children to feed on the fees of marginal small-town practices. In 1922 he had to move to Salisbury, Pennsylvania, and work as company physician at the stone quarries. Men could get smashed up doing that work. There was trade. But the quarries petered out. Dr. Morrow moved his family again. He bought his practice in Centre Hall from a Dr. Longwell.

My father and I stopped on a ridge overlooking Centre Hall. I had not seen the town since that summer years before when we came from Danville with my stepmother. My father and I stood in the cold morning air looking out across the valley. The town lay below us, like a sweet American primitive, like a Grandma Moses. It lay in handsome, motionless winter.

Coming up the mountain, we had passed an enigmatic little home-made shrine fashioned from wrought iron. It was a roadside memorial that a father named Ripka had erected to his son Larry, who died, the tablet said, in 1977, at age eleven. Did the boy die along that stretch of mountain road? An accident? Had he been hit by a car? My father and I passed the odd memorial several times that weekend. I started to look for it each time we drove up the mountain. I found it unsettling and somehow moving: I pictured the father grieving for the son, clumsily, obsessively stricken, trying to appease his grief—or institutionalize it—with the jerry-rigged shrine.

My father and I descended toward the town. He told me about the day he roller-skated down this mountain: 60 miles per hour. (Perhaps the Ripka boy was doing that; perhaps he flew off the side of this small mountain like a ski jumper gone disastrously off his track, and went pinwheeling endlessly down through the air toward Centre Hall until he crashed in the forest.) My father said that years ago truckers sometimes lost their brakes and came screaming down the mountain stripping gears and bawling on the air horn.

"I had a beautiful life here," my father said. "A small town. A mountain to climb all over. The only tragedy in the whole damn town was the day one local minister came to Dad and said, 'Doctor, my wife has run away with a pipe-organ salesman.' She came back, though. They let her figuratively wear an A for a while."

Once a boy on the high school soccer team stole a visiting player's wallet from the locker room during a game. The boy was caught. My father shook his head. "Out of just plain shame, he shot himself in the head with a .22 rifle. The whole class of 1933 went to the funeral." Then, as if explaining the theft: "All of us were poor. It was the depths of the Depression."

There were other shadows, Spoon River stories. A sort of golden boy in the class went wrong somehow. In later years he was seen dead drunk in the stands at a Penn State football game, and people shook their heads. No one knew what was wrong. Or no one would talk about it. There was another boy who was a homo, almost publicly so, and seemed perfectly happy with his life.

I sheepishly prompted my father about the past. His eyes alternated between being flattered and being uncomfortable. We were riding in my Saab sedan. My father drove. He enjoyed the car, which was almost new. I was chagrined to find that he drove it badly. He worked the clutch wrong. He shifted into third gear when the car was going only 15 miles per hour, and the engine would lug. I could not understand it. My father had always been the best driver in the world, with a perfect ear for the engine, a kind of elegant sensitivity to the machine. Why was he mistreating my Saab so badly, using the wrong gear at the wrong speed? He had inexplicably lost his touch. (I had felt something of the same bewilderment several years earlier when my mother—the mother of seven children—picked up my son Jamie, still an infant, and fumbled him so badly that I feared she would drop him. I took him from her.)

"I was closer to Dad than to Mother," he said, shifting into fourth gear at 20 miles per hour. I jammed my right foot onto the floorboard as if there were a gas pedal there with which to relieve my poor engine. "Once I started getting out into the cold cruel world, I was closer to Dad. He taught me to hunt and shoot. We went deer hunting. I wounded a deer once. We tracked it for miles, following the blood, but never found it. It was a nightmare. I had a .30–.30 carbine. Dad had a .30–.06 Winchester, with a box magazine and Lyman peepsights."

Dr. Morrow was a great man for the road. When he finished seeing his patients at nine or ten at night, he would get all the children out of bed and pile them into the car and start the eight-hour drive to Philadelphia to visit relatives.

"In a sense," my father said, "I was raised in a pretty Victorian family. I never heard Mother and Dad have a quarrel—except once. On that occasion, all I heard was Dad shouting, 'You bitch!' And I rushed to Mama, and Mother was sobbing, 'He never speaks to me like that.' Mother was having the vapors, and all the children were clutching around her skirts and staring at Dad, as if to say, 'You brute!' But otherwise, whatever their frictions were, they were remarkably skillful at not involving their children."

We pulled onto the main street of Centre Hall and parked. We walked for half a block. A man in his late sixties saw us from across the street and hurried over with an air of surprise and discovery. "You're Punk Morrow!" he said to my father.

They pumped each other's hands in reunion. It was Carl Burkholder, who owned the hardware store. Almost immediately he pulled down his left eyelid and showed a scar. Fifty-four years earlier, he told us, he was in a car accident, and Dr. Morrow had stitched up that eye.

We drifted around Centre Hall all afternoon. When he was a boy, my father told me, he kept a trapline for skunks. He would get up at five in the morning to inspect his traps. He would sell the skins for fifty cents per pelt.

"Once," he said, "I got sprayed. In fact, our school's characteristic smell was skunk. There was always at least one member of the class being sent home to change clothes and bathe."

My father showed me where Mitterling's poolroom had been. He had spent a significant part of his adolescence hanging out there, he said, watching a local bad boy named Spike shoot pool for money. I saw that he cherished the raffish Americana of the memory. "Years later," he said, "I was a newspaperman in Lewisburg,

Pennsylvania, and I was doing the usual police reporting. The
sheriff said, 'There's a fella here says he knows you.' So I went to
visit Spike in jail. He was in for a little dalliance with a local maiden,
an adultery charge, I guess. I walked in and he says, 'Hello, kid.
Got any cigarettes?' I went out and bought him a carton of Camels.
In memory of his great educational services in Mitterling's poolroom."

My father's memories of Centre Hall were light enough: wholesome, small-town, American. But sometimes a peculiar darkness
would play on the story. Perhaps the darkness was merely all the
years that had intervened. Perhaps it involved the way that the
childhood had ended.

My father said that once, Dr. Morrow had a chance to open a
large practice in Baltimore. But he did not. He moved his family
from town to town in central Pennsylvania. He stayed in Centre
Hall through most of the twenties and into the thirties. But when
the Depression came, his patients, never wealthy, could hardly pay
him at all. Dr. Morrow was getting into his sixties.

"Then," my father told me, "a certain Dr. Light appeared in
town. He was young, and new. It was the kind of community
where you needed all the practice you could get in order to make
a living. A lot of Dad's old patients, especially those who owed
him money, flocked to Dr. Light. Dr. Light wiped out Dad's practice. Dad had to pack up and leave. The last thing he did as he
was leaving town was to deliver a baby."

My parents were first cousins once removed. They were still
almost children when they married. He was twenty-one. She was
fifteen. "It was just barely legal, my boy," my father told me with
his jaunty irony.

The details of their marriage remained obscure to me for many
years. There seemed to be something shameful involved. It was
not until they'd been married for ten years or so that my father
bought my mother a wedding ring. The ring was extremely ugly:
white gold worked in a thick pattern.

The shame involved was not pregnancy. There was a different
sort of compulsion involved: my mother's father, Tom Vickers.

All my childhood, my mother referred to her father only as "that monster." He was, I knew, the cause of her epically unhappy childhood. My mother would fall into dark rages about her father, but she never gave details. They came to me over the years like rumors that refugees bring when they struggle out of an unthinkably violent country.

When my mother was born, her father was a prospering steel broker in Pittsburgh. He also traded in plumbing supplies and published the *Plumbing News*. He lived in a mansion in Sewickly. He drove a huge Pierce-Arrow with headlights on the fenders. He bought the car because it was the kind that his hero, Andrew Mellon, owned. Tom Vickers had gardeners and cooks and upstairs maids. He put his money into Citco in the twenties, and he flourished.

His brother was George Vickers, who was my father's grandfather. "As they say in dog-show circles," my father told me, "it was close breeding," but still legal. George Vickers, my father said, was a 350-pound item of Americana. He worked for a time as a journalist. The family lore had it that it was George Vickers who informed Theodore Roosevelt that he was President of the United States; William McKinley had just been assassinated in Buffalo. George Vickers had bought the old *Evening Herald* in Philadelphia, an afternoon paper then deeply in debt. He brought the paper out of the red and then back into it again. The family had that talent for working both sides of the American dream—the handsome success would presently slip into folly and bankruptcy. Perhaps there is some deeply coded family memory of such things. I have always been vaguely haunted by a premonition of American disaster, a fear of failure and disgrace, of the furniture piled on the sidewalk, a life defunct, nowhere to go. George Vickers' brother Tom was to come to that himself eventually.

George Vickers seems to have moved through his life with a portentously rounded nineteenth-century air of bombast. He wrote epic poetry—about the Battle of Gettysburg, for example—which he sometimes published in his newspaper.

I gather that George Vickers liked to drink. He was a diabetic. My father said ruefully that it was from George that he inherited the disease. "It always skips a generation, you know." My father remembered that George Vickers, a massive and stately man, kept a bottle of Old Grand-Dad bourbon on the washstand as he shaved in the morning. When he emerged after shaving, his face would be patched here and there with wads of toilet paper. He had an elaborate chiming pocket watch that seems to have been my father's most vivid memory of him. "A perfect grandfather's watch," my father said.

"If I was emulating anybody," my father said, "I suppose it was my grandfather Vickers. I enjoyed him. He was almost a W. C. Fields character. I guess he was a son of a bitch with the women in the family. He had a literary quality about him—bush-league literary."

My grandfather Tom Vickers had some of the same pretenses, the same slightly theatrical air. He had, in any case, a talent for American tragedies. In 1931 Tom Vickers lost almost everything he had in the catastrophic market. He moved his family out of the Sewickly mansion, into a rooming house in downtown Pittsburgh. That event, that move, was the first primal catastrophe of my mother's childhood. The world she knew disintegrated.

Tom had wanted a boy. He raised my mother in some ways as he would have raised a son. He taught her Shakespeare. He behaved ambiguously sometimes, as if he expected her to become a leader of men. In a way, that is what she was. She was a brilliant child, and willful and spoiled. Her father was, I gather, a flustering American autocrat. When he took her once to a stage production of *Hamlet*, he looked around the theater and loudly demanded, "What are all these people doing here?"

His wife was Hildegarde Wuesthoff. Her family, cosmopolitan, intellectual, came from Alsace-Lorraine. My mother would remember her with a worshipful and stricken face. Her mother was artistic, fragile. She had a romance of some kind, it seems. When Tom learned of the affair, he threw Hildegarde and my mother out of the house. They moved into a rooming house. Disasters compounded. That was the second and crushing event of my mother's childhood.

My father told me, "Tom was a short and stocky man. When

he and Hilda separated, any relative he'd run into, he'd say, 'Have you heard of my tragedy?' He couldn't understand why some of us just burst out laughing."

The tragedy, of course, was not his. He was, I gather, one of those brute narcissists who smash up other people's lives and then moan bitterly, luxuriously, "Why me? Why me?"

Hildegarde's sanity was fragile. Now it broke. Tom had her committed to a state mental hospital. She was diagnosed as a paranoid schizophrenic. In 1945, she died there. Tom Vickers remarried and lived on for years. I never met him. My mother's side of the family was to me a menacing blank.

My parents were married in 1937. It was an odd romance. My father went to visit the Vickers' family in Pittsburgh. His cousin Elise was a precocious adolescent. She was an intellectual, forceful child-woman, I gather. The cousins began a romance. One of my aunts years later told me, "They were a beautiful couple. They were so glamorous, so young and golden."

Tom Vickers learned that they were sleeping together. He had a gift for moralistic dudgeon. He hired a private detective to drive across Pennsylvania to fetch my father and bring him back to Pittsburgh. There he found the irate father and the waiting child-bride. My father made it sound as if he had been brought before the justice of the peace in handcuffs. He said with a heavy ruefulness, "Elise, with a little help from the law, acquired a husband,"

My father was running the Lewisburg, Pennsylvania, news bureau then. He earned about $60 a week. Lewisburg is in Union County, on the north branch of the Susquehanna River, near Sunbury. My father worked as a correspondent in that part of the state for the Associated Press, United Press, International News Service, the Philadelphia *Inquirer*, the Williamsport *Sun*, the Sunbury *Daily* and the Harrisburg *Evening News*. He gave each a separate story on any event in the area that was worth reporting.

My father and mother moved into an apartment on Main Street in Lewisburg, over Hartz Drugstore. My mother remembers the drugstore's lunch room, which had a jukebox. In the evening Glenn Miller and Tommy Dorsey music would drift up from the jukebox to the tiny office-apartment. A year later Hughie was born at Dr.

Morrow's house in Loysburg, Pennsylvania. Dr. Morrow delivered him.

My father started work at the Philadelphia *Inquirer*. I was born, my father told me with a satirical smile, "in a disreputable little hospital favored by abortionists. Right around the corner from our apartment."

It was September 1939. Hitler had marched into Poland earlier in the month.

"I vividly recall my first glimpse of the Infant Lance," my father said. "The nurse brought you and was holding you under a naked light bulb. You were making little snorting and sucking noises. You got the nickname Snuffy."

My father told me, "You looked exactly like Winston Churchill."

They moved into a small country house out in Bucks County. My father had no car. The finance company had repossessed his 1933 Ford cabriolet. It didn't really matter. The wartime gasoline rationing would soon make it hard to use a car anyway. He took a bus and then a subway to commute into Philadelphia. He worked the 2 P.M. to 11 P.M. shift at the *Inquirer*. He came home at two in the morning and slept until almost noon.

My earliest memory is of my father's absence. I stand in the middle of the bare dirt yard in Bucks County, under a tree, and I am alone. The farmhouse is in the background, and a sepia light encroaches upon the edges of the scene. I was, I think, three years old. I look for my father, but cannot move. In my recurring image of myself as a child, I stand like that in the middle of an open space, immobile, under a dark gray sky.

4·A Citizen of Their World

Jung thought that children dream their parents' dreams. Hughie and I dreamed our parents' dreams. We wanted their lives as well. We wanted to take possession of them, to have them, to inhabit them.

They were young and beautiful: Hugh and Elise. They were myths to us. They forever receded from us. They vanished into taxi cabs, into the rainy night.

It was a peculiarity of our childhood, that almost unnatural longing. It was a secret of ours. The family was centrifugal, compulsively fleeing, incoherent, in a literal sense: it would not cohere.

There would be a shattering, like fireworks bursting, and then a subsiding into black space. The universe worked on that psychic model.

The family was covertly violent, and oddly formal. My parents were both writers, and yet a family of dumb beasts could have communicated their emotions more articulately than we did. Words, my parents' professional medium, forever failed. Injury and anger gusted inarticulately through the house. The spirit bore a bruise, a grievance: the bruise was mysterious. It came to us as we slept. We could not explain it, we could not assuage it.

Twice the bruise was actual. The blows were astonishing. In a way they were a kind of relief. In each case the offense was verbal.

My parents were strange about words. They sometimes thought words more powerful, more dangerous than deeds. To my mother, words had primitive force. Books to her were vaguely sacred. That was one thing, at least, that her father had given her. And she taught it to me. The mere presence of books today gives me a pre-rational, sensual comfort. I go to bookstores when I am unhappy. The sight of so many volumes in new bright dust jackets soothes me. I dip into them, browsing and anticipating, and buy, and come home with a sackful, and still draw from them, after so many years, the unmistakable glow of my mother's pleasure, her mystical book-worship. I hear her slightly histrionic voice (a cello playing Elgar, throbbing with certain evening tones) as she reads to Hughie and me from Walt Whitman: "There was a child went forth . . ." A sappy sort of Ben Shahn watercolor decorated the Whitman poem: a stylized American child, a seraphic Tom Sawyer dreamily gazing down upon an American village.

There were elements of fraud there. The reading was a sort of dramatic excess: a certain excess was my mother's style. And Hughie and I were not seraphic, not dreamy. We were borderline savages. We expressed ourselves most vividly by destroying things. We were inventively and relentlessly destructive children. Strangers some-times pronounced us disturbed, in need of psychiatric help. Dead End kids. Sociopaths. My Uncle Bill came back from Europe, from fighting under George Patton. He shook his head at me and Hughie, and said, "Why are you boys so violent?"

We hurled rocks at passing cars. We gouged holes with knives in the living-room walls. We shattered windows. Hughie carried a twenty-pound hunting bow, with which he almost killed a neighbor child one day. Hughie chased the boy, a preacher's son, to his house and fired a hunting arrow after him, through the window in his front door. The preacher came around to our house shaking the arrow in his fist. He told my father that Hughie and I were under the influence of Satan.

Somehow these acts did not communicate much meaning to our parents.

My parents had bought Hughie the bow for Christmas. They also bought him a Gilbert's chemistry set with which he could build little parodies of the atom bomb in the basement—with small, perfect mushroom clouds. I marveled at Hughie's bombs. There, in the basement shadows, halfway between the hot-water heater and the washing machine, there came the flash, and the little smoke mushroom rose and then stretched up into a vertical pillar, with perfect rings around it: a miniature apocalypse. It looked exactly like the vivid rotogravure pictures of the Hiroshima bomb that came in the Sunday *Times-Herald*, wrapped around the comics section.

Once in an especially notable rage during a visit to my grandmother in Baltimore, Hughie and I took an uncle's .22-caliber rifle and live ammunition and barricaded ourselves in Grandmother's bedroom. We loaded the rifle. We pushed a dresser in front of the door. We announced through the door that we were not coming out. We found Grandmother's cold cream and smeared it on our faces like war paint. We were six and seven years old at the time.

Hughie tells me this story at dinner now. As always when we discuss such things, the memory comes to him with an immediacy that I can read in his eyes. It is right there, exactly so in his mind, and I see the sheer wonder he feels at being so suddenly transported back. I search my mind, but I do not remember the incident with the rifle at all. It has vanished from me. Hughie shakes his head at the memory—his hair and beard turned grayish now—and rolls his eyes, and then sighs "Ah, well!" and drains his wineglass.

Hughie went to MIT and studied metallurgy and married twice and had seven children of his own. He has ended up single again and is working in New York. I see him often. Hughie feels the reverberations as often as I. We have sat sometimes at a restaurant in New York for hours and wandered back across the territory of our mutual childhood, a territory that seems to both of us to be haunted and spookily still. The past is always accessible. It is not irretrievable. It is merely irreparable. It left in each of us, and in my younger brothers and sisters as well, a distinctive ache.

But it was not our acts of vandalism that stirred our parents. It was words.

The word "fuck," for example. I learned it one morning in 1945 when I was playing with Bert, an infectiously corrupt seven-year-old in the neighborhood. My family lived in a semiattached house on the outskirts of Washington—the only house my father could find during those years when Washington became the boomtown headquarters of the wartime government.

I was five. Bert and I knelt in the dirt beside Benning Road. We threw his jackknife into a wooden telephone pole. As we withdrew the blade we would pry it sideways to gouge out small chunks of gunky wood that smelled of creosote. Bert taught me "fuck" that day, but without explicit instructions on its use. He employed it mostly as an adjective. He told me to "get the fuckin' knife out of the fuckin' pole."

It seemed to me a word of quality and power. It had a resonance, an adultness even, and a certain swagger that I found irresistible. So I tried it on my father.

We were riding in a Ford convertible that my father had borrowed from a friend. We did not own cars in those days. My father rode around Washington in a procession of borrowed cars, or else he and my mother took cabs. They were always telephoning for cabs (Veterans cabs, Yellow cabs, Diamond cabs), and then pacing around the living room and little hall, waiting for the honk from the curb.

Now we drove in the borrowed convertible down Benning Road toward the center of Washington, along a scruffy boulevard overhung with telephone wires and a lattice of electrical cables for the trolleys. Hughie and I rode in the back seat in silence. My father talked to my Aunt Sally, who sat beside him in the front. As we came to the Anacostia River I remarked loudly, "Hey, look at this fuckin' bridge."

My father wheeled in his seat and regarded me for a split second with surprise. Then he reared back and twisted in his seat, and struck me with a blazing slap on the face.

Sally and Hughie were shocked, and said nothing. I was stubborn, with the child's stoic defiance. We drove another block, past an enormous trolley barn.

"Hey," I said again, "look at all those fuckin' trolleys."

My father wheeled and slapped again, hard. I could feel the clear aftermath outline of his fingers on my cheek.

The silence was longer this time. I do not remember crying. As we drove down Pennsylvania Avenue from the southeast and saw the Capitol ahead, I leaned forward and, articulating each word, said loudly, "Well, there's the fuckin' Capitol."

Sally turned and looked at my father and then at me, with an expression of near-panic on her face. My father seemed confused and thwarted. He behaved now like a man who waves wildly at a bee that returns repeatedly to menace his ear.

He stopped the car, in the middle of Pennsylvania Avenue, stopped it for leverage and emphasis, and turned and slapped me again. My face burned. I finally subsided into shame and silence.

My father never explained why he had slapped me. He resumed driving, toward, I think, the National Press Building, downtown. His profile was impassive as I watched it. He had never hit me before, and he never did so again.

But I'm not sure I understood what was forbidden to whom, and why. Three years later my father stood in our living room in a new house we had moved to, on Mount Pleasant Street. It was early evening. My father had a friend there, with whom he was talking. My father had a drink in his hand, and he gestured with it as he spoke. He looked histrionic. They were talking politics. My father said, "Something's got to be done about this fucking business." Then he saw me and Hughie standing in the doorway, and in his elaborately courtly, satirical voice, raising his glass to us with a half-smile, he said, "Excuse me, boys."

The other word was "nigger." I hate it still. Whenever I hear it, it bounces clattering around my skull like a grenade that someone has tossed into the window.

We had a cleaning woman, a colored woman, as one said then, to watch me and Hughie and take care of the little house on Benning Road.

Bert taught the word to me and Hughie at the same time. Again, the word seemed powerful, with an almost invitingly evil sheen on it, a smack of inexplicable malice that I recall savoring. Hughie and I rushed inside to try it on the cleaning woman.

We found the maid making the bed in my parents' room. We started chanting in a singsong: "Look at the nigger woman making the bed." She looked at us for an instant in disbelief, eyes empty, then on fire. She burst into tears and fled downstairs.

We pursued her, chanting: "Look at the nigger woman running down the stairs!" She fled into the kitchen. She was shocked. We taunted in high, childish malice: "Nigger, nigger, nigger, nigger, nigger, nigger!" Then we ran outside again to play with Bert. The word, we saw, worked well. Amazing.

Bert's father had a strange occupation. He made Purple Hearts. He manufactured the medals that the armed forces pinned on all the wounded boys from Anzio and Normandy and Iwo Jima. Bert that day took me and Hughie to his house. Upstairs, from a metal case in his parents' bedroom closet, he withdrew a beautiful tray of Purple Hearts. They lay in the tray like expensive candy in a box, like sugary lavender mints decoratively attached to bright ribbons. They looked so rich and sweet that I reached out my hand to touch one, to take one. I would have given Bert anything to have a Purple Heart. But he slammed the case shut, and suddenly scared, he replaced the medals in the closet.

When Hughie and I arrived home that afternoon, the cleaning woman was gone. I could feel a change in the air pressure of the house. When we were just inside the door, my mother came at us. She came in a fury, almost demented. Her face was all rage and teeth.

Hughie and I raced down the basement stairs. I hid myself in a small marble-topped cabinet that was stored in the shadowy dark. Hughie sought refuge behind the hot-water heater. From my hiding place, I saw my mother drag Hughie out by his upper arm, his legs and arms windmilling and struggling. She beat and slapped and pummeled him up the stairs, shrieking at him, *"Monster! Monster! Monster!"*

I waited. Then she came screaming after me, and found me and beat me. Her rage felt like the surprising burst of heat from a fire when you open the door to a burning room. She tore me from the marble-topped cabinet where I hid and beat me up the stairs, with wild roundhouse cuffs and swats. I wrenched free and fled across Benning Road into the woods. I stayed there alone, fugitive, hiding out, until long after dark.

It was not a progressive way to teach ethics. On the other hand, I never used the word "nigger" again.

It seemed that Hughie and I could conjure up my parents by sounding vile. That became our tactic. And still they went on resolutely and almost abstractly fading from us. They seemed to appear and disappear clothed in their mythic nimbus, in their utter preoccupation, their eyes fixed somewhere off, elsewhere.

If I could not have my parents' world as completely as I wished, I struggled at least to become an honorary citizen of it. Hughie chose to keep more to his own world, in a dignified exile. I, being younger, abjectly eager to please, set about precociously trying to absorb their culture: their songs, their gestures, their slang, their politics, their prejudices and intonations and favorite words. Once they had beaten the two items of vocabulary out of me, I began to approach language with both an elaborate discretion and a kind of hunger. In any case, the natural cultural transmission and absorption between parents and children, the long, complex process of attraction and repulsion, imitation and rebellion, became in me intensely and unnaturally foreshortened: I rushed to be a parody of them.

The effect could be both funny and slightly haunting, I suppose—something like the sight of a ten-year-old who can light a cigarette exactly the way that Bogart did, squinting, and inhale an expert lungful. When a child manages to assume that air of adult cynicism and élan, then nature is alarmed. A form of moral clowning has occurred. Funny maybe, but a little sinister. (The effect sometimes works in the reverse direction: I once knew a man of forty-five who wore a banker's suit and a homburg, a distinguished gent, except that he was retarded. He had the mind of a four-year-old. His handsome clubman's face would suddenly erupt in an idiot grin. This sport, with the face of an ambassador, drooled like a teething baby. He played with himself on buses.)

I sought my parents' power, their secret, in their gestures. V. S. Naipaul wrote about witnessing the effect in certain former colonies in the Third World. The European, vanished, left behind a complicated and complete idea of a culture, the abstract, the ghost of a culture. But in the hands of the natives to whom it has reverted (is this another way of saying, years later, "Nigger, nigger"?), the culture becomes essentially parodic. They parade around in regimental kilts, to bagpipe music, or sit in the old British club drinking brandy and soda, going "Eh, wot?" and "Jolly good" all afternoon, or else shuffling papers briskly as the white administrators once did, thinking that the sheer shuffling itself was the magic of power and empire.

I became a citizen of that kind in my parents' world. I learned to make their drinks for them. I was good at dry martinis. My mother had picked up a repertoire of Yiddish expressions, which she used because they seemed intellectually stylish. As a result, I gave up "fuck" for a while, and started saying *"Oy vay!"* My father had a way of using French. He would raise his eyebrows in a Gallic way and purse his lips, and with an air of elegant surprise, he would say, *"Zut alors!"* or *"Quelle délicatesse!"* Or (this with a more American air, rolling, satirical and wide-eyed at once): *"Toujours gai, Archie! Toujours gai!"*

I took books out of bookcases in our living room and pretended to read them, rolling my eyes over the texts and making a show every few minutes of getting stuck on a word. I would carry the book to my mother and ask her what the word was. She thought this was adorable. Hughie's face would cloud and blacken with anger. He hated the stunt, and the fond look my mother gave me when I staged it. There was too little of that fondness to go around. Hughie sat in the corner and stared at me with wild black eyes. Heathcliff.

I breathed in their atmosphere: the psychological aftermath of the Depression, my mother's thirties Communism (card-carrying, even) and World War II. I absorbed the touching (if slightly tinny) democratic impulse that caused my father to ride in the front seat of taxis, with the driver, or caused my mother, for a time, to order her taxis only from the Veterans Cab Company.

The earliest intrusion of a public event: I was in Children's Hospital in Washington in 1945, having my tonsils out. I counted back from 100 through the ether fumes and got to 92 . . . When I woke up, my mother and the nurses and nurses' aides were standing and weeping on one another's shoulders. Franklin Roosevelt had just died.

But Washington always had its public contexts. My parents were journalists, writers, and their talk was of public things. I came to see that their ideal of success depended precisely upon the degree to which the public merged with the private: the degree to which their private lives were associated with power, the degree to which they knew its workings and went to dinner with the senators and Cabinet members and ambassadors who held it. Public lives and public power were the medium in which they sought to function.

Years later, when I had two sons of my own, my mother sent to them, quite unexpectedly, an article that *Newsweek* magazine wrote about her in its Press section in the issue of October 6, 1947. At the top of the Xerox copy she wrote, in her distinctive, emphatic penmanship: "Years ago! Your grandma!"

At the top of the article was a wonderful glamour shot of my mother, in her mid-twenties, quite lovely in a forties way, rather haughtily and stagily holding a telephone in her left hand and a pad and pencil in her right. Her eyes are looking sidelong at something offstage. They have almost a flamenco dancer's sexual challenge in them, and her lips are quite red and full. There is something of a Lana Turner quality in the picture. It was startling to see my mother so young and so aggressively sensual. The article began:

> Twice a week the pert and tiny (5 feet ¾ inch) Elise Morrow whips the frosting off Washington's upper crust and lays it bare in "Capital Capers." Three weeks ago, Mordell Features discovered her column in the Philadelphia *Inquirer* and by last week had planted it in the St. Louis *Post-Dispatch* and John S. Knight's four dailies—the Chicago *Daily News*, Detroit *Free Press*, Akron *Beacon-Journal*, and Miami *Herald*.
>
> These news customers are pretty far from the capital's cocktail beat, but the farther the better, Mrs. Morrow believes. Often her column is as much a rib of her society-reporting sisters in Washington as it is of the capital social whirl itself. But few of Mrs. Morrow's colleagues see her stuff. "If they did, I'd be tarred and feathered," she says.

Newsweek quoted some of my mother's prose. She had some wonderful words about the Washington hostess Mrs. Evalyn Walsh McLean: "Swaddled in pink marabou and satin and ostrich feathers, with ropes of diamonds from her wrists to her shoulders, with too much rouge on her face, screaming and crooning by turns, she was absolutely unique." Then *Newsweek* went into my mother's biography:

Mrs. Morrow has been turning out her column for only two years, but has been writing ever since a precocious childhood. Born in Sewickly, Pa., just outside Pittsburgh, in 1922, Mrs. Morrow barely finished the eighth grade, but read voraciously. At 15, she was married to her husband, Hugh, now assistant to the Washington editor of the *Saturday Evening Post*. When she was 16, she and her husband ran a news bureau in Lewisberg, Pa., and after he was offered a job with the Philadelphia *Inquirer*, she stayed behind to handle the bureau.

She quickly created a minor scandal when she tried to expose bad working conditions in a local furniture factory that had just declared a 100 per cent capital-stock dividend. The mayor, the local bank president, and the local editor wouldn't stand for her candor, and Mrs. Morrow and her bureau were run out of town.

Then Hughie and I made an appearance.

For the next two years, she raised her family (two sons, now 7 and 9) in Philadelphia. In 1945, after the Morrows had moved to Washington, her husband went into the Navy. Mrs. Morrow decided to take over his column. *Inquirer* editors were dubious, but she talked the Washington bureau into teletyping an opus with this at the bottom: "Elise Morrow wrote this."

Mrs. Morrow started writing for the *Saturday Evening Post* before her husband joined it. Her first piece was on K. C. Adams, editor of the *United Mine Workers Journal*, and last week with her *Post* story on Springfield, Ill., she became the only woman contributor to the magazine's series on American cities. Her ambitions are to write bigger and better stories about the miners and someday to run for Congress.

She did not accomplish that. My mother had a sometimes intimidatingly powerful mind. Her gifts of observation and recall amazed me. She read hungrily.

She studied with Hannah Arendt for a time. She and my father were long since divorced. She lived in Chicago then, married to a businessman named Robert McCormick. He was one of the Chicago McCormicks and my mother took from him a sort of proprietary sense of the city. The McCormicks were the Rockefellers of Chicago. She enrolled at the Committee on Social Thought at the University of Chicago. She tried to lose that old shame of leaving school when she was fifteen. She took courses with Saul Bellow and read Thucydides and Kant.

In Washington, when I was a child, great issues—the war and its aftermath, politics, elections, chicaneries—flowed through their private conversation, but always discussed in an intimate idiom, a knowing, slightly cynical vocabulary marinated in Scotch and cigarette smoke and the journalist's bonhomie of what they called the Tampax Room (the lounge off the front lobby of the National Press Club where women were permitted to join the men for a drink). Hughie and I belonged to a truly private world that they did not often see, off at the end of Benning Road, next to the Maryland border.

Large events flowed by. Prisoners of war were hauled in open trucks ("POW" stenciled in enormous white letters on their shirts), and their faces were lost and confused but somehow not foreign-looking. At night, while the war was still on, my parents hung blankets over the windows, but even with the blankets up they kept off the lights, and I would feel my way in utter darkness in the middle of the night toward the bathroom.

V-J Day arrived. I absorbed the news, this time, through a thoroughly childish medium. The Kellogg's cornflakes box yielded up a V-J Day button, which Hughie and I took turns wearing. The papers showed the Bomb, and then the triumphant new Pentagon building, miles and miles of corridors, the embodiment of what America had invented to win the war: serious central bureaucracy of the superpower class.

Then they came home. I associate the house on Benning Road with uniforms and disasters.

Down the street lived a houseful of nurses who worked at the Veterans Hospital. On Saturday nights they gave parties. I have a sort of hallucinatory memory of them, the facts of what I actually witnessed mixed up with stories I overheard later from aunts and uncles. From the edge of the nurses' yard, I could watch the early stages of the parties: the house aglow in the early evening, the soldiers and sailors piling out of cabs. Something was wrong with almost all of them: arms or legs gone, a hand missing, a cane, a crutch, a limp. They were loud and a little nihilistically wild when they arrived. They would get drunker, and louder and randier, lurching for the nurses however they could manage. Their wheelchairs made traffic jams.

I was fascinated and terrified. The amputees were grotesques with dangerous resources of hilarity and rage in them. Their drinking and groping were desperate. Through the window, their laughter (muffled by the glass, disembodied), their heads thrown back, their teeth, their vivid uniforms and service stripes and patches, all formed a bright, strange frieze, like an orgy of monsters in an aquarium.

One afternoon a carload of soldiers, probably drunk, went screaming out Benning Road toward the Maryland line, which was just at the top of the hill beyond our house. The car flew out of control. It smashed full speed into an oak tree across the road from our house. Bodies lay everywhere across the grass beneath the oak tree. The bodies were strewn at all angles, in all poses, like the battlefield dead in photographs in *Life*. The car was black and shattered, mashed up against the large, unyielding tree.

The air was filled with an astonishing smell, which came to be, to me, quite distinctly the smell of death: alcohol and motor oil and antifreeze, and a thin, sharp smell I cannot identify. Desperate medicine and blood, I came to think, all the smells of things and people ripped open. Later I always smelled that smell whenever I passed the oak tree and saw the great kidney-shaped scar, the gash in the bark, that the car made when it hit.

From Benning Road, I remember also a sense of terrible and inescapable cold. A Washington winter is not especially harsh. Yet the winters then, or my memory of them, still chills me now when I smell the first Canadian weather coming down in the fall. I own eight parkas and overcoats. They hang in my closet. Certain characters are hereditarily warm. They do not feel the cold. They plunge into the bitterest weather wearing only a jacket and tie.

They came through New England prep school winters with only a scarf wrapped around the neck. Cold always feels to me like abandonment.

The cold I remember was almost metaphysical. Once I was walking alone to school through the woods across Benning Road and then across a large pond. It was utterly frozen, solid. Hughie had gone on ahead of me. I stood in the center of the ice and did not, could not, move. I imagined that my suave and jaunty father must come for me. I almost froze. Hughie turned and came back for me at last. He irritably jerked me off the pond.

Hughie and I proceeded with our lessons in manhood from Bert. Bert's father smoked Pall Malls. He kept cartons of them in his car's glove compartment. Bert would steal them, a pack at a time, and we would withdraw to the woods across Benning Road.

We would huddle in a clearing. Each boy—Bert and Hughie and I—would draw a Pall Mall, one sacramental tube, from the pack that Bert held. Then Bert would cup it in his hands, and we would all three light up at once, puffing up a common cloud in the center of our circle.

When I tried to inhale, my five-year-old lungs of course recoiled. I came home from smoking rituals very green and sick. But we persisted. When Bert's father discovered the cigarette thefts and locked up his cartons, we smoked "Indian cigars," the pods of a tree that grew in those woods. Or we tore up brown grocery bags and twisted the pieces into cigar shapes and lit one end, which smoldered like a smudge pot or else flared and threatened to set our hair on fire.

I loved the glamour of my father's smoking. He smoked Camels, endlessly, one after another. The wondrous blue smoke that curled up from him, that swirled around him, that shot in twin jets from his nostrils or else popped from his mouth in staccato bursts as he talked after inhaling—that smoke was part of his essence. His incense. I always thought the smoke smelled lovely, when it came from his cigarette. Yet when I smoked one myself, it tasted quite different. It then became dangerously internal, part of me, a poison inside. My body hated it. But emulation was stronger than revulsion. I kept at the cigarettes and homemade cigars for months.

Their allure as a prop of manhood was powerful. I saw myself as my father when I smoked.

My father went away. Because he was in his mid-twenties and married, with two children, the draft board did not call him until fairly late in the war—1944. He joined the Navy. Because of his age, the eighteen- and nineteen-year-old kids at the Great Lakes Naval Training Station called him "Pops" or "the Old Man." The Navy offered him a chance to go overseas, to see combat even. But he had a good job editing a Navy newspaper in the Loop and decided to wait out the war there. He had friends in Chicago—newspaper reporters, photographers, people to drink with.

Just at the end of the war, I started kindergarten. The first day, my mother escorted me there—to a long, low, prefabricated building recently erected on the far side of our smoking woods. My mother wept over her "baby" leaving home. It was the only time she took me to school, however. Hughie usually did that.

I remember nothing of the inside of the school. Only that I wanted to be out, to be playing guns, to be talking sex with Hughie and Bert and some of the older boys. They all possessed the usual precocious and preposterous wealth of information and mythology on the subject. One lean nine-year-old reported back from somewhere with an item of anthropology about cock-sucking. It was actually done, he said. The thing went into someone's mouth. They sucked it. Dares began. One boy said he was not afraid to do it. But not now. He would do it Saturday morning, in the woods. We wondered for several days if he actually would. Saturday came. The tribe filed into the trees for the solemn occasion. The designated boy brought out his penis, small and red, and the other boy beheld it, and shrank back himself. Everyone waited. The dare had been made, accepted. So the boy who had accepted the dare crouchingly advanced. He opened his mouth with an agony of fastidious care. With a peculiar darting of the head, like a fish ambivalently going for bait of which it is (justly) suspicious, the boy made an instant's contact with the other's penis, and then almost reeled backward, wiping his lips in disgust. The dare had been satisfied. Honor had been redeemed. But the boy had gotten off on a technicality.

. . .

The cleaning woman whom we had so injured never came back. She was replaced by a younger, vaguely dangerous woman. We would never have called her nigger. Arlene had a boyfriend who was in jail. One day he called her and said he was out. He was coming to get her with a knife. My father, of course, was away in the Navy. Arlene sat in the kitchen and cried. My mother was genuinely afraid. It was the first time I had seen such a vulnerability in her, the first time it had occurred to me that her rage might sometimes fail her and leave her defenseless. I was confused and thrilled to learn that.

Hughie had the wit to be frightened. I leaped into a show of male swagger: I seized a Coke bottle and announced that if that son of a bitch showed up at our front door, I was going to cave in his skull. Hughie gave me that black, despairing stare of his again. The boyfriend never came.

Money was one of the central controversies of my parents' marriage. Neither of my parents seemed to know that money could be saved, could be managed, that investment could make it organic and induce it to grow. They were infantile with money. When it came, it was like a holiday, and the money would be spent as rapidly as possible. They were extravagant and improvident, like some tribe that makes a spectacular kill and feasts for a day and a night, gorging on the animal, and lays nothing by against the longer haul. It was as if they had some faulty conception of the future, some incapacity to imagine that more days were in prospect down the line. They lived at the mercy of nature, financially naked: aborigines.

One morning when the mail came, my mother shrieked—in pleasure, this time. It was a check from the *Saturday Evening Post* for $500. She had sold her first freelance article. She cashed the check at the bank and came back with five $100 bills, which she flourished, fanned out in her hand like a royal flush. She had made a kill. We would feast. She took me and Hughie to Best & Co. and bought us clothes.

I am chastened now to realize, again, how young she was—twenty or twenty-one. Elise and Hugh in those days must have lived a good deal on their élan and energy and nerves and youth and panic and confusion and a certain amount of alcohol.

In those days, I was deviled by a feeling of nonentity. I was outraged by a sense of insignificance, of unworthiness.

I began to wish to be Jewish. A Jewish family next door took Hughie and me in. They saw that we were in business for ourselves. They let us wander in and out of their house, silently, most of the time, wondering at the strange flavor of the place. The grandmother was a shriveled *baba* out of old Russia who drank dark tea from a glass and spoke only Yiddish. She looked at me with a complex gaze that mixed her affection for children, her pity for us, and her suspicion of goyim. The language of the house was Anglo-Yiddish, spoken in New York accents, mostly. But the family possessed a wonderful directness of spirit, a readiness of affection that was unprecedented. In the house I knew, emotions were sidelong and somehow wounded. They were kept resolutely, nervously hidden, most of the time, lest they burst into flames, lest they come screaming out of the black box and kill us all.

Hughie and I regarded emotions as mortally dangerous. The Jewish family did not. They were demonstrative and vivid. They looked right into our eyes and told us we were hungry and made us eat. They touched us. They ruffled our hair. They squeezed our cheeks. This was unheard of. Hughie and I flinched a little at such unthinkable intimacies, but we always returned gratefully to them. Eventually one of the household, Jeanette Simon, married my Uncle Chris. Jeanette was exuberant and direct, and perfect for the Morrow male she married.

My father finally came home from the Navy. My mother and Hughie and I went down to Union Station to meet him. There he was, stepping along the track through the spurting train steam (an image out of a movie of the time). He swung his sea bag, looked lithe and heroic, heroic and faintly ridiculous in a sailor's uniform, with the square front fly-flap on the trousers and the small-boy's sailor cape and the bright white sailor's beanie, with the brim flexed and dented just so on the sides.

I had never been happier. My father was home. He had brought me and Hughie each a bagful of uniform patches—badges of service and rank. Their threads had an opulent military gloss. The war had been on for all of my life. I had been born just after Hitler marched into Poland in 1939. My entire childish world had been filled and formed by the war.

I remembered Aunt Sally and Aunt Virginia singing a ballad called "Roger Young" (". . . stands the name, Roger Young,/ Fought and died for the men he marched among") about a hero who died in the Solomons. Uncle Bill had gone to France. Uncle Rowland landed at Anzio. Uncle Chris wore a Navy uniform just like my father's. We'd saved coffee cans full of bacon grease and turned them in at the grocery store down the road. Almost all of the men I'd seen all of my life wore uniforms. The uniform patches that my father brought home to me were badges of membership in his world.

All the way home out Pennsylvania Avenue I stroked my bright patches, my heart jumping. The cab arrived and stopped across Benning Road from our house. I leaped from the cab. I ran around the front of the cab and started across Benning Road. I heard my mother scream.

After that, nothing. Today, almost the most vivid image in my memory is the ring of faces to which I awoke that morning on Benning Road. They were in a perfect circle, standing over me as I lay on the roadside gravel. Each face wore precisely the same expression: utter suspension, just at the edge of fear and curiosity. There was a sort of Norman Rockwell sweetness in the scene: an American anecdote.

I had been hit—hit hard—by a car going about 40 miles per hour. The woman driving the car had considered going on—hit and run. She drove on for several hundred yards before she stopped. She fought with her conscience in that space. She thought she had killed. She almost had. But the fender of her Chrysler (that bright, carnivorous grin of chrome) had hit me at a lucky angle. I woke up to that ring of faces.

I began to imagine, at the age of five, that I was immortal.

5·Charles Creek

I carry fixed in my memory the image of my father's borrowed blue Nash sedan disappearing down a dirt road in southern Maryland in the summer of 1949. Scrub-pine trees line the sides of the road. Here and there the ruts and dips of the road have been repaired with a fill of oyster shells that crackle under the car's tires.

Now the dust rises as the Nash—Hilda Cloud's Nash, a 1942 model, light blue, with rounded lines, like a robin's egg—goes quickly down the long, straight road. I watch the blue cartop clipping along just above the stunted pines, followed by its whitish dust plume. Then the car is gone.

The July afternoon is densely still. The long line of dust cloud that my father made hangs for a little while in the air, and then it almost imperceptibly thins and drifts away and vanishes.

We came to southern Maryland that summer—Hughie and I and Aunt Sally, who was then nineteen—to a remote point in Charles Creek, on the western shore of Chesapeake Bay. The cottage we stayed in was owned by one of my father's friends. No longer married, he never seemed to use the cottage anymore. It sat near a clump of trees beside a large plowed field. The cottage contained two tiny bedrooms and a living room and a screened porch. It was set in the middle of an overgrown lawn. Once or twice a summer Henry, the tenant farmer on the property, hitched his white plowhorse to a grass mower and clattered over to the house to saw down some of the shaggier grass.

But the place was unmistakably headed toward abandonment.

In the lawn not far from the house, so thickly surrounded by the encroaching grass that it was invisible from twenty feet away, lay a ten-foot by fifteen-foot swimming pool. It was empty. Weeds grew through its cracked concrete, which was painted a chipping, chalky blue.

The first time I came to the place, I started running toward the creek, which was visible through a low stand of trees a hundred yards beyond the house. I almost fell into the empty pool. When I saw it, I was struck by the sadness of it, by its air of ruin. But perhaps that is merely memory being melodramatic. I now imagine that I visualized earlier summers there: the lawn trimmed, the people down from Washington stretched out on the short grass, or sitting around the edge of the pool in bathing suits on summer afternoons, drinking. I think that I wondered if there would have been women there. The place was now suffused with an air of aftermath and even, obscurely, of emotional wreckage.

I had a precocious sense of such things, at any rate, a sense that was part of my childish effort to absorb the terms and textures of my parents' world. I did sense that the house at Charles Creek was a bit of the rubble left by a divorce, some ugly, wounding business now past.

My father had borrowed those ruins in order to get his children out of Washington for the summer. The vacation was not designed primarily for our benefit, Hughie's and mine. My mother wanted us gone. She told my father she could not cope with us, with her life, with everything. We went down to Charles Creek with a jumping sense of the adventure and, at the same time, a sharp ache of banishment.

We had no electricity or running water. We pumped up our water—from a rusty hand pump fifty yards from the house. We kept our perishable food (a stick of butter, a pound of hot dogs, bologna, a loaf of bread, mayonnaise, half a dozen eggs) in a small turn-of-the-century cabinet icebox, blond wood and white porcelain, that stood, as if just evicted, on the ground beside the water pump. The ice blocks we brought from Billy's roadhouse several miles away melted within three or four days. As the week wore on, our food in the icebox grew warmer. The bread and hot dogs developed molds. The morning would come, Thursday or Friday, when the food was inedible. I would come down from the house in the cool of the morning and unclasp the icebox door and find the temperature inside warmer than out, and our food fringed with little diseases of spoilage.

There were no grocery stores for miles. Every Saturday morning my father drove down from Washington with a load of supplies. On those days, as early as eight in the morning, Hughie and I walked down the dirt-and-oyster-shell road to the blacktop. Sometimes the shells cut our bare feet. We climbed a pine tree and sat in its branches for three hours or more, waiting for the blue Nash.

No traffic passed—nothing except sometimes a pickup truck laboring west into the countryside with a load of oysters from Charles Point. Hughie and I waited, our eyes fixed on the bend in the blacktop that would eventually reveal my father. Then we would scramble tumblingly down from the branches and pile into the blue Nash, and my father would drive slowly up the dirt road toward the cottage.

But he stayed for only a short time. An hour maybe. He needed to get back to Washington. One day we unloaded the bags of groceries (hot dogs, Ritz crackers, mayonnaise, bread, milk, tuna fish, Fig Newtons, eggs, potatoes) and he said goodbye almost at once and drove away.

The owner of the cottage seemed to have been a gambler. Hughie once told me that the man liked to light cigars with $5 bills. Then Hughie told me that he once used a twenty to wipe himself. I did not ask Hughie where he had learned this, but somehow the gestures fit my idea of the character. He also liked to take fistfuls of dimes and toss them to the tenant farmer's children, the pickaninnies, as he called them. The children would scramble for the dimes in the dirt.

I imagined that the owner was fat and drank too much. His breath, I thought, would smell of whiskey. His fingers would be yellow from tobacco. His cottage, a white wooden frame structure outside, was lined inside with a fluted dark wood that was a color two shades darker than bourbon. The centerpiece of the furniture was a large round poker table covered with green felt, its perimeter outfitted with trays for chips and sockets to hold each player's glass. The chairs were worn brown wicker. Decks of cards and poker chips—red, white and blue—were strewn around the room. The overall effect was gloomily masculine, with a muzzed intimation of the alcoholic, of failed and forlorn carousal.

I sometimes wondered who had come to Charles Creek: more Press Club gamblers and drinkers, undoubtedly, the owner's cronies. All of those characters of my father's generation would describe themselves, at any given time, as being either "on the wagon" or "off the wagon." The distinction was a comprehensively descriptive shorthand. By knowing whether a man was on or off, you could infer most of what you needed to know about how he felt and how he might behave. I later came to be mildly amazed by the enthusiastic lack of embarrassment with which my father's friends discussed their drinking. The knights of the Press Club bar took a binary view of the world: a man was either drinking or not drinking. The distinction was meaningful, significant even, but morally neutral. My father used to savor a story about one Press Club drinker of heroic reputation. A young member entered the Press Club bar one afternoon and found the great boozer drinking a glass of beer. The young man asked, "Well, Charley, you tapering off?" The old man glared and replied, "No, tapering on!" My father told the story with an odd relish, tilting his head back to mimic the man's defiant and even dignified folly.

One Saturday when he brought the groceries to Charles Creek, my father stayed. That night, after dinner, we lit the coal-oil lamp that hung over the poker table, and my father undertook to explain to his sons how to play the game. Hughie and I were enthralled. My father liked to handle cards with a faintly satirical svelteness; he would abruptly and smoothly fan them in his hands, then with the magician's flourish of pinkies and air of elaborate innocence, he would sweep them into a neat little stack again and reach down to his pile of chips, and offer his bet to the pot in a little fluster of self-deprecation. I loved all of this. When queens showed in a hand of stud, he would chime with a sort of burlesque surprise, "What's this!? A pair of ladies!?"

That night Hughie and I learned all the hierarchies of poker, the ascending authority of pairs and three of a kind and full house and four of a kind. We learned to call the threes "treys" and the twos "deuces." We discovered that some jacks have only one eye. That aces and eights is a "dead man's hand," with a historical footnote about how Wild Bill Hickok was holding that hand the night he was killed in a saloon in Deadwood, South Dakota. (It is an oddity of recall that tonight as I write this in New York City, three decades later, the exact date of Hickok's death drifts back to me—August 2, 1876—and the name of the man who shot him, Jack McCall.)

We stayed up half the night playing five-card draw and five-card stud and seven-card stud. The brown room glowed dimly and smelled of coal oil. An item of insect night life now and then flew into the lamp's chimney and perished there, sometimes with a small sharp crack of detonating carapace, but more often in a moth-wing wilting, shriveling silence, exquisitely remote, an inaudible extinction like the death of a star.

As the hours of the night passed, the air in the cottage hazed and blued with the smoke from my father's Camels. The butts accumulated in white, ashy mounds in the tin-dish ashtray at his elbow. My father's cigarette smoke sometimes gave me a headache, but tonight it did not. The round poker table, the cigarette smoke, the coal-oil lamp, the chinking poker chips, the pattering card-game monologue that my father maintained ("ten-a-clubs, no help . . . pair-a-jacks . . . dealer bets five . . ."), the sharp and faintly debauched smells of the house (spilled drinks, a bitter varnish, long saturations of cigar smoke in the furniture, something unshaven in the air of the place)—all seemed to my nine-year-old sense of manhood a ceremony of welcome into the world my father inhabited.

I loved the way he lit a cigarette: he struck the match and squinted and cupped both hands like a sailor in a high wind, like a man intently bent on performing some hasty, dangerous task upon which a great deal depended. Grace under pressure. It took only, say, three seconds, but the abrupt concentration of the act always amazed me. All thought and conversation were suspended until it was accomplished, with a smooth blue exhalation. Then the game resumed.

Years later I played poker in the middle of the night in a farmhouse in Kansas. I thought of my Saturday night game with my father on Charles Creek. I had come out to Kansas to go dove-shooting with a friend from Harvard, Wayne Nichols. I was infatuated with Wayne's sister—with his entire family, in fact. Wayne's grandfather, J. C. Nichols, had been a minor American entrepreneurial genius. In the twenties, foreseeing the change that the automobile would bring, he built the first American shopping center, the Country Club Plaza in Kansas City. It was, as shopping centers go, a remarkably elegant affair: reconstructed fountains from Spain, expensive European tiles on the walls which later, in other suburban malls, would be gaudily decorated with plastic logos. Something in me was drawn to the Nichols' Midwestern solidity (as I imagined it), to their roots in the place. They seemed armored and safe and coherent in ways that my family had not been. For a time, I wistfully courted them.

Out west of Kansas City, in the countryside near Olathe, they kept an old farm. When we went dove-shooting there, we slept in a low, dark Quonset lodge, all one room, outfitted with a kitchen and a primitive bar and half a dozen double-decker bunks.

We played poker all night. I was nineteen then. I lost all night, smoking and drinking and playing for dimes and quarters, and borrowing more.

The game left me broke and tired. At dawn I walked out into a lovely blue Kansas light. I thought of my father and the game that night at Charles Creek: my father's bets, his sweet ceremonial presence there with Hughie and me in the middle of the night, in that remote glow, his voice, something lost. A sudden sense of bereavement came up. I looked back at the Quonset. Through the window I saw the other players, three of them now, still playing, though slow-motion, in a clustered glow, huddled over their chips and the round green table. It seemed to me I was outside the cottage at Charles Creek, in the cold dawn, and the ceremony went on, with different players, and I was excluded from it.

That day in Kansas I shot a dragonfly. I stood with Wayne's sister by the pond, in the morning before the dove-shooting. I held a Browning 12-gauge over-and-under shotgun, and in an abrupt fury I aimed at an air-skittering blue dragonfly four feet away and fired, and obliterated it from the clean late-summer morning air.

"Well," said Wayne's sister. "You're quite a hunter."

We walked out along the country roads for several miles, half a dozen of us strung out in a line, watching for the doves that look like musical notes as they sit on the telephone wires, and then leap off in their dodging, erratic flight that makes shooting them the equivalent of getting a hit off a good knuckleball pitcher. In a mean, destructive mood, I blew a rain crow out of a tree where it was perched. I liked the gunblast, the kick, the bruise on my shoulder, the smell of powder. I was ashamed of myself. I let the rain crow fall into the brush, and I hurried away.

I got no doves. Toward afternoon I walked with Wayne along a fenceline, our shotguns on safety. I felt low and exhausted. We suddenly flushed quail: a flustering explosion of feathers thirty feet ahead. They flew a radical angle toward the right. I snapped the shotgun off safety, aimed at one bird, swiveling my barrel to follow its flight. I pivoted, watching the bird, until my muzzle had swung almost in Wayne's face, and then I fired, and he felt the blast go by his nose so close that had I not jerked back the gun for one thousandth of a second before the trigger-finger's spasm, his entire head would have been gone. Neither of us spoke. We stood in the road not looking at each other. We never discussed that gunshot, ever.

Years would pass before I went hunting for doves again. Then one early fall when my first son, Jamie, was seven, I took him out to West Texas with me when I was working on a story for *Time* magazine. A rancher I knew, Joe Mertz, invited us to go dove-shooting. We drove out across the range, among the mesquite, just before sunset. The air was sweet and cool and utterly clear; still in daylight, there was a full moon in the eastern sky, as clean as a dime.

We installed ourselves beside a large pond where the cattle came to water. Joe Mertz walked to the other side. Jamie and I waited beside a stand of mesquite. We waited in a lovely silence until doves began skittering in for an evening drink. They came singly, or in pairs. Joe Mertz took the first one. We could not see him through the mesquite, but heard his 12-gauge booming, and saw the birds crumple and tumble down.

Then two doves knuckleballed in on my side of the pond. I lifted the shotgun, a 20-gauge, and knocked one down. The bird fell with the sudden weight of lifelessness, into a black tangle of mesquite that had been burned over. Jamie watched this with a sudden delight and wonderment. He had never seen a life shot down like that, just picked out of the air and canceled. I saw in his eyes a gruesome childish male pleasure at the spectacle of shooting and killing something. I could see that the shooting struck him as handsomely final and efficacious: the way that a man ought to do business.

Later, after I had knocked down seven or eight birds, I went out to collect them. One bird lay on the range grass, bleeding and still alive. I picked him up, ashamed of myself. I would have to knock his head against a tree to finish him. Jamie stood at my elbow, and watched me. I turned my back to him, concealing the soft bleeding gray bird from him. He moved around to see. I asked him to move away, but he would not. I walked to the tree and whacked the bird's head twice against it, and he died, messily, at last. Jamie watched all this with the cruel and matter-of-fact eye of a child. I could see that he admired me for the business.

I stood among a litter of spent shotgun shells. I asked Jamie if he wanted to fire the gun. The sunlight had faded off to a clear red glow to the west, and the light of the full moon had begun to mingle with it. I propped up a target, a thick stick of wood, in some mesquite, and then held the 20-gauge against Jamie's shoulder as he aimed. The gun kicked him hard, the target vanished. Across Jamie's face there dawned a look of the initiate, a fierce little illumination of his masculinity.

The game that night at Charles Creek ended in a drowse of happiness. Hughie and I fell into our sleeping bags well past midnight and slept late in the morning. At breakfast my father was still in the spirit of the night before. He greeted us with the bombastic dignity of the confidence man: "Mornin', boys. Would you care for a game of chance? Would you like to examine the books of the Black Pussycat Café?"

That was always a favorite Fields line. Hughie and I will repeat it now, years later, imitating our father's voice imitating Fields. We will recite it, for no reason in particular, in the middle of the third or fourth glass of wine, intending it, I guess, as a vague homage to our father and, in a buried but quite specific way, to that poker game in southern Maryland in 1949.

That morning my father, in his good spirits, also sang with great drooping baritone mock solemnity some Press Club drinking buddy's version, derived from the Great Depression, of "The Song of the Volga Boatmen":

> They say, we are Cossacks,
> But those are not the facts.
> We are creditors
> of Goldman Sachs.
> We put our money in the goddamned trust.
> All of a sudden that old trust went bust.
> Caught with our pants down,
> caught with our pants down.
> Phooeee, phooeee, Goldman Sachs.

He warmed to it. He sang his version of "Deutschland Über Alles":

> Life presents a gloomy picture,
> dark and dismal as the tomb.
> Father has an anal stricture
> Mother has a fallen womb.
> Uncle Hans was just deported
> for a homosexual crime,
> and the housemaid's just aborted
> for the forty-second time.

My father told me years later that a writer friend of his had learned the song from the President of Panama during a night of carousing. I taught the song to Jamie, and we sing it sometimes on long car trips.

In 1949, Hughie and I did not understand the lyrics very well. The fact that they were vaguely dirty, in some sophisticated and even clinical way, and the fact that he sang them for *us*, gesturing operatically, made us lavishly grateful.

But then we had breakfast, and then he was gone. The irony that he used on us, even to say goodbye, suddenly came to seem an infuriating instrument with which to keep us at bay until he made his getaway.

"Well, my boys," he said, still in the part, "remember what your old dad has told you." And he laid a hand on our heads in a Micawber benison. We stood in the thick grass beside the car in the hazed and entirely empty Sunday morning. I felt a sharp panic of anticipation and inevitability. Something would be taken away. Then he got into the Nash and turned it around on the dirt road, and drove away.

I felt like an exile from their lives. I lay for hours in the grass beside the empty, ruined swimming pool and watched the clouds passing. I was acutely, precociously aware of the passage of time. Time seemed to me even then a vast and unthinkable tragedy. It was not that I thought of death. No one in our family had died within my lifetime. Death had no concrete meaning or menace to me. What I seemed afflicted by was a vague, heartbroken sense of the inexorable. I even took a certain melodramatic pleasure in all of this faintly Slavic sadness. Lying in the grass, I watched the banks of cumulus clouds riding distantly by, and I imagined myself forsaken.

Twenty feet away, Aunt Sally lay sunning herself in her jeans and bra, her eyes dreamily closed in a sunbathing obliviousness that I found incomprehensible. She was not asleep. But her face was still, serene. She had my father's face, the Morrow nose, turned to the sun now, but blond hair, like my grandmother's when she was young. She could not be thinking. A grasshopper made its way in two leaps across her bra. She frowned and brushed herself vaguely, but did not open her eyes. I rose in disgust and headed down the road to find my brother and Charles.

Charles was ten years old, Hughie's age, the second of the tenant farmer's seven children. Charles was large for his age, larger than Hughie. He insisted that his dimensions were exactly right to be a jockey. He assumed, without much conviction, that he would not grow any larger, for that would spoil things. He even smoked cigarettes to stunt his growth.

Charles was forever slapping the back of his thighs with his hands to make the sound of a horse galloping. He made himself canter from place to place. He reined himself in with a "Whoa!" and a backjerk of the head when he arrived somewhere after a gallop.

He had a real horse, or his father did—a white mare named, for some reason, Bill. Bill was a squat, phlegmatic, long-suffering animal built low to the ground. She seemed most at peace with the world trudging up and down Henry's small tobacco field before a hand plow. When the farmer set us to plowing, Charles and Hughie and I complicated Bill's work. One of us would grip the handles of the plow and try to guide it in a more or less straight furrow. Another would hold Bill's reins and walk diagonally behind her, like a water skier slow-motioning in the pluming dust. (Normally, the farmer simply looped the reins behind his back while he guided the plow with his hands.) And the third got to ride on the broad swaying table of Bill's back.

When Bill was unhitched and padded stolidly toward the pasture behind Henry's house, Charles would leap aboard and crouch in the aggressive fetal tuck of the jockey. He dug his heels into Bill's flanks and hammered them dat-dat-dat-dat-dat-dat as he clutched the mane and bent low forward and urgently whispered, " 'Mon, mare, 'mon, mare!" into Bill's ear. At last Bill would break lumberingly into a trot and even, if Charles badgered her enough, into the brief halumpf-halumpf-halumpf of a gallop. At those moments, Charles's fantasy took off. His eye gleamed wildly. His body was all tucked into a black capsule, a bullet, atop the smooth white acreage of Bill.

When she slowed to trotting, the illusion died, for the jockey then began to bounce uncontrollably, in a rapid rallentando, and he might end with his body sliding ignominiously off one side with no hold on the horse but his handfuls of mane. Bill was too old for this. She took it with a grandmotherly forbearance, but sensed that it was undignified.

Bill was our only transportation. Every morning, Charles and Hughie and I mounted her, one behind the other, all three, and rode her at a walk to Billy's roadhouse, to place our penny bets on the numbers.

The journey could begin only after a morning ritual of numerology. Leona was Henry's wife—a large, kind woman of considerable force. She, Aunt Sally, Charles, Hughie and I would sit on the porch of their unpainted two-story farmhouse, with its dirt yard and its chickens, and contemplate our bets. Leona sat massively in a straight-backed chair. Her children hung from her and snuggled to her like puppies. She sat abstracted, and considered.

She had not bet her sister's birthday for six months. She might try that again. That particular sister carried luck in the numbers. Several years earlier, she had hit, and come home with more than $600. The memory of that win would legitimize the daily playing in Leona's family for years to come.

Aunt Sally chose her number. I chose. Hughie chose. Charles worked by a complex formula that involved his own birthday in relation to the present day of the month. As we chose our numbers we wrote them with a stubby pencil on a piece of notebook paper. Charles folded it and placed it in his pocket, along with the sums bet—usually four or five pennies each. Then we set out for Billy's.

The errand could consume the better part of a morning. It was a slow plod, sweetly rolling in our loose conversational jounce on Bill's back, the three of us rocking with our easy separate motions, like three camel riders on the same beast. The journey took us through the low-standing scrub-pine woods, past a small lumber mill long since abandoned and left, dark gray boards in the evergreen woods, to rot and tumble apart.

Past the mill, a deserted black sedan sat in a small clearing. It rested on its axles, which were vanishing now into moss. Its windows were all gone. The back door was open. I was troubled by the ghost of the idea that the door had been opened for someone, a woman, and that it now waited to be closed—there was a sort of haunted incompleteness there. I could see the seat cushions, their fabric rotted away, and the springs poking out here and there, rusted brown.

One day Charles and I, prowling through the woods, pretended that the car was a tank full of Japs. We crept up to toss a grenade inside. Charles made the sweeping motion of the grenade lob, his arm going through the window and into the car, and as he did so, a black snake exploded from the seat and struck at his arm—the black rope suspended in midair.

I was impressed that Charles, when he fled, even faster than I, was still jockey enough to slap his thigh as he galloped away.

When the three of us on Bill came to the end of the dirt road, we turned right, onto the asphalt state road. The pine woods beside the road were taller now. Keeping to the gravelly shoulder, we rocked along toward Billy's. Sometimes we stopped at a still, brown pond in the woods, a little off the road. The side of the pond served as the garbage dump for Billy's. Henry, who earned a dollar or drinks by hauling away the roadhouse's empty bottles in his wagon, would bring them here. Giant Henry would stand in the back of the wagon and with his shovel cascade out hundreds of dark brown National Bohemian beer bottles, Four Roses and Seagram's and I. W. Harper, all clattering and smashing down the pond bank, which was now itself a dark junkish slope of defunct bottles. The water in the scummy, still pond must have approached 50 proof.

When we stopped there, Charles and Hughie and I sometimes hunted for toads. Out of sheer bucolic malice, we hurled beer bottles at them. We always missed. Charles said you had to get them with a long flat board.

When we came to Billy's, we tied up Bill to a pine and entered by the door for "Colored." Charles handled the money. He stood stoically at the tiny window, cut in the wall, that opened to the back of the bar. Through this window, with its small counter, Billy served his black customers.

The colored section was the back room of the roadhouse, a slummy but somehow comfortable place with a few tables and straight chairs, all worn, unpainted, brownish-gray. Its only brightness radiated from the jukebox, a Seaborg which lighted with a bubbling glow of rainbow colors, one of those unexpected American fantasies, a kind of miracle, a small extravagant Christmas in the corner of the nigger bar.

The jukebox was dark in the mornings when we came to bet the numbers. Bright sunlight shot through one window but left the rest of the colored room in shadows, the dust motes hanging in the air. The room had a sour morning-after smell of beer and cigarettes. Chairs stood upended on tables. Hughie and I hung in the shadows. Billy let Charles stand for a time—the racially significant time. The small schedules of humiliation were coded into Southerners, the precise time necessary to establish who was boss. Did Charles have to wait longer because he was a child? I doubt it. It was his blackness that must wait, not his youth.

At last Billy, a balding man with a pencil-thin mustache, a sort of redneck Bud Abbott, would saunter to his colored window and say, "Bettin', boy?"

Charles would say "Yessuh!" and push his accumulation of pennies and his betting slip toward Billy. Billy would snort, but he would ceremoniously accept the bets and then vanish from the serving window. Charles would turn with a certain triumph and lead us back toward the horse.

"Today's my day," Charles said every morning. "I know today's my day."

Hughie and I spent all of our days with Charles. After several weeks on Charles Creek we began spending our nights with him as well. Henry and Leona took us in. If they looked at us at first as proprietary whites come to occupy the owner's cottage and therefore suspect and worth treating carefully, they saw before long that we were as angry and unhappy as orphans there. We began eating our dinners with Charles and his family, usually after our own week's supply had gone bad.

Leona made us welcome. She set a coal-oil lamp in the middle of her dining-room table. With some formality she ladled out the dinner: a lumpy and sweetly delicious concoction of kidney beans cooked in a thick soup of sugar.

We sat in the evenings in Henry and Leona's living room reading the Montgomery Ward catalogue. We joined Charles in dreaming moonily over the pages that advertised cowboy boots. Charles was almost unhinged on the subject. He needed those boots. The Montgomery Ward catalogue became a sort of encyclopedia of his longings. He would dream over it, and Hughie and I would enter into the dream, the three of us turning the pages under the coal-oil lamp: "Man, I sho' would like that pair. Ummm!"

As we did this, the smaller children stood silent just outside the round primary glow of the lamp, and when I looked at them in their private little shadows, their faces regarded me with a solemn, peering, mute intelligence.

Henry and Leona accepted us with a grace that impresses me still, after thirty years. Leona fed and protected us. We loved her with a spontaneous, instinctive reciprocity.

In that isolation on Charles Creek, no one else knew about us. It seems odd to me now, but we knew no neighbors. From the owner's cottage, we saw no other houses—only, in one direction, the creek, and in the other, a wide expanse of tobacco field, a line of trees, and in the distance, the tenants' house, Henry and Leona's, standing up harshly and matter-of-factly in the flatness.

We settled into their family and its routines. We pumped water for them and used their outhouse. Once when Charles's teen-age sister Margaret was preparing herself for a date, she sat on the porch in a straight-backed chair, and Leona used pomades and red-hot curling irons to sculpt her wiry hair. It seemed to crackle. I was fascinated by the smell of that singed hair and by Margaret's sweet stoicism. I tensed to watch those hot irons twisting through her hair, so close to the skull. It seemed a strange enterprise, like combing one's hair with an acetylene torch. But Margaret sat with a patient, expectant look on her face. Leona bustled about her with a massive concentration.

Early one morning, a Sunday, Leona announced that we would visit her great-grandmother. We would take the skiff that was kept tied to the tumbledown dock near the owner's cottage.

Leona settled into the stern seat with two small children. Charles and I rowed. Hughie and Margaret sat in the bow. The skiff, with its erratically thunking oars, slid wanderingly out into the creek.

The "creek" was one of those many estuarial fingers that reach inland from Chesapeake Bay. The network of them is vast and complicated, and the waters both shallow and quite broad in places. In summer the bay is liable to abrupt, violent storms. The sky turns an ominous copper color and grows still. Then a black squall bangs down.

The air as Charles and I rowed that morning was the more usual moist bright Chesapeake haze, the windless midsummer heat rising. Leona directed me and Charles across the waters, around points, up creeks. Now and then an oysterman would move across the waters, far off, or a skipjack working crab pots, slow-motion, somnambulistic in the distance. The shores of the creeks seemed deserted.

We came at last toward a point on which we saw a handsome sweep of grass up a hillside, and almost at the top, an unpainted wooden farmhouse, deep gray from a hundred years of weather. I was surprised by the sheer remoteness of it, a remoteness not only of place but of time. It belonged in another century.

We pulled the skiff up to the mud shore. There was no dock. We debarked and all fell in behind Leona as she marched up the hill toward the house. One of the qualities in Leona that I admired was her sense of ceremony, the dignity and formality with which she invested certain occasions: her impressive courtesy. This visit, I detected, called for some ceremony.

Leona halted before the door of the house. She called. Waited, then called again, not expecting an answer, evidently, but simply announcing herself, us. Then Margaret stepped in front of her and carefully opened the weathered wooden door. Leona led us in.

After the morning sunlight, the house inside was a sudden shadow. It took a moment to see. In a rocking chair, with her back to an unlighted stone fireplace, sat great-grandmother. She smoked a corncob pipe, sucking it with toothless cheeks. Her skin was gray-black and shriveled and inconceivably old. Her head was topped with a cirrus of white wispy hair. I suppose she was close to a hundred years old: a tiny, intent black bird, all bones and black hide and eyes, which, despite their intelligence and comprehension, seemed to watch us rheumily from a very great distance.

She nodded to us as we came in and rocked as she nodded and sucked on her pipe: a complicated series of geared movements that made her seem a small, intricate mechanism, tightly and precisely wound. Leona went forward kindly, murmuring after the old lady's health and holding out to her a packet of Beechnut pipe tobacco. Great-grandmother's shining black hand, like a claw, rose to accept the gift. The hand did not shake. She accepted the gift and withdrew it into the folds of her dress. Her face wore a sort of chronic scowl of old age, but there stirred in it a faraway sneaking undercurrent of recognition and even of momentary pleasure.

Leona leaned to give her a little squeezing hug. Then Margaret came forward to be greeted, and then Charles and then the younger children. The children did not hug the old woman, but stood silent, peering at her, watching her. For a moment the idea of the children seemed to exhaust her, and her eyes unfocused and blurred. But then, as abruptly as it had clouded, her gaze cleared and locked upon the two white boys standing just inside the door of her house.

The sight of the great-grandmother shocked and moved me. I had never seen anyone so old. And her race, her color, with its almost metaphysical dimension of age, its unthinkable reach backward, seemed to me a new way of seeing blackness. Surely she had once been a slave, a child of slaves. I did not speculate on all this at the age of nine, but I did sense it. Neither Leona nor Charles nor anyone else in the house had ever talked about slavery or color. The eyes with which the old woman saw me were eyes that had first opened in roughly the year that Dred Scott went to court in Missouri for his freedom.

But when she saw me and Hughie, the old woman's face lost whatever flickering warmth had stirred there for her family. She stared at me and Hughie with the frank, flaming hatred of the very old.

Leona saw it too, and tried to mend the moment. She said to her great-grandmother with a gentle haste, "Grans, thiz Mistuh Lanny. And Mistuh Hugh, come from Washington . . ." She had never before called us mister.

But the old woman's stare was fixed and unappeasable. We stood where we were for a painful moment. Then Leona shooed the children outdoors to play. Hughie and I skittered off, bewildered and obscurely ashamed of ourselves.

That afternoon we all rode the skiff back to Charles Creek in silence. As we tied up, at the owner's cottage, the sky turned that telltale copper, the air close and heavy. The storm struck us as we reached the road to the cottage, the first raindrops falling fatly, like meteorites smacking in the thick, dry dust, making craters. Then it all came down in a drench. The sky blackened. The wind tore at the trees.

Hughie and I ran for the shelter of the cottage and yelled at Charles to follow. But he would not. He and Leona and Margaret never crossed the threshold of the cottage. I knew that they were afraid. Hughie and I watched them as they walked hurriedly out of sight, down the road toward their house half a mile away.

One morning Henry hitched Bill to his wagon and started off for Charles Point, a small oystering town ten miles away, to do hauling and other errands for the white oystermen. Charles and Hughie and I pleaded to go along. We climbed into the back of the wagon. Henry, in order to talk to us, sat sideways on his seat, his right hand idly managing Bill's reins, the left hand gesturing as he talked.

Henry was a large and gentle man—except when he was drinking. He had a high, wild sense of the satirical, and his eyes when he told stories took on a bulging, desperate mirth. As we rode slowly toward Charles Point he told us that the night before, a black man at Billy's had gotten drunk and threatened to shoot another black man "right in his ass." The other man, also drunk, said the first man didn't have the nerve to do it. So the first went home and got his shotgun, and the second, still daring him, went outside of Billy's and pulled down his pants and stuck out his ass.

The man with the shotgun backed off a good distance—"didn't want to *kill* him nohow, ya know," Henry explained with his soft, wondering chuckle—and let the buckshot fly. The man with his pants down leaped and hooted and danced away down the road with twenty or thirty pellets embedded in his ass. Henry laughed, shaking his head. "One *crazy* nigger," he said. "And one *sorry* nigger."

Charles laughed too, and even repeated his father's final phrases, imitating. Hughie and I looked at each other and looked away. That word. We had never heard it spoken by blacks before. It was a strangely dislocating thing to learn, like walking into someone's bedroom accidentally and finding something private and best kept secret.

We were used to the whites "niggering," of course. The drinkers at Billy's, when we came there to bet the numbers, would see Hughie and me going into the colored door with Charles and would remark, by way of explanation, that we were "stayin' with the niggers over across the way." We were from the city, and we were children, so the arrangement did not seem to upset the social order unduly. They never saw us. We were strangers.

But sometimes in the evenings Aunt Sally and Margaret would bring Hughie and me to Billy's, and the girls would dance in the colored section to the music from the bubbling jukebox. Hughie and I sat to one side, behind a crowd of black drinkers, the men in overalls, the women in cotton dresses. Sally would treat us to a Coke. And she would dance the "Hucklebuck" or "Ballin' the Jack" with Margaret:

> First you put your two knees close up tight,
> Then you sway 'em to the left,
> Then you sway 'em to the right . . .
> Stretch your lovin' arms straight out in space—
> Then you do the Eagle Rock with style and grace . . .

Sally's bright white face would shine, her blond hair flinging and waving in all of that crowd of black folks, who looked at her wonderingly. Now and then I saw the white drinkers' faces peering, staring through the little window that Billy used to pass through drinks to the colored. The white faces bobbed in the window like hallucinations, full of a cracker smirk and curiosity and lust.

One night early in the summer one of the hallucinations followed us home to the owner's cottage. It ghosted past Sally's window, then ours. Then at Sally's again it rose like a small moon, gray-white in the light of the coal-oil lamp.

Sally screamed. The face vanished. We sat up most of the night around the poker table, clutching butcher knives and listening to the night and swiveling suddenly now and then toward a window as if to surprise the face before it could get away. The next morning we were exhausted. We moved to Henry and Leona's house and slept there for the rest of the summer—Hughie and I in sleeping bags on the parlor floor, Sally upstairs in Margaret's room.

When we told Leona about the face in the window, she seemed to know whose it was. But she said only, vaguely, "Just some trash . . ."

Several days later Hughie and I were exploring a path that ran a quarter of a mile up the creek bank behind the owner's house. We broke suddenly out of low, thick woods into a small clearing. In the dead center of it stood a gnarled and stunted tree hung with green apples. All around beneath the tree the ground was carpeted with hard green apples the size of golf balls. Hughie and I picked up a couple of them and bit them experimentally, and when we started to spit them out, we saw that hallucinatory face again. It appeared at the edge of the clearing; it watched us from the low bushes.

In the daylight we saw the face clearly: long and thin, unshaven, with sparse, dirty hair on top. Hughie and I were about to turn and run when the man stepped out into the clearing and spoke: "Hi, boys."

The voice stopped us. So did his eyes, which were round and sad and alcoholically red. The man was hardly larger than Hughie— a crouchy, almost emaciated figure. He was dressed like a Chesapeake waterman, but in a tattered way, his old khakis stiffened with grease.

"You boys stayin' in the house there?"

". . . Yes."

"I'm Cap'n Tom."

We nodded.

"Don't eat them green apples now," he advised. "Give ya the runs."

We threw them down. We paused, then backed out of the clearing and ran to tell Charles.

Hughie and I got to know Tom, in a way. He came by the honorific "Captain" because he had run an oyster boat out of Charles Point at one time. But something happened. He lost the boat. He lived in a shack now, hidden in the trees down by the creek in an out-of-the-way corner of the property. Tom begged drinks at Billy's and sometimes even earned them by clearing the tables there. The white drinkers all knew him and scorned him, with an easy contempt. If they called him "Captain" Tom, they meant the title ironically.

Hughie and I developed a taste for the green apples. Or perhaps it was simply that the apple tree became one of the stations we visited on daily wanderings, a place to get to.

One day when we stopped there, Tom came out of the bushes again and said he had something to show us. We followed him up the path several hundred yards. We came to his shack that sat low on the creek bank. The shack had been made from driftwood boards and tar paper and a window frame that had been cannibalized from a real house somewhere and grafted onto Tom's. In the creek mud beside the shack was a midden of discarded tin cans and half-pint whiskey bottles.

Captain Tom crossed the narrow gangplank laid over the mud to his front door, and he gestured for me and Hughie to follow. "C'mon, boys," he called, and in a remote way he sounded like my father doing Egbert Sousé in *The Bank Dick*.

We followed. The shack was surprisingly cozy. It had a close, small, littered warmth of home about it: a kitchen table with oilcloth cover (red checks), a jumble of cans and bottles in a packing case that served as a cupboard, a naked black iron bedspring topped by a prison-stripe mattress with an army blanket crumpled on it. Tom's walls were papered thickly with yellowing newspapers, some of which reported battles in France and the South Pacific, and the siege of Stalingrad. The newspapers were his insulation.

Tom had invited us there to show us something. From the wall above his sooted coal-oil lamp, he took down an old photograph. It was now much faded and cracked.

"Look a-here, boys," he said, handing the picture to us. It showed a young woman in a cotton dress standing beside a house. She looked at the camera, smiling. Standing beside her, holding her hand, was a little boy with a surly face, squinting.

Hughie and I studied the picture for a moment because Tom obviously wanted us to do so. We had no interest in it. We were puzzled, although of course we formed from the photograph a quick, vague, bewildered sense of Tom's prehistory. Tom watched us hopefully as we looked at the picture. We handed it back to him.

"He was a little younger than you in that," Tom said, nodding to me.

Tom never explained what had happened to the woman and the boy. But I knew, in some vague way. He had lost them as he had lost the oyster boat, probably to drink. There would have come a morning when she had moved out on him—packed up the boy and two suitcases and gotten on the bus. He would have awakened in his mess of hangover and remorse and found her and the boy gone. Some empty drawers. No note, nothing of ceremony. Just the ripping and the absence, like a death. He would have gone on a four-day drunk.

Something in me, even at that age, sympathized with Tom. It was a complicated transaction, I suppose. He was a father who had lost a son. I was a son who had, in some sense, lost a father. Misplaced him, anyway. I felt superior to Tom, a nine-year-old who felt morally and even physically superior to this father. I felt with Captain Tom, I think, the ghost of the connection between father and son, and even a ghost of the rivalry. As I reproduce the photograph now in my memory, I feel, quite close, for an instant, a small stab of pain. The stab amazes me: to traverse so many years and still feel the loss dealt once to a southern Maryland bar bum. I wonder where the child in the photograph is now.

As a rule, Hughie and I rarely saw Tom. He took private back paths through the woods. He seemed to have a beaten track from his shack to Billy's, but we never found it. He avoided even the dirt-and-oyster-shell road that passed by Henry and Leona's. He lived and traveled like a small riverbank creature, noctural and secretive, a mole, a muskrat. In his cringing and ruined way, he was a remarkably self-sufficient man.

Eventually Hughie and I betrayed him. Leona hated Captain Tom. One day she heard Hughie and me using "shit" and "fuck." She drew us firmly into her kitchen by the black wood stove. Leona was a southern Maryland Catholic, a puritanical woman, though with soft edges.

She asked where we had learned such language. It could not have been native to us. It must be some evil local influence. Leona felt responsible for any moral contaminations that we came down with. Hughie and I spontaneously hit upon the most convenient plausibility: Captain Tom had taught us those words.

Now Leona rose up. Her eye was lit with an indignation that I had never seen before. "Come on, you boys," she commanded. She stormed massively out of the house and marched into the corn field opposite, in the direction of Captain Tom's shack. We followed her, in a parade: Hughie and me and Charles, and after us, four or five of her other, smaller children, leaping and scrambling to keep up with us, capering like puppies behind the dense, indignant black cloud of Leona moving across the field.

When we came to the creek side, to Captain Tom's, Leona planted herself before the gangplank, hands on hips, and shouted at the shack, "Tom! Tom! . . . Come on out here, you white trash!"

The moral authority of a black woman calling out a white man surprised me. I wondered if Tom would come. And if he did, which of them—man or woman, black or white—would prevail. Some odd reversals had occurred.

We all waited, the children crouched behind Leona in a frieze, waiting for something to happen. All of us were titillated.

Leona called again. At last Tom's door opened a little, cringingly. Leona shouted. Tom appeared now, barefoot, his eyes red from liquor and sleep.

Ordinarily, I think he would have retreated back into his shack. Leona was much too heavy to make it across the gangplank to his shack, so he was safe from her there. But the sight of Hughie and me, the white boys, suddenly puzzled Tom and imposed a duty on him. Retreat would be too shaming. So Tom, with a little grumbling swagger, unsteadily came across the plank.

"Now, woman," he said, as if trying to muster up some Kluxer menace, some of the sneering racial command presence practiced around Billy's. "Now, woman, what the hell you want?"

The "hell" probably did it. Leona raised her huge arm and cuffed Tom hard, on the side of his head. He stumbled, surprised, down onto one knee. With her great hand, Leona banged him again, on the other side of his head, and Tom collapsed, rolling onto his side, and then came up onto both knees, surprise and humiliation quivering on his face.

Tom tried to stand, but Leona loomed over him and menaced him down as she poured forth a furious sermon on the innocence of youth and on words that should never reach children's ears from the mouth of such trash as Tom. Leona ranted for several minutes. Then, finished, she bowled Tom over again with a blow to the head, and she turned, with virtue triumphant, and led her parade back across the corn field. She did not look back. When I did so, I saw Tom on his feet, waving his arms, railing soundlessly after Leona.

It is possible that Hughie and I, being white, being from Washington and guests of the owner, legitimized Leona's attack on Tom—Tom being not even a working tenant on the land, but a squatter. It did not occur to us to wonder why it was Leona who administered the beating and not Henry. But even that, I think, we understood in some distant, unspoken way.

When matriarchal Leona delivered the beating, the entire affair was safe, a domestic detail, colorful, even funny, something the white old boys at Billy's could laugh about, shaking their heads. Imagine old Leona getting so worked up about some dirty words. But if Henry had done the beating, the black man humiliating, punishing the white man—why, then . . . Our words would have stirred up killers.

Henry understood all of that, I know. He was a powerful man. He was an animated storyteller. But he was also a brooder, distracted, preoccupied, often silent. He would withdraw, emotionally and physically. Sometimes he would disappear for several days at a time. I liked him better than his own son Charles liked him. But he seemed to avoid his own house. I think he feared Leona.

Henry hauled empty bottles for Billy. He took his wagon to Charles Point to haul for the oystermen. He hitched Bill to his hand plow and sometimes in the hot afternoons we would see him in the distance across one of his fields, scratching a furrow for tobacco or corn, the plow blade kicking up a light plume of dust.

Sometimes he would come home drunk from Billy's. He would smash things then. A rage radiated off him, almost in waves. Once it happened in the afternoon. He pulled his wagon into the dirt yard in front of the house, and he jumped down swayingly. The children all came out onto the front porch and watched him like an audience. He announced almost incoherently to Charles and me and Hughie that he was going to "break" Bill, that he was going to break her like a cowboy would.

Henry unhitched poor stoic Bill and led her into the middle of the yard. He leaped aboard her and landed hard, heavily in the middle of her back. The abruptness of the mount, the weight of the rider, made Bill jump and crane her neck with a wild eye to see the sudden animal on top of her.

Henry dug his heavy brown ankle-high plow shoes into her sides and yanked savagely at the rope bridle. Bill suddenly rioted. Her hindquarters bounded into the air, amazingly high, and kicked. Her body arced twistingly around the yard, gyrating, thumping, forelegs straight and stiffened while the hind end rotated in a thumping buck, trying to loose herself from the flailing big black man on her back.

Then, as she fought, from her hindquarters streamed a bright yellow coiling rope of piss, a vivid helix of it spiraling out behind the horse and rider. The children stared wonderingly at that. It seemed such a beautiful, violent piece of magic that we all clapped our hands and cheered.

For some reason, I cannot remember how the ride ended. Bill did not throw Henry. I would have remembered that. I think that Henry had his way, that Bill eventually bucked herself out and came to a surly, defeated halt. Yes, and then Henry dismounted and gave Bill a furious kick in the ass with his boot. He had demonstrated his manhood in front of his children. And Leona was very angry. Henry disappeared into the woods and was gone for two days.

My mother never came to Charles Creek. That did not surprise us. But Hughie and I never understood why we were there. We accepted it. We missed Washington. Mostly, we missed my father. One Saturday morning when he came in Hilda Cloud's Nash with the groceries, we begged him to take us home with him. Sally stayed, and my father drove me and Hughie to Washington. My mother was away from home. Late on Sunday afternoon he told us it was time for him to take us back to Charles Creek. He had already returned the Nash. This time we hitchhiked.

The ride that night with my father has mostly blurred and vanished. I remember walking outside a roadside restaurant somewhere near Washington: bright lights from the restaurant, gas pumps of a filling station attached to the roadhouse. My father negotiates with three sailors in uniform. They have been drinking, and my father in a joking way pleads for a ride for himself and his two boys. We climb sleepily into a dark sedan. My father and Hughie and I crowd into the back seat and ride in silence. It seems unnatural that my father is not driving. Something is wrong. The sailors smell of drinking. I fade off.

Somehow, we got there. The next morning my father left again, hitchhiking back to Washington. He behaved as if some harrowing drama were occurring there, out of our sight, as if we had been so elaborately transported to Charles Creek just to be out of all of that for the summer.

Our last ride out of Charles Creek came on an August night. We said goodbye to Charles and Henry and Leona around dusk. But something had changed between us all. My father was there, the owner's friend, a white man with a large car, and the whole family retreated into a coloredness, a forbiddingly remote subservience that left me hurt and angry for a moment.

But that passed. We were going home. My father was there. Hughie and Sally rode in the back seat of the Nash. I got to ride up front.

On the way out, my father stopped for a drink at Billy's. We waited in the car for what seemed a long time. When my father came out of Billy's, he smelled a little of Scotch. He started the car and checked the gas gauge, squinting, having trouble seeing it in the dim light from the dashboard. Then he counted his money. Sally asked anxiously if he had enough gas to make it to Washington. He said he thought so. His money amounted to only a dollar in change. Sally did not reprove him, but she rode in a tense silence.

I think sometimes of our ride home that night from Charles Creek. The roads were black and narrow and curving. I leaned forward, my face almost pressed against the windshield. Sudden blinding lights of oncoming cars would erupt out of the night, explosions of twinned lights, and then vanish. I dimly saw the side of the road. I watched that, and I watched the speedometer, and I watched my father's face.

He lit up one Camel after another. To do so, he would wait for a straightaway, then jam his elbows into the steering wheel and steer the car with them for a moment while one hand struck the match and then both hands cupped the flame for the cigarette. The cupped hands beamed the light for a second onto his face. I saw a strange light in his eye. He was driving 75 miles an hour on those back roads—driving beautifully, artistically, shifting gears with the flowing and alert grace of a thoroughbred horse in full stride. And the Maryland night shot by outside: the lights of cars and occasional towns blew by like meteor showers. My father had gone into some mysterious and beautifully coordinated trance—an odd performance, at once spirited and removed and dangerous. None of us said a word.

One morning in December of that year, Hughie and I persuaded my father to drive us back down to Charles Creek. Mainly, we wanted to see Charles. We stopped at a Kresge five-and-ten to buy a Christmas present for him. We selected a small plastic case filled with bright pencils, outfitted with a translucent 12-inch ruler that slid in to become the top of the pencil box.

The weather was dark, gray, sleeting. Hughie and I were excited to be going back. A few months, at that age, were sufficient to invest Charles Creek for both of us with a sense of adventure and nostalgia.

When we pulled off the blacktop onto the dirt-and-shell road to the owner's place, the landscape all seemed changed. The trees were leafless, the dusty summer road was now puddled and dark with mud. The sky was low and close and cold.

We pulled up to Henry and Leona's house and left the big Nash in the muddy yard. It, and we, were out of place here. Leona came out hesitantly onto the porch. She was remote and polite and subservient. She called me "Mister Lanny." We stood in her dining room and she lit a coal-oil lamp in the wintry afternoon grayness.

Charles stayed in the shadows until we asked if we could give him a present. We handed him the pencil box, and he took it without a word. He seemed angry, sullen. We were embarrassed. We wanted only to get out of there, to get away.

Charles had grown. He was taller and heavier now. He was now, irredeemably, too big to be a jockey.

6·An Access to Power

My father covered the Capitol for the Philadelphia *Inquirer*. When I was six or seven, he took me and Hughie to the Hill sometimes on Saturday mornings. We rode the streetcar down Pennsylvania Avenue, then walked into the Senate Office Building and took the elevator down to the subway. There we waited for the monorail subway car that ran through the bright yellow tunnel between the Senate Office Building and the Capitol.

The little open car had seats of varnished light brown wicker. It got up just enough speed on the run (less than a minute) to make the wind blow through our hair as we screeched and whirred through the curving tunnel. We fancied ourselves in a kind of projectile, though one that was oddly mannered and antique. The operator sat amidships. The car did not turn around at the end of the line; the front simply became the back as it set off for the return trip.

Usually we had the car to ourselves on Saturday mornings. Hughie and I would ride back and forth several times, until the operator began to scowl and wave us off.

Sometimes a senator got on the car with us. We learned to recognize senators. They were not difficult to spot. Each carried himself with a distinct individual bearing, an odd combination of physical presence and remoteness that put me in awe. I had never before encountered the abstracted self-consciousness of the public man: the senator moved through space with the air of a man being observed by crowds, even on a Saturday morning in the empty Senate subway. A senator's flesh would seem different from the flesh of ordinary men. It had either a higher color or, conversely, a sort of marmoreal whiteness. It seemed somehow fixed and vivid in a way that most flesh did not, and the relationship between the flesh and the bones beneath was tighter: a better fit. A senator's face generally had an unmistakable mark of character, a distinctive stamp.

I liked the old Southern senators the best, for they came costumed. Some of them in those days still wore wing collars and string ties. I think I remember one in a frock coat, with a pince-nez dangling from his breast pocket. My father clearly enjoyed the Southerners as well. When they were out of earshot he would identify them to us, his voice falling into a heavily satirical Southern accent.

My father would nod to the senators when we met them on the subway, or exchange words with them. My father had a way of saying "Hello, Senator!" that combined respect and a light, burlesquing irony—as if my father were bestowing the honorific on someone he knew perfectly well was an impostor. He said "Hello, Senator!" the way that he might say "Hello, Doctor" to a colored waiter at the Press Club. I think my father's tone with the senators must have played engagingly in their ears for an instant. The tone insinuated that he knew about them precisely what they knew about themselves: that there was in the public man the lightest touch of the fraud. He used a hint of bombast in the greeting, too, so that the burlesque was on himself as well, and therefore somehow disarmed.

My father took Hughie and me up to the Senate press gallery. He greeted friends and elevator operators and fiddled with his newspaper work for half an hour.

I loved the Senate. Even the smell of it was distinctive. It may have been the wax on the burnished corridors. I loved the dark old leather couches placed in niches, and the air of richness, the nineteenth-century fixtures of the place, and all the heroic statuary that was the furniture around which great daily business proceeded. I sensed tremendous resonances of power and tradition and chicanery and character there.

My father was at home in this world. He moved easily in it, his step and reflexes light, ironic and certain. He owned it in a way that I delighted in. He took it just right: detached and shrewd and yet obviously fond of all of it. He knew the element.

When I was thirteen, my father brought me into this world. A Republican senator from Michigan, a paraplegic war veteran named Chuck Potter, had an opening in his patronage for a page boy during the summertime. His regular page had asthma. He had to return to Michigan when the Washington summer set in.

As soon as I finished my school year at Gordon Junior High School on Wisconsin Avenue, I bought several white shirts and a dark blue tie and dark blue slacks and began work as a Senate page.

At first I was lost. A page from Massachusetts became my mentor. He was a bright boy with virulent acne. It required sunburn treatments that made him look as if he had been boiled. He guided me through the labyrinths of the Capitol. He taught me the secret corridors through the basement, showed me how to sneak up to the top of the Rotunda.

He instructed me in the rituals of floor duty. The pages sat on the bottom steps of the Senate rostrum. A senator would snap his fingers, and the first page in our line on the steps would spring up and make a brisk, dexterous leap up the aisle to the senator's desk, receive murmured instructions, and then be gone on the errand.

On the third day of my duty there, the junior Senator from Minnesota, Hubert Humphrey, put his arm around my shoulder and led me off the Senate floor into the ornate lobby behind the Senate chamber. He asked me to sit in a black leather chair beneath a crystal chandelier.

"Now, son," he said, "I know this place can be confusing." I was astonished by the sheer earnest focus of his attention on me. I stared at the rug, bewildered and pleased. He went on, "I want you to remember that if you ever have any troubles, any questions, any difficulties, you can come straight to me. No matter what else is going on, you just come straight to me. All right? You have a good time here, son, but remember, I'm always here if you need me."

I never did seek him out that summer, or the next either, when I returned to the Senate. But I thought of him thereafter with a kind of filial affection. Some twenty years later I was working on a story for *Time* about Minnesota, and I spent a long evening with Humphrey in Minneapolis. The governor, Wendell Anderson, had a dinner party for all of us (me and my wife, *Time*'s Chicago bureau chief, a local judge, the Humphreys) at the governor's mansion. At first, through cocktails and dinner, the talk was all political anecdote and analysis.

After the coffee, more drinks began arriving, and the time wore on to midnight and beyond. Humphrey fell into reminiscence. The dialogue became monologue—not unusual for Humphrey, of course. But this soliloquy had none of Humphrey's old exuberance and high, flushed, Rotarian humanity. This was Timon of Athens. Humphrey spoke with a venom I had not imagined to be in him. He was drinking beers, one after another, and his mind kept drifting bitterly back to 1968 and what had happened to him then, to the anti-war demonstrators who vilified him and the turmoil that had cost him the election. "They were scum!" he said. "Just scum!" At last, very late, at one or two in the morning, he sat brooding and depleted, and his wife led him away.

When I wrote the long story on Minnesota, a cover story, I did not mention Humphrey—an odd omission, in view of Humphrey's role in the state's political history. I am not sure now why I slighted him so stupidly. I heard later that he had picked up the magazine and begun thumbing through the piece, that he skimmed it with a gathering outrage until at last he was tearing through the pages and yelling, "Where am *I*?! Where am *I*?!"

As a page, I came to find some of the senators faintly ridiculous. The Southerners had their thick air of local color, and their string ties and florid manners. Hooey of North Carolina wore wing collars. Burnet Maybank of South Carolina kept up a sort of background chorus during all debates. He would sit stolidly at his desk in the first row of the chamber on the Democratic side and demand: "Vut! . . . Vut! . . . Vut!" He meant that the Senate should shut up and vote. No one ever paid the slightest attention.

The Southerners were amusing. The conservative Midwestern Republicans had a darker, heavier air. They had none of the Southerners' flair for self-satirizing bombast. Jenner and Capehart of Indiana managed to be both fatuous and menacing at the same time.

Echoes of the know-nothing snarl would sound in their voices, a native American meanness. Their interests were bewildering sometimes. One day in the Senate cloakroom I overheard the two of them arguing for twenty minutes about the price of a hamburger at Burning Tree Country Club: "No, goddamnit, Homer! You're dead wrong!"

Joe McCarthy of Wisconsin, on the other hand, had resources of charm that have since gotten lost in the historical record of his career. He was a darkling lout, of course. His eyes were shadowed by kohl-like bags; they were drinker's eyes. Yet he had a politician's gift of ingratiation. He could work a human encounter with a lightness and agility of spirit, the pol's way of making eye contact and moving up close, squeezing the flesh. I remember when McCarthy, in his early days, still hunting for an issue, would haunt my father's office on Jackson Place, on Lafayette Square, trying to sell him articles for the *Saturday Evening Post*.

Once my father had written a profile for the *Post* about Alexander Wiley of Wisconsin. I knew Wiley, an enormously round man who wore white suits, as the loudest and least embarrassed farter on the Senate floor. He would tilt his body in his handsome nineteenth-century chair and unleash thunderclaps. His flatulence approached the status of rhetoric. It amazed me. His face, after each explosion, wore an expression of infant innocence, of infinite pink well-being and self-satisfaction. The pages sitting on the rostrum steps would lurch and squirm in a pantomime of hilarious, pop-eyed disbelief.

There were follies there. Some senators kept gin in medicine bottles in their Senate desks. But I thought of the Senate as the home of gods. I was a child at large in their world. I savored the resonances of their power and magic. They reminded me of my father. Or else they were my father, done in larger terms, the terms in which I thought of him.

The page boys had their rituals of hazing. They liked to send a new boy on snipe hunts. They would ask him to go upstairs to find a "left-handed bill-stretcher." He would innocently hurry up to the "Senate Doc" on the gallery level, the vastly cluttered document rooms containing copies of thousands of bills and resolutions and *Congressional Records*. He would stand at the counter there and apply for the item, like a man ordering a fan belt at an auto-parts store, and the young documents clerks, mostly ex-pages themselves, would smirk and snigger and dispatch the newcomer across the Capitol to look for his bill-stretcher in the House Documents Room.

Once, being the youngest and newest, I was given the mission when Senator Margaret Chase Smith of Maine wanted someone to go to her office and bring back her purse. It damaged my sense of dignity to walk through the endless corridors and then ride the subway car to the Senate clutching a woman's purse. When I arrived with the bag on the floor of the Senate and walked down the aisle to present it to Senator Smith, the other pages giggled behind their hands. They flounced the limp wrist at me. One of them wet the tip of his little finger with his tongue and smoothed his eyebrow with it, as if he were finishing his make-up.

We set up the Senate chamber for the day's business in the way that acolytes and deacons prepare the altar of a cathedral for solemn high mass. We moved in the reverend setting with a casual, bantering familiarity of which we were proud. While we arranged the senators' desktops in the mornings, placing copies of the pending bills and of yesterday's *Congressional Record* just so on them, the tourists in the galleries watched us. We moved with an offhanded self-importance.

At ten, or eleven, or sometimes at noon, the chaplain of the Senate came and opened the session for the day with tiredly fervent prayer, a homily with a sort of off-key relevance to the news that was in the Washington *Post* or the *Times-Herald* that morning.

On many days Vice President Nixon would appear to preside over the start of the day's business. He would stay for half an hour or forty-five minutes, sitting in the presiding officer's chair, and then, unless something important was going on, he would hand over the gavel to some senator and stroll out through the rear doors of the chamber. He had no other real duty as Vice President, of course, but I understood why he did not stay for the rest of the day's business.

It was mostly a droning, desultory routine. The chamber was never more than one-third full, except when a major bill was being voted on and the parties' floor leaders were getting out their troops.

The Senate worked along most days like a fairly stately engine room.

Lyndon Johnson spent long hours in his chair, working the engines, getting the bills through. He sent Bobby Baker skittering here and there around the Capitol during the day, rounding up votes, troubleshooting. Across the aisle from Johnson sat Senator William F. Knowland of California, a heavy-faced, heavy-voiced, saturnine man who was the Republican leader. Knowland many years later committed suicide. He blew his brains out while standing beside the Russian River in Sonoma County.

One learned routines. Knowland would snap his fingers and mutter "White Rock!" That meant: Go to the cooler in the cloakroom and bring a glass of White Rock soda water. Johnson sometimes wanted vanilla ice cream. He would pull from his trouser pocket a silver money clip crammed with an enormous wad of bills, and peel one off. I would fly down the marble back stairs to the Senate restaurant and then fly back up with the small dish of ice cream. I loved the way that the summer tourists would watch me on these missions. I imagined that they were awed, standing in their clusters, as I shot through the tiled corridors. I never looked at the tourists. They were a different class. They were outside. I was inside. I had come into my father's world and belonged there. I was very pleased with myself.

My first summer, I worked on the Republican side of the aisle. A page worked not just for his patron senator, but as part of a general pool. The second year, I went over to the Democratic side. My boss then was Bobby Baker. He was the assistant to the secretary of the majority of the Senate, and ridiculously young, barely out of adolescence himself. He was Lyndon Johnson's protégé. In the sixties he was convicted for income-tax evasion and conspiracy to defraud the government. But then he was still a slick boy from North Carolina—sinuously thin, with a weak but shrewd country face, and heavily oiled hair that he combed back with a little mound of pompadour. Bobby wore a silk necktie that was polka-dotted and pleated and squared off at the bottom. I had never seen one like it.

Bobby knew everything. He knew who was drunk. He knew

how to trade votes and delay roll calls and make deals. We pages gathered around Bobby's desk in the Democratic cloakroom every morning, where he would joshingly hold court. He was still wide-eyed and dazzled and ready for anything. One morning he told us, with undulous, hubba-hubba gestures, that he had seen the junior senator from Massachusetts, John Kennedy, coming out of a movie on G Street with a blonde the night before. She was stacked. She was six feet tall. When Bobby talked about women, his face fell into a dumb, lecherous, slack-jawed grin, and he would peer at each of us in turn and wink. But sometimes on Monday mornings Bobby would tell us that over the weekend he had been down home, "down in God's country." His face would mime a little transport of heaven.

A page was a boy brought intimately into the shrines of American political power and permitted to witness history up close, mixed with farts and gin. The experience produced odd and sometimes unlikable effects. A boy developed the sort of premature worldliness and cynicism that Fagin's street thieves brought back to their den. We tended to become presumptuously knowing squirts, little Dead End Kids loose in the democracy's headquarters. We were paid too much, and that added to our illusions about ourselves.

I earned $60 a week, the same salary that my father made in Pennsylvania when he married my mother. I collected my money in cash every two weeks from the Senate Disbursing Office. Some of the pages asked to be paid in silver dollars, as a kind of joke. They walked out of the Disbursing Office with their trousers so weighted with coins that they were practically falling down. I always took my salary in crisp new $20 bills. It was more money than I had ever put in my pocket.

I was the youngest of the Senate pages. I was barely at puberty. I was innocent enough to be awed. Sometimes history would suddenly be standing in the middle of the routine of the morning. It belonged there, of course, but it startled me. One day Herbert Hoover appeared at the rear of the Senate chamber: an apparition. He looked bristlingly old and healthy and American and anachronistic. He looked as if he had just arrived in a buggy. He stood for a moment, until he was announced by the presiding officer.

Then all heads in the chamber turned, and everyone rose. The chamber filled with a complicated applause that amounted to a spontaneous referendum on Hoover and his role in American history—the Republicans beating their palms with a defiant and truculent approbation, and the Democrats making grudging, minimal pitterpats and returning to their seats almost immediately.

One morning all the Republicans rushed out of the Senate chamber and into the lobby behind the rostrum. They crowded around the wire-service machines there. Then they broke away, shaking their heads. Some of them wept a little. Robert A. Taft had just died.

Even in a chamber filled with prima donnas, there was one young man whose presence could cause silence and long looks of curiosity. He rarely came to the chamber. During one of the seasons I was there, he was recovering from an operation. He had to walk on crutches. But one afternoon he appeared. I had never before witnessed the galvanizing force of star quality. John Kennedy came into the chamber through the main door at the top of the center aisle, and he slowly made his way across the back of the chamber toward the Democratic cloakroom. He'd lean on his crutches and stop to talk. Some wandering speech proceeded like background noise. No one paid attention. Every eye in the chamber followed Kennedy. It was an astonishing effect.

When I worked as a page, it was high Washington summer. The city's metabolism slowed to a deep summer torpor. Washington summer was thick and damply hot. I always liked it. Sometimes I came home late from the Senate. One night I rode an almost empty streetcar back up Pennsylvania Avenue toward home. Senator Henry Jackson of Washington was the only other passenger on the streetcar. I thought that our professional relationship, our professional comradeship almost, justified my sitting down next to him. We worked together, after all. I felt I knew him. I had sometimes played softball with him at Georgetown Playground on weekend afternoons. Jackson would not recognize me from that, I knew. He liked to get into pickup games there with Georgetown types and neighborhood kids. He played an earnest, workmanlike second base, always in a crouch, low to the ground.

So I sat down with him on the streetcar. He was startled. He could see by my white shirt and dark blue tie and blue slacks that I was a congressional page. He was polite but distracted. Mostly he looked out the window. I kept up a line of congressional patter, by turns rueful and expansive, as if I were a politician waving a cigar.

Jackson responded with distant vaguenesses. At last, in Georgetown, with a look of relief, he muttered "Good night" and hurried off the streetcar. It screeched on up Wisconsin Avenue in the summer night.

The Senate had been in late session. I was filled with a tired sense of peace and well-being. I got off the streetcar at Macomb Street and walked the long way around to our house on Newark Street. (Since the city was planned by a French rationalist, L'Enfant, the gridded streets run in alphabetical order—Macomb, Newark, Ordway, and so on.)

The night was as hot and thick as Alabama. The tall trees over Newark Street softened the street lamps and diffused the light. The night was filled with a rich stillness.

Up Newark Street, I saw our house. All its lights were on. My parents were giving a party. The house glowed. It was as bright as a diamond. I watched it for a time from a distance, through the summer darkness.

The Senate was having a filibuster that week. It was an intrusion upon the usual formless summer rhythms of the place. We worked in shifts, around the clock. Senators slept on couches in their offices.

The substance of the debate was incomprehensible to me. Dixon Yates. Something to do with power projects. It was not surprising that I did not understand the issue. The point of a filibuster is to talk about precisely everything except the matter at hand.

The most durable long-distance speaker was Wayne Morse of Oregon. He was a party-switching loner with a grim Cromwellian fire in his eye. A dark passion would come over Morse's face, a strange, single-minded fury, and he would rant like a circuit-riding preacher. He could speak all night without sitting down. The pages claimed that he had a tube running down his leg to a flask that was strapped to his ankle. That way he could relieve himself without missing a sentence. I never found out if it was true. If it was not, his bladder was heroic.

I loved a filibuster. It was a sort of crisis of boredom. But it was peculiarly exciting. A filibuster seemed an archaic ceremony, like a medieval fair, like a joust.

The usual schedule was broken. Sometimes I came out of the Capitol at six, into the cool, sweet summer morning, when the dawn was coming up pink and touching all the white Washington stone—statues and Capitol and Supreme Court—with a light rose glow.

Sometimes my father would drive to the Capitol in the middle of the night to pick me up and take me home. He would talk to me with a sleepy humor about the rituals of filibuster. I detected that he liked them as much as I did. In those days they were a fairly frequent occurrence, and a common tactic of the Southern bloc. The spectacle amused my father—grown men, the nation's leaders, reading to an empty Senate chamber from the telephone book, from Gibbon, from seed catalogues, from anything. The filibuster made an exquisite hoax and joke on the politician's rhetorical arts. It was nothing but great gobs of insensate rhetoric hefted like medicine balls and heaved into utter emptiness.

The sheer meaninglessness of the words was a satire on politics. It was an invitation to reflect that there might not be all that much difference between the filibuster and the usual political process.

As we drove home in the middle of the night through Rock Creek Park, I told my father what wonders of the pointless the Senate had accomplished during my shift. He was an editor at the *Saturday Evening Post*, and no longer came to the Hill very much anymore. I gave him news from the world he once inhabited. I eagerly told him things he did not know, and that brought me close to him. For years afterward I would use political talk with him for that purpose.

That night, I told him, in great detail, about Pastore's leap. The senator from Rhode Island, John Pastore, had spoken earlier in the evening. He was a tiny man: a smart, electric, mustached little character who always drew himself up to an inch more height than he was entitled to. And when the full rhetorical passion seized him, usually at the instant he ended a sentence, his right hand would flail abruptly down and his entire, electrically stiff body would leap off the floor. He would bounce. He would levitate. He would clear the carpet by a good three or four inches. He looked as if someone had sent a jolt of current through the floor.

But in the leap, his face remained just as it was—as if to say that he would remain unshaken, no matter what turbulence might knock his body about. And when he hit the floor again, the effect was to make his entire body an exclamation point.

I told it as elaborately as I could. My father laughed. We got onto the subject of Wayne Morse. My father said with a smile, "You know, Clare Luce says that Wayne Morse was kicked in the head by a horse, and that's why he acts that way."

I considered. Massachusetts Avenue was empty now. My father was speeding as he usually did when he had the chance. We shot past the British embassy. I drew myself up a little, sitting there in the darkness of the car, trying to sound like a crony at the Press Club. I said, "I don't know. I think Morse is a prick!"

My father nodded slowly. I caught no irony in his profile as he wheeled, too fast, through the right turn onto 34th Street, and fired toward home. He said at last, "Well, you may be right. Morse is sort of a prick, at that."

I wished that my father would come and sit in the press gallery and watch me work: watch me hurry into the chamber from the Senate cloakroom and down the aisle, and whisper something into Lyndon Johnson's ear, and then spring off again, all business.

One day I was sitting on the rostrum steps waiting for the snap of a senator's fingers. It was a dull morning. The Senate's schedule was almost vacant. The clerk droned the number of a few special-interest bills that senators introduced to get their constituents small dispensations. We had been paid that morning. Vice President Nixon sat in the presiding officer's chair a few yards away from me, over my right shoulder.

Another page, Steve Rosenfeld, walked down the aisle and told me that a man who said he was my father was in the hall just outside the Democratic cloakroom and wanted to see me. Steve took my place on the rostrum steps.

I was surprised. I walked out and found my father. As I came out of the Senate chamber, a group of tourists swept by him and down the hall, and left him standing by himself on the worn tiles of the corridor. He looked sheepish.

He stammered for a moment. Then he got to the point. He needed some money. He asked me to lend him my salary. I took the six twenties out of my wallet and handed them over. My father said "Thanks," quickly, and said he would see me later, and vanished down the marble back steps.

I had never felt more light-hearted in the world. I borrowed $2 from Rosenfeld for my lunch.

7·The Jesuit Fathers

It was not long after that that my mother first introduced the subject of God. My father never understood it at all, I think.

Fervently, with a dreamy ardor, my mother converted to Catholicism. The *Saturday Evening Post* had assigned her to do an article about South Bend, Indiana, and the most interesting thing to her about South Bend was Notre Dame University. She fell in with the faculty there. She entered the Catholic orbit, and became enchanted. There were other reasons for it, I suppose, reasons that I did not understand until much later. In any case, she began instruction in the faith. She was baptized.

One day soon afterward, she dragged me and my father to mass at a parish church on Pennsylvania Avenue. It was a cold, rainy Sunday, and the church was crowded. The Mystical Body of Christ, on my first inspection, seemed a damp, unintelligible business— all of the faithful in the pews while the priest, in green robes of the sheening, opalescent kind I had seen before only in women's cocktail dresses, paced on the altar with his back to us, murmuring on in a strange tongue.

But the words were sometimes mysteriously beautiful. I was drawn by the ritual, so highly developed, so impenetrable and hieratic. I came to understand it only later. It had such effects: the chalice and the quick-shaken, almost Chinese handbells of the consecration.

The church resonated with powerful and unknowably remote, exotic drama. Yet it drew the people into its mysteries, and they were thereby oddly transformed. They held black books that dripped with bright streaming ribbon place-markers; they answered the priest's Latin with Latin of their own. I liked the vaguely voodoo way in which they crossed themselves. I noticed a gesture that they made once with the right thumb: a swift little plus sign etched on forehead, then on lips, then on breastbone—a surreptitious, elaborate series of gestures that looked like a hurried fending off of the Evil Eye.

One ceremony especially moved me, even when I did not understand its purpose. From time to time a parishioner would make his way—usually it was her way—toward a front corner of the church. In the shadows there, tiers of little candles flickered in many-colored jars, like a small bright treasure discovered in a cave. The candle flames were fitfully busy; the banks of colors wriggled and twinkled with a life of their own, like a bright miniature crowd restlessly waiting for something. A parishioner would walk to the candles in a slightly bent and sorrowing way, her form now outlined dark against the candles. She would drop a coin into a metal box beside the candles. The coin would fall with an inappropriately loud, hollow *clonk!* Then she would draw a long stick of matchwood from a black iron box, ignite its end on one of the already lighted candles, and with slow piety touch the flame to one of the jars hitherto dark and still, and it would light up brightly and flicker with a life of its own.

I asked my mother, in a whisper, what the ceremony was all about. She answered with a short explanation, huskily whispered, that sounded like a line of Tennessee Williams: "Candles for the dead!" For the ill also, I later learned, for any soul in distress. But my mother had a melodramatically dark turn of mind sometimes.

When the time came, my mother advanced to the communion rail wearing an expression of excruciating piety, hands folded before her, eyes downcast, her cheeks drawn in and face elongated: an icon, a Madonna. My father took all of this in with his ironic eye, a complicated half-smirk on his lips.

My father had too keen an eye for the bogus—too keen, because it robbed him of some subtlety of appreciation. He could be too quickly dismissive. He was never savage or intolerant about it, but he was bound to regard religious intoxication with a Menckenesque disdain. Such contempt was a reflex and a pose of his generation. My father could spot the con. It was, I suppose, an item of his masculine pride that he could do so. God did not acquire easy entrance to his soul, especially not a God tricked up in all the stagecraft and mummery of the Catholic Church—the muttered Latin, the ardent transubstantiations (Watch closely, this bread is now in fact the Body . . .), the medieval abasements performed in such ostentatious gowns, the agony of Christ worked opulently in gold in the cross above the altar.

It was not the Church itself that roused my father's irony. It was the spectacle of my mother's conversion to it. My mother's genius for self-dramatization being extravagant, her ego a kind of pagan religion in itself, he reasoned, why then, what histrionics would attend her conversion to the most theatrical of churches. Two thousand years' experience and exploration had equipped the Roman Church with elaborately detailed knowledge of all the territories of ceremony and sin. My mother would be drawn to a system at once so patriarchal, so forgiving, and so professionally capable of understanding her.

She would be drawn by the sacrament of confession, with its ritual details both Roman and vaguely Viennese. The loosely clenched fist swinging from the wrist like a small bell clapper, strikes a light thump, thrice, in a rhythm dolorously slow and measured, to the breastbone: *Mea culpa, mea culpa, mea maxima culpa.* Her face would progress through the Act of Contrition like the Old Vic doing Lear, like an interminable close-up of Garbo. My mother's most profound artistic resource was a very nearly Tolstoyan knack of pitching herself body and soul into different dramatic parts at different times. It was not an ugly or false talent; my mother possessed a gift of pure sympathy, an almost self-annihilating capacity to imagine other lives, other realms, and to cast herself into them. She was a magnificent actress—and should have practiced the art professionally. She always believed in the part. In any case, any spiritual gaudiness toward which the Roman Church might tend would surely lead my mother to the excesses of pietistic gilding for which converts are famous.

I suppose my father accepted my mother's Catholicism as a cross he must bear. (That's the kind of thing he would have said about it, anyway.) In fact, it required little of him. The cold and rainy Sunday mass on Pennsylvania Avenue was the only Catholic service, I believe, that he ever attended with her. Her Catholicism may have seemed to him merely a new form of an old phenomenon. Once, some years earlier, my mother had become bored while recovering in a hospital from some minor female surgery. She had a hairdresser come to screw down and frizz her hair into the "poodle cut" that was popular that year. What was worse, she had her hair dyed red, or what she expected to be red. It turned out pink. My father said her hair had become "pink shredded wheat." I think he regarded her embrace of the Catholic Church as the spiritual equivalent of what she had done to her hair: a fad, a woman's mildly screwball restlessness, probably temporary. In a sense, he was wrong. My mother drew her children into the Church with her, so the effects reverberated unpredictably into the next two generations.

There were, or are, at least two branches of the American Catholic Church: the Church Ethnic and the Church Intellectual. (There is also the Church Aristocratic, which amounts to a kind of native American branch of the Church Ethnic, or else, from another point of view, a vaguely Romish sect of High Church Episcopalianism.)

The Church Ethnic is the vigorous Catholicism of the Irish and Italian and Polish settlements in America—the Church of the parochial schools and nuns and blue-collar neighborhoods and Saturday-afternoon confessions and the Legion of Decency: bingo Catholicism, the Crosby Catholicism of *Going My Way*.

Fulton Sheen tried in the 1950s to reconcile the two branches, but he proved too wholesome and popular in the television way to attract much profound loyalty from the other wing, the Church Intellectual. That branch was the Graham Greene, *Commonweal*, Thomas Merton sector of the faith.

My mother entered the Church Intellectual. She liked, I suspect, the complexity and tragedy of the faith therein, the deliciously ripe sense of sin to be cultivated, luxuriated in, plucked, savored. That sense of sin was subtle and perverse, which added to its joys both intellectual and sensual. It could attain an opulent aridity, for example, in a soul like Graham Greene's. My mother disliked Greene's novels except at moments when she was drunk and maudlin. I read them as well, at a precocious age, and without much judgment. I reveled, as she sometimes did, in Greene's exquisite wastes of guilt and betrayal, the divided mind, the flayed conscience. I was especially fond of the whiskey priest in *The Power and the Glory*.

Greene's seemed to me, admirably, a grownup's God—a Being that took account of all the stained and smoking complexity in which adults lived, from which children were excluded. The whiskey priest meditated: "God was the parent, but he was also the policeman, the criminal, the priest, the maniac, and the judge." Or else he thought: "Man was so limited he hadn't even the ingenuity to invent a new vice; the animals knew as much. It was for this world that Christ had died; the more evil you saw and heard about you, the greater glory lay around the death. It was too easy to die for what was good and beautiful, for home or children or civilization— it needed a God to die for the half-hearted and the corrupt." I admired the world-weariness of that, in somewhat the same way I admired a man with a hangover. The condition seemed gallant to me. In the yearningly romantic way of early adolescence, I'm sure I even believed that a hangover was like a temporary form of crucifixion. I sensed that both had something to do with redemption through suffering.

Catholics born into the Church Ethnic are apt to regard their religion as a repetitious and even somewhat banal fact of life, no matter how pious they are, or how comforting and valuable their religion may be to them. It is, to them, a sort of spiritual appliance, no more surprising than, say, a house equipped with electricity. It is miraculous, of course, and luminous, but it comes to seem after so many years to be mainly, merely, utilitarian.

In those days, in the reign of Pius XII, before Pope John and Vatican II, the Church Ethnic was rigidly predictable in all its mechanisms. Grace flowed through certain sacramental circuits with a reliability so profound as to seem eternal, like the peasant passages of seasons, reaping and sowing. Sins venial and mortal were remitted for certain acts of contrition, certain penances, and then

were recommitted routinely, and then reconfessed, and then re-
forgiven: grace pulsing back and forth endlessly in the wires. Priests
sat at the switches, middle-aged Irishmen and Italians in Roman
collars in the dusk of the confession booth, their hands inevitably
spread like a porch roof shading their eyes, in a gesture of discretion
and weariness and covert disgust (not disgust at the sins so much
as at the drudgery of hearing them, the interminable procession of
soiled underwear that they must inspect, for an instant or so, and
then splash their sacramental grace upon): always, the priests in
profile through the small rectangular wire grill; their voices low and
businesslike and compassionate in a murmurous official way. "How
many times?" they inevitably asked. "How many times?" Confession was like making a slightly humiliating application for a bank
loan, being forced to endure the wait on the bench outside, and a
moment's abjectness before the small reward of relief, of grace,
would be granted.

I never quite believed in the psychotherapeutic benefits of penance: it was my least favorite sacrament, probably because I came
late to the Church, was not used to confiding my secrets to strangers,
or granting strangers the power to forgive me. It seemed to me
embarrassing. I was instinctively, from a very early age, a very
lonely Calvinist—and profoundly covert.

My mother loved the Church Ethnic as well as the Merton and
Greene and Jacques Maritain and Ronald Knox branch. She was
no snob. If anything, she romanticized the Catholic workingman,
the labor movement, the warm and enduring authenticity of im-
migrants and their families.

Her own family was centrifugal, violent, unreliable. Her father
was strange, remote, high-handedly brutal in a nineteenth-century
way. It made emotional sense that she would be infatuated with
strong immigrant family tableaux. My mother had ideological reasons as well. As a teen-ager, for something less than a year, she
was a member of the Communist Party. In the summer of 1939
she wrote a letter resigning from the party. The day after I was
born the letter was returned to her. Across it was scrawled: "ENEMY
OF THE PEOPLE?" When she began her career as a magazine
writer, she wrote several profiles of labor leaders, men like John

L. Lewis and Phillip Murray. For years she kept up her subscription to the *United Mine Workers Journal*. She used to sing an advertising jingle from the coal fields: "Did you ever hear of Miss Anthracite? She never smokes or goes out at night." My mother adopted the American labor movement—an emotional adoption that amounted to a thorough and, I thought, admirable passion. So some of that passion naturally extended to the Church, to which so many of her beloved workingmen belonged.

My mother told those awful, endearing little Father O'Malley and Sister Theresa jokes that once went around to prove that even the clergy, even the pious, could enjoy a little laugh—the sort of laugh that might be described as "merry." The state of grace, in this genre, was suffused with innocent mischief.

One of the more elaborate and precociously ecumenical of my mother's jokes had a Jewish man visiting the Pope and amiably greeting him: "Good yontif, Pontiff. What's nius, Pius?" That joke appealed to me because of its sophistication—it presupposed an acquaintance with Yiddish, after all—and its implicit cosmopolitanism and tolerance. A touch of the Church Intellectual, and a reverberation of its traffic with Jewish intellectuals in liberal circles. It was told by a Catholic with a small twinkle of self-congratulation. I wonder about that twinkle, now. The Jew in the joke, with his cute Yiddishisms and tailor's accent, would not have gone to the Vatican to visit that particular Pope. Knowing Pius XII's record during the Holocaust, in any case, the Jew would certainly not have gone there to joke.

The Church, to the convert, was a magnificent novelty, a fresh and complicated discovery: a dramatic new civilization. When my mother entered it, she drew me along after her. I went in part because the same novelties appealed to me that attracted her.

In many ways my mother knew more, and felt more, than my father ever did. She quested in ways that he did not. She was almost entirely self-taught, and yet her range of knowledge was astonishing, and still is. She reads more extensively and intelligently than anyone I know—huge portions of history, mostly, the records of whole continents and periods. Her father was in awe of learning and books.

It was my mother who led me to the Catholic Church. But I went also because, in some roundabout ritual way, I was looking for my father there, in larger and more reverberant form. I may have sought the patriarch in patriarchal structure, all of those laminations of authority that rise imposingly to the papal pinnacle and then leap like an electrical charge into the upper air, to God.

In what sense is the longing for God and His totality a search for the father? God created man in His own image. The son fashions a God out of his intuitions and fears and passions for his own father. And at the same time creates an idea of his father out of some deeper model of God—almost a cultural memory of God.

Yet it was under my mother's influence, not my father's, that I went into the Church. I began with Father Schellenberger, a round, pleasant assistant pastor at St. Anne's, our local parish church on Massachusetts Avenue.

Tuesdays and Thursdays, at four in the afternoon, we met in the living room of the rectory, a room furnished with pastel stuffed chairs and couches that were covered with clear plastic, like a fastidious house in the suburbs. Even the pastel portraits of the Virgin seemed to match the colors of the rugs and chairs. The room was dark in the late afternoon.

Father Schellenberger and I progressed through a mild catechism, a chapter at a time. I understood it, I thought, but I did not ask questions: I was not concerned with the fine print of the religion. The general idea suited me, and even more, all of the outward costuming and ritual: the intricate filigree work of feast days and ember days, and holy days of obligation, daily masses and novenas and vespers, and the dense population of saints, each with some strange heroism to tell and some highly specialized power of intercession. The Church possessed a systematic totality, all new to me, that seemed, I suppose, like an appealing edifice, a home. It wished to embrace me.

I was baptized one sunny Sunday afternoon at St. Anne's. I tilted my head over a baptismal font of light green marble and I abjured Satan and all his works. Father Schellenberger, with his solemn and flushed amiability, pronounced: "*Ego te baptismo in nomine Patris et Filii et Spiritus Sancti.*" My godfather, in absentia, was a professor of journalism at Notre Dame, the nephew of a cardinal, a friend of my mother's. I never saw him after my baptism.

We returned to the house on Newark Street, where my mother served sandwiches and a cake that was iced in those same pastels, a heavenly pink and heavenly blues and whites. Father Schellenberger and several other priests moved in their black suits and white collars through the sun-bright dining room around the table. The Catholic Church began to acquire for me a sort of abstract color scheme: a wrought-iron clerical black, the highly polished sunbursts of gold, the chalice, pyx, patin, all the bright altarware; and the Virgin's dreamy light blues and whites.

Now that I was baptized, at the late age of thirteen, on the frontier of adolescence (and thus, in the nick of time), my religious education formally began. A clerical friend of my mother's, Monsignor George Higgins, a figure in the Catholic labor movement, recommended Gonzaga College High School, run by the Jesuits down on North Capitol Street. Father Higgins had jarred my sense of the way a priest behaves; he came to our house one evening and with considerable relish joined my mother in knocking back small glasses of straight vodka, chilled; after a couple of them, he told the joke about a man whose doctor has prescribed suppositories ("Take these daily") and who returns in two weeks complaining, "Doc, for all the good these have done me, I could have shoved them up my ass." Father Higgins, a "meat-and-potatoes Catholic," as my mother said, liked Gonzaga partly because it was in a bad section of town, a black slum, and because the students came from working-class families: smart kids who had to pass the entrance exam to get in, but tough. They commuted there from blue-collar neighborhoods all over the city. Gonzaga was emphatically not Georgetown Prep, the Jesuit academy for the upper middle class, for the Church Aristocratic. Georgetown Prep was for the Buckley or Kennedy class of Catholic. Gonzaga was for Studs Lonigan.

The difference sometimes shamed me. Georgetown Prep, on the outskirts of Washington, all trees and ivy, was a sort of Catholics' Groton. I played a tennis match there once, when I was number two or three on the scruffy and incompetent Gonzaga tennis team.

Tennis was not Gonzaga's kind of sport. Gonzaga boys did not grow up spending their summers at Burning Tree or Chevy Chase Country Club.

Few of us knew how to play it at all. I was a fancier character than most Gonzaga boys. I had learned tennis on the concrete public courts on Q Street in Georgetown.

The day that we played Georgetown Prep on its courts on a May afternoon, I came up against a breezy boy with country-club strokes, a sunny mama's boy with a tennis sweater tied around his shoulders. He enraged me. His father, I suppose, would have been something like a career Foreign Service officer, and would have worn tweeds. The boy would grow up to drive a yellow MG home from college, would have a camel's-hair polo coat and tassel loafers, and would drink gin until he was rosily drunk and fell asleep in the sweet pink daze of his parents' house, his parents' love.

He beat me. My tennis strokes were always balletically correct, even impressive, but they somehow had no control about them, and the ball driven on a beautifully sculpted forehand would sail twenty feet past the baseline. There was even something a little demented about my game. I looked like a first-class player who was suffering some attack of private hysterics. The classiness of the strokes and the compulsive inaccuracy of them made me look like an interesting but probably pathological flywheel. Every game felt like a breakdown. My one real weapon was a homicidal first serve which, if it happened to land in the service court, was unreturnable. I won, I think, two or three games from the Georgetown Prep boy in that way. He absorbed my game from his supercilious distance. When we shook hands at the end of the match, he gave me a quizzical, superior look, and strolled away.

Gonzaga was on the other side of town entirely—a different world. It took me almost an hour to get there from our house on Newark Street in Cleveland Park. First I took a trolley down Wisconsin Avenue through Georgetown, and on down Pennsylvania Avenue to Lafayette Square across from the White House, where I transferred to a bus. In winter I started the morning trip in darkness, the streamlined trolley sliding and screeching like a bright capsule through the silent, bluishly dawning streets, until the White

House appeared, glowing moth-soft in the first light, General Eisenhower upstairs somewhere shaving.

Gonzaga boys always hauled immense loads of books when they rode to school. We never used book bags, but like expert waiters hefting six full dinners on a tray, we piled the textbooks upon the loose-leaf notebook, which served as the foundation, and tucked the whole load under one arm. Managing these books, all of them clad in their shiny purple-and-white Gonzaga book covers, seemed at first a feat akin to that of a native woman carrying an immense water jug on her head.

Gonzaga boys wore coats and ties, but looked recklessly uncomfortable in them. The tie, the knot of it jerked to one side as if the boy had just walked out of a bar fight, was like the leash with which the Jesuits would lead them—us—to excellence and submission. The boys were tough. The Jesuits were also tough. Gonzaga in those days had about it, I thought, an air of bruised defiance. The outer world had certain forms of privilege and power to which we did not gain admission. Both class and religion burdened the school and the boys who went there, and gave them a little of the anger of the excluded. My father would have understood that sort of anger perfectly. If he thought about it much, he may have liked some of the rawness of Gonzaga. Whatever else the place was, it was not phony.

There were puzzling contradictions of status there. The Jesuits were a Catholic élite, Gonzaga had the Jesuit virtues, a mental toughness and energy. By contrast, the Christian Brothers ran a military academy across town, St. John's, at which the boys dressed in cadet uniforms. They fooled no one. We were infinitely more militant than they, and smarter than they. Gonzaga had a kind of élitism about it, too.

Encased in every Jesuit I knew then was (I thought) a spiritual core that was as hard as a stone, an intellectual will that seemed to me grim and impressive: a hard bright black rock with blue flame flickering around it. The Jesuits walked the halls in black cassocks, and they walked fast, the cassocks flapping around their legs: blackbirds. They taught an aggressive sort of humility. Belligerence and even arrogance would bulge like muscles beneath the smooth doctrinal surfaces. Yet under the arrogance was a black and alert kind of anger. The Jesuits transmitted it to us.

They taught peace and grace with a punitive fire in their eyes. They taught us as if they were mercenary officers hired to take savages from the ethnic tribes, dangerous children, and turn them into literate soldiers with neckties, officer material, suburban husbands and fathers, FBI agents.

The grace of God was not enough. A Catholicism of the servant class had consoled generations of nannies and hod carriers with the knowledge that in eternity the last shall be first, and the Holy Communion that the maid takes at 6 A.M. mass is the feast of grace that makes the roast beef she served to her Protestant employers the night before seem vain and pitiable.

But restless, mobile characters like the Jesuits could not still themselves to such a peasant's trance of rosaries and visions of their posthumous revenge upon the rich and powerful. They were not instinctively servants, but they were not masters either, at least not by birth. They saw a larger world, this world, not the next. They possessed the intellect and energy to master it, and yet they felt obscurely inferior to it, resentful, excluded. They armored themselves in black cassocks and the tremendous encircling spiritual legitimacy of their parents' Church. They preached eternity, but bristled with intense temporal ambitions. The friction of so much ambivalence and aspiration—the claims of their own ambitions and of their parents, of the world and of their Church—sometimes made them angry. It made them grim.

The Jesuits must have been an extraordinarily complicated kind of manhood. Ignatius Loyola was a soldier; the spirituality that he taught his order was not so much sweet contemplation as a soldiering of the soul, an armed struggle. The battleground was all interior; the mind could grow black and desperate with combat.

Yet the Jesuits were not really soldiers, either. We called them Father (the ones who had been ordained) and yet they were not fathers, or husbands. Their sexuality was also part of their interior warfare, the battlefield forever afire. Those militant fantasies, unrelieved by discharge into reality, were bound to make such men grim and tense. Soldiers without firearms, fathers without wives, without children. They were less than ordinary men but also more than ordinary men. This was a hard conceit for them to enact, I think, a rather elaborate self-definition, not always convincing, not natural. At last, when Pius XII died and the new Pope, John XXIII, and Vatican II and the sixties brightened and rehabilitated and trivialized the old Church, many Jesuits abandoned the conceit of their priestly manhood. They flapped off in new plumage, in civvies, in beads, to girl friends and wives and radical politics.

I began my career at Gonzaga in a state of convert's zealotry and awe at the newness and strangeness of it; I was simultaneously impressed and terrified. My mother, when she entered the Church, had acquired an interesting new wing to her cultural life. But I had far more serious business with the Church, with the Jesuits. I entered their daunting structure of authority, and was both shocked and comforted by it. It was an utter novelty in my life. Hughie and I had been raised without any religion whatever—we had invented our own paganism. My father's family was Episcopalian. But until my mother's conversion, my parents practiced a devout worldliness. The sudden entrance into a consuming relationship with God and the painful submission to his earthly ministers was a shock to my cultural system.

If my own father had seemed to me elusive—the admirable and vanishing man for whom I felt all through my childhood, intermittently, an almost orphan yearning—then here, abruptly in my life was a procession of Fathers: God the Father, Jesuit fathers, all of them insistently present and demanding, monitoring my behavior, inspecting my sins, such as they were, hearing them whispered through the grillwork on Thursday afternoons in the lower church—the basement church—of St. Aloysius, censuring me, exacting penance. And ordering all my weekdays from before dawn until late at night.

Gonzaga was a four-story brick and stone building on Eye Street, just off North Capitol. The school was attached at the North Capitol end to the red brick Church of St. Aloysius Gonzaga. It stood across the street from a long row of slummy red brick houses with small front yards of packed dirt. One of those houses was a black whorehouse, which the police raided regularly. One day during the morning religion class the cops came and marched the whores out in their slips and housecoats and ushered them into paddy wagons. The black women were angry and sullen and jerked their arms away from the white policemen who led them out of the house and through the yard and past their broken little black iron fence. I was sitting beside the window and watched all of this out of the corner of my eye. In the desk in front of me a boy named John Balducci, an exuberant priest-baiter, turned and stared raptly at the scene, muttering "Yeah! Yeah!" Father Tucker, our religion teacher, a short and normally kind priest who had served as a chaplain in Korea, stole up behind Balducci and smashed him on the back of the head with a hard-backed Baltimore Catechism: a resounding blow, a forehand stroke that Father Tucker repeated over and over as he bore down on the flinching boy in a monotone: "Something interesting, Mr. Balducci? [*whack, whack*] What are the Sins That Cry Out to Heaven for Vengeance, Mr. Balducci? [*whack, whack*] Pay attention, Mr. Balducci! [*whack*] *Age quod agis.*" (*Age quod agis* . . . "Do what you are doing," in other words, concentrate, is a Jesuit motto that in later years I have kept posted above my typewriter.) John Balducci regarded Father Tucker with servile loathing and then dropped his eyes, and sniggered for all of us when Father Tucker strolled away and commanded the class beadle to lower the shades.

The school was as austere as the ritual Church (the vestments, the gold, the mass) was sumptuous. I was as surprised by the hard, black puritanical energy of Gonzaga's routines as I had been by the elaborate magnificence of the Mystical Body as a whole. Gonzaga was another culture shock. I was accustomed to the slack and vaguely demoralized atmosphere of public schools, their casual, slouching drift from one grade to the next. The Jesuits moved briskly, with a sense of destination. Their classrooms were as ascetic as a monk's cell. A crucifix hung above the teacher's desk, which stood on a platform before the class. There were blackboards. Otherwise the rooms were bare.

The classroom rituals were all novel to me. An atmosphere of discipline just on the amiable side of grim prevailed in all classes;

the Jesuits liked to maintain a certain edge of subliminal menace in the air. We rose as a body when the teacher entered the room, and remained standing for an Our Father and a Hail Mary before starting the class. All our test papers came on pages headed AMDG—*Ad Maiorem Dei Gloriam*. When the teacher called on a student for an answer, the student would slide out of his chair and stand in the aisle and say, "Yes, Mister," or "Yes, Father."

Despite their militarist discipline, I liked the Jesuits. They were mostly quiet and earnest men. Some were funny. My sophomore Greek teacher, a scholastic (meaning a Jesuit not yet ordained a priest) named Mr. Bakiris, was a wispily thin and rueful man; he treated us with the amused tolerance of a man who knew that we were God's punishment upon him for his sins. If one of us pushed him too far, he would, without a word, open the window of the classroom and point to the fire escape outside. The boy would climb through the window and sit on the fire escape and pull the window closed behind him. I remember Bob Rhinehart spending an hour sitting out there as the snow fell down on him and turned his hair and shoulders white; he peered through the window at us with a look of dumb wounded dignity. Mr. Bakiris also liked to hurl blackboard erasers at us; he would coil his emaciated body like a baseball pitcher and even lift his leg a remarkable height under his cassock as he prepared his delivery, and then he would let fly a strike at the head of a boy who had gotten the second aorist wrong.

The teachers regarded me as an oddity when I arrived at Gonzaga. They knew that I was a new convert to the faith. This was interesting to them, but puzzling. When I joined the Freshman Sodality and came to the first meeting, the proctor, Mr. Greene, S.J., stared at me intently for long moments, as if trying to discern exactly what kind of soul he was dealing with. I thought he was scanning me looking for evidence of the devil's influence. I was uncomfortable under his gaze. He stood in a corner of the room during that Sodality meeting, a slight man with a clean, scrupulous face, and peered at me through his thick, clear-framed glasses. I felt then, perhaps for the first time, the force of the Jesuit personality—its aggressive inwardness and self-possession.

I felt out of place at Gonzaga. The school had its fierce drive and inner logic, but it seemed an alien place to me, a large and faintly dangerous secret, a cult and a penitentiary. Soon after I arrived there, I stood for an eternity at the top of a flight of iron stairs near the chapel; it was almost evening, the corridors were empty and beginning to darken. I felt lost, as if I had been abandoned there, far from home, among strangers, in the clutch of a punitive God. I felt paralyzed and inconsolable at the head of the stairs.

I believed in God. But my faith was an act of will, and therefore possibly not much more than an attitude that I struck on demand. The Freudian might be right if he said that I joined the Catholic Church in order to make myself seem so dramatically good that my parents would have to love me.

But I worked intensely at it. I got up at four in the morning, like a young Trappist. I dressed and took my schoolbooks silently down to the kitchen table, where I studied for two hours.

The house on Newark Street would be utterly still. The predawn hours were a kind of hideout for me. I made coffee and fried two eggs, every sound in the kitchen utterly clear—caused by me. My mind as I studied religion or Greek for the Jesuits, with the day imperceptibly blued and whitened through the windows, was as lucid and serene as it has ever been in my life.

One morning at four when I came down, I found my father working at the bottom of the cellar stairs. He sat at a card table installed under a naked dangling light bulb near the furnace. I saw him through a dense blue fog of cigarette smoke, unshaven. He might have been a killer on the lam, or a counterfeiter surreptitiously engraving his plates.

His fingers through the banks of smoke twiddled in the air above the typewriter keyboard, his hands in a sort of sveltely nervous ballet as they waited for the next phrase or clause or paragraph to arrive from his intelligence. He held his cigarette in his lips, raked up jauntily (like FDR, but without the holder). His eyes squinted in the spiraling smoke, like a gangster, and his head tilted back to one side with a swaggering, speculative air. I always liked my father's style when he was writing.

It had been an all-night run. He was just at the end of an article for the *Saturday Evening Post*. I had not heard him at first when I entered the kitchen. But as I started the eggs I heard down below that busy, muffled clattering, the sleepless, subversive noise of words, in clusters, being smacked onto the page. I walked halfway down the cellar stairs. My father finished his phrase, and then looked up, the cigarette in his mouth, and gave me a small grin mixed with his odd, self-deprecating irony—an irony I have never been able to understand, even when I have detected it in myself. "So, my boy," he said in his W. C. Fields voice. "You would like to examine the books of the Black Pussycat Café?"

He trudged upstairs dandling his jumble of yellow copy paper, the manuscript he'd accumulated during the night. "You want some eggs?" I asked. He looked surprised. "Sure." He smiled wearily. He sat down at the table with a curious formality, waiting to be served. He held his manuscript in front of him and tapped the pile of papers edgewise briskly, evening the pages on the white Formica tabletop. The room was filled with the smell of the coffee, then with the other breakfast smells—the brief, faintly sickening whiff of gas from the stove before my match ignited the burner, then butter and eggs frying, and toast. We were companionable. The first light started through the windows.

"How's the Greek?" My father did not touch my papers spread on the table—the text of Xenophon's *Anabasis*, the vocabulary book, the exercise sheets—but nodded at them with a courteous detachment.

I worked the eggs around the frying pan. "Okay. We're doing Homer after this. You finish your piece?"

"Oh, brother!" Meaning yes, but it was hard.

My father was vaguely impressed by this highly developed monk's routine of mine, the slightly fanatical discipline I had unpredictably developed. I had become a sort of incipient Jesuit myself, and was therefore slightly foreign to him. He did not know quite what to make of it, any more than he knew what to make of my Catholicism or my mother's. He respected it, in me at least. In any case, he had found me in my pre-dawn hideout. I had startled him in his furtive basement labors too. It disconcerted us both. Our night-traveling capsules had butted into each other. We were like two cat

My father posed for this gag shot when he was in the Navy in Chicago in 1944. COLLECTION OF HUGH MORROW

Hughie (left) and I boxing with my father at a beach in New Jersey in the late forties. COLLECTION OF HUGH MORROW III

Hughie and I at the wedding of a family friend in the late forties. Aunt Sally is in the background. COLLECTION OF HUGH MORROW III

My grandfather, Dr. Hugh Morrow, in his office in Williamsberg, Pennsylvania, 1917.
COLLECTION OF HUGH MORROW

My father with his son Davison in Bronxville, 1967. BERT SMITH

My brother Michael in the mid-sixties, before his final illness. PATRICK MORROW

Vice President Rockefeller and my father confer at the U.S. Capitol in 1975. COLLECTION OF HUGH MORROW

My father in the middle of a fracas between Rockefeller and a New York State Democratic leader in the New York Hilton in 1969. NEW YORK POST

Above left: *My father announcing Rockefeller's death to the press in 1979.* ASSOCIATED PRESS

Above right: *Lance Morrow with Justin, the Christmas of his first year.* COLLECTION OF THE AUTHOR

My father with James, Justin and me. *SALLY MORROW*

My father with Justin at his house summer, 1984.

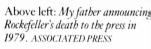

burglars who have suddenly discovered each other intently looting the same house in the dark.

So we fell back on professional courtesy. My father's internal instruments, as always, steered him resolutely toward the normal, or appearances of the normal. That tendency endowed him with a sweet fatalistic dignity, but also with a watchfulness, a remoteness that his children came to find discouraging, even maddening.

When I put the plate before him, my father thanked me. We fell silent. My father ate the eggs in his rapid way. He ate intensely, with his eyes down, preoccupied. My father had an odd way of drinking his coffee: he took an ice cube from the refrigerator and dropped it into his steaming black brew, let it melt a moment, then drank down the entire cup so abruptly that it seemed to have been inhaled. When he had drained the cup, he banged it down on the table with an exhaled "*Yah!*" The entire rite required only a few seconds, and yet it always seemed to remove my father so utterly, into such a sudden inaccessibility, that it alarmed me. For that instant, he psychically vanished: his soft brown eye as he reared back to swallow the coffee whole filled with an animal blankness: like the eye of a bolting horse, a stricken, slightly wild gaze, remote and terrified at the same time. His eyes rolled abstractly toward the ceiling, his mouth gulping.

The sight of it set me off on a nervous line of patter. I told my father with offhanded pedantry, "The Greeks had a system of phonetics that made it almost impossible for them to make ugly sounds with their language. The rules were built in." Why was I saying this? "Certain sounds could not follow other sounds, because the combinations were thought to be too ugly. If they used an ugly sound, it was deliberate. Like '*blapto*.' "

"*Yah!*" The coffee cup hit the table.

My father's vanishing moment was immediately past. His eyes returned. They looked at me—steady, amused, remote: " '*Blapto*' sounds like flatulence. Onomatopoeia, is it?"

"No. Or a little. It means hurt, harm, weaken, strike, damage . . ."

. . .

I timed my trip to Gonzaga in order to make the daily seven o'clock mass in the lower church of St. Aloysius. That mass was an oddly keening and elegiac ceremony. Those who found daily mass necessary or comforting were, as a rule, more sorrowful than others. In all of the lower church, there would be gathered thirty or forty worshipers: a few workers from the Government Printing Office a block away, a Gonzaga student or two, usually only me. A couple of nuns from the house that the Little Sisters of the Poor maintained a few blocks away (whose windows we sometimes washed on Saturdays as part of our Sodality good works). Mostly, the mass attracted the slow, shuffling elderly of the parish, the last white remnants in a neighborhood that had been turning black for years.

In the dimly lighted basement, with its pastel-and-gilded plaster bas relief Stations of the Cross lining the walls, the old people sat, a few couples, but mostly widows alone—bent over in their pews as if the weight of the low ceiling above them were pressing down. Everyone was in mourning. Everyone wore black. The banks of colored candles for the dead and ill always flickered more densely there than in any church I have ever seen. Almost every candle was burning, like a burst of Christmas lighting in the surrounding misery.

The priests moved matter-of-factly and incredibly fast through the daily masses. One advantage of the Latin was that a priest in a hurry could unreel a low mass in a stream of accelerated syllables (like a tape recorder on Fast Forward) unintelligible to all but himself and God. No one in the congregation would judge him impious, or even know the difference. One priest, the prefect of discipline at Gonzaga, could do the low mass in nineteen minutes. I admired the way he worked; the mass is an intricate business to do so quickly without missing steps, missing crucial readings or gestures.

I wondered sometimes what the spiritual wattage of such a speedy mass would be as prayer—how much true supplication and fervor could be conveyed by such a short-order performance. I thought idly about the same point sometimes during recitations of the rosary. During May, the Month of Mary, the entire school would assemble in the parking lot behind the school, and there, lined up like platoons of soldiers on a parade ground, we would proceed in a cadenced rumble (not a joyful noise) through long rounds of the Sorrowful Mysteries and Joyful Mysteries. Sometimes, as an officer of the Sodality of Our Lady, I was delegated to lead the prayers. I stood on the fire escape overlooking the parking lot and led the prayers like a general addressing his men.

We charged through the Hail Marys in the way that a man puts his signature to a pile of fifty traveler's checks before he goes on a trip: eventually, only the first letter of each name is legible—the rest of the word is a scribbled undulation. So with the Hail Mary, We recited it like this:

HAIL MARY fullofgracethelordiswiththeeblessedartthouamong womenandblessedisthefruitofthywombJESUS.

HOLY MARY motherofgodprayforussinnersnowandatthehourof ourdeathamen.

And yet the mumbling did produce deeper spiritual effects—at least in the church if not in the parking lot. The rosary delivered me into a soothing, trancelike state, and at such moments my soul came as close as it ever has to a state of prayer. I liked the click and tactility of the beads, and my thoughts drifted through the church in a floating haze, a small meditative wandering.

Almost twenty years later, after I had a heart attack, I tried to buy a rosary in New York City. I wanted a rosary like the heavy one I had used at Gonzaga, one with a silver crucifix and worn black wooden beads. I remembered that almost trancelike state of prayer. I wanted a rosary to hold in my pocket and finger when the coronary panic would descend on me, when I was certain the black fist in my chest was going to clutch into a hard ball again and stop my blood. I had that panic for months. When it came, I would finger my small bottle of nitroglycerine in my pocket, as if it were my only connection with life. I thought a rosary might serve the purpose. I became obsessive, looking for the rosary. Mary-worship had gone so far out of spiritual style by the mid-seventies that a rosary was almost impossible to find. When I asked a nun about one in a Catholic bookstore near Grand Central Station, she looked at me as if I were a religious fanatic. I received the same look, mixed with contempt, when I later tried to find a Baltimore Catechism of the kind we used at Gonzaga every day. I never found the rosary. Eventually, the heart panics passed.

In those years at Gonzaga, I was not cynical about worship. Once, the rector of Gonzaga assembled the entire student body in the upper church, the grander sanctuary that was used for special occasions, while the lower church served the daily business of the school and the remnants of the parish. The occasion was unusual. We were to do reverence to a relic of a Jesuit saint, a fragment of bone from his foot that had been brought to us from Rome in a much worn golden case that looked like a woman's compact. We filed in long lines to the altar rail and knelt, and—in a brief instant of piety and repulsion and curiosity—we kissed the flat round golden case, presented to us at arm's length by a priest in vestments. After each kiss, the priest wiped the gold surface quickly with a soft white linen cloth, and then thrust the relic out again to meet the next boy's half-pursed lips. We kissed it like small children acting on a dare. One of my classmates, a descendant of Studs Lonigan, afterward claimed with a leer that he had "frenched" the relic.

I had never encountered the native, defiantly anticlerical punk before, the scourge of nuns, the baiter of priests. To me, priests possessed an impressive and even faintly terrifying authority. The Studs Lonigan boys at Gonzaga, raw and smart, were inventively sacrilegious. One day during Lent, our class gathered in the chapel for the Adoration of the Blessed Sacrament. A Polish boy, a sullen, sneering character who was nearly electric with defiance, was the first of our class to drink, and drink heavily. Sometimes when he came to school in the morning, he actually smelled of beer.

In the chapel, the boy edged toward the vestry at the side of the altar. There he found the cruets, the small jars in which the water and wine for mass were kept. He seized the little jar of red wine, and as we watched horrified, he drank it down: the blood of Christ, or what would have been the blood of Christ at the next transubstantiation. Then the kid smiled his idiot grin, his bad teeth showing, and allowed a squirt of red wine to dribble onto his chin. He wiped his mouth with the entire forearm of his jacket sleeve, and grinned again. The priest obliviously went on with his incantational Latin.

Boys like that never let any opportunity pass to bait or mock a priest, to ridicule his authority, to diminish him. The boy had drunk the altar wine, I suppose, as a way of exposing the priest: Hey, Father, fuck you! Strike me with lightning! There was a lot of immigrant defiance in it, a strutting of manliness against authority—and especially against the authority of these men in black dresses who never got any pussy (that we knew about) and yet claimed supernatural, dictatorial powers. Those boys had grown up chafing against the Church, giving nuns the finger behind their backs. To me, such contemptuous blasphemy seemed incomprehensible. I was too new to the Church's embrace to wish to defy it, to repulse its fierce clasp.

Some of the Jesuits returned violence with violence. There were legends about that. There had been one priest once, the story said, who was only a little more than five feet tall and almost grotesquely muscled, with biceps that strained the sleeves of his cassock. He looked round and hard and lumpy and always angry enough to kill. The rector and the headmaster seem to have known that the priest was given to irrational rages. In a precaution designed to soothe him, the school pumped a continuous stream of classical music into his office, a gentle in-house Muzak that no other member of the faculty enjoyed.

The force-field of anger buzzed around him, nevertheless. It terrified the students. But it seemed only to arouse and challenge the priest-baiters. One Polish boy's face was lightly dusted with pimples, which he tried to conceal under a thin, wispy beard, more like dirty down than whiskers. The priest warned him to shave. He warned him several times. He sent the boy to Jug each time— the Jesuits' after-school detention. At last one day the priest found the boy unshaven still, in the corridor outside our classroom. The priest seized him, clutching a fistful of the boy's shirt and tie, and dragged him into his office. There, with the classical music piping softly and unavailingly, the priest took a Gillette safety-blade razor to the boy's face and shaved it without soap or water. He emerged from the office dabbing his bloody cheeks with paper towels, his pimples all decapitated.

I heard that another priest had once taken a boy out onto the handball court behind the school. The story said that the boy had told the priest to go fuck himself. The priest removed his cassock and Roman collar, and like a union goon, he jolted the boy around the handball court with hard body punches.

I went back to Gonzaga one day in early November twenty years later. I flew down from New York on the shuttle. We landed in bright sunshine, but the sky looked like histrionic March. Wonderful gunpowder-dark clouds blew fast behind the Capitol dome and the city's other federal marbles, all white and splashed with sunlight. Red and gold leaves still hung on Washington's trees. The sky's sheer urgent motion made the city seem to rotate. My eyes took it in as if by time-lapse photography. Washington lies low upon the horizon; its sky is vastly larger than New York's or Boston's. It is possible to feel in the air in Washington sometimes a kind of nineteenth-century sense of history, the imminence of events of size and drama.

Days like this there had always made me ache with a deep, vague longing whose object I could never identify: a large sense of wistfulness and loss. I enjoyed the sensation. It brought tears to my eyes. I suppose that Washington, D.C., is an unlikely city for anyone to love—a transients' city, furnished with bureaucrats and marble and vast dreary semi-slums and a pervasive mediocrity of spirit that sometimes seems deliberate and even ideological (something to do with the American flirtation with the lowest common denominator, with the rule that if you want to get re-elected, you don't offend the voters out there by going to Washington and getting elegant and witty). Yet I loved the city, and whenever I return there I feel that ache of familiarity and home and the irrecoverable loss of the years I'd spent there.

I had called the headmaster's office from the airport. I explained that I just wanted to see the school again; might I come by and walk around? The secretary told me to come ahead. The taxi brought me down North Capitol Street past the Government Printing Office. As we approached Eye Street and the Church of St. Aloysius, I saw that the entire block that had once held the whorehouse across the street from Father Clements' Latin class was gone. A football stadium stood there—something that Gonzaga had not had when I was a student.

But the school looked much the same. I went inside and found that the rector, Father Bernard Dooley, was expecting me. We wandered together through the school for an hour or more. More blacks attended the school now. The pews in the chapel had, for some reason, been replaced by Breuer chairs, which gave it a pleasant airiness; the chapel did not seem as regimented as once it did when the football team would lumber in before a game wearing their uniforms, the cleats clacking on the linoleum floor and denting it, and kneel to pray for victory in a ceremony that always reminded me of some brute Visigothic rite on the outskirts of Rome before the slaughter.

Father Dooley, and Gonzaga, had clearly been brushed by the sixties, by Vatican II and the astonishing process that had so deeply changed the Church. As we stood outside the chapel now, a hulking sixteen-year-old stole up behind the Jesuit rector and grabbed him around the shoulders and horsed him playfully across the hall.

I was stunned. In my generation, I would as easily have brought in a pistol and shot the rector as contemplate such physical liberties with him. Father Dooley just laughed good-naturedly and wrestled loose and gave the boy a playful mock punch on the shoulder— doing all this without missing a beat in his conversation with me. Just a normal, pleasant moment between the rector and a student.

Father Dooley invited me to have lunch in the rectory. I was still in my own mind time-traveling, and somewhere I found it inconceivable to be having lunch with these priests and scholastics in their dining room—which had always been as intensely private as the rest of their lives—and listening to their faculty gossip.

Across the table from us was an old Jesuit who had spent many years in the missions in India, and was evidently just visiting in the United States. He had a thin, pure, tragic face with oddly glazed eyes, the color of cobalt. I was introduced to him, but I seemed to make no impression on him whatever. His mind was utterly elsewhere. Father Dooley treated the man with a gentle deference, as if the priest were ill or had endured some immense sadness. The sadness, of course, may have been simply India.

As we ate lasagna and plain, overcooked vegetables, I told Father Dooley how astonished I had been by the boy who grabbed him around the shoulders. Father Dooley looked at me for a moment, and said softly, "Ah, yes. This place really ran on fear when you were here, didn't it?"

It was during the annual retreats that the fear was virtually formalized. During the first three years, the retreat was held at the school itself. We heard sermons in the upper church, we meditated, and so on, but we did not actually withdraw into seclusion.

The Jesuit retreat sermon is an art form that has probably been lost forever since Vatican II. James Joyce had the prototype perfectly in *A Portrait of the Artist As a Young Man.* The Jesuit retreat masters at Gonzaga all had their distinctive styles, their favorite metaphors. One of them conducted our retreat in the chapel during the sophomore year. He was a raw Irishman with a crew cut and a tough, slightly wild look in his eye. I liked him very much. His best retreat parable went like this:

"So, boys, I was sitting in the hold with the fellas as we come in toward the beach at Iwo. Well, they were scared, and they were thinking about their girl friends and their mothers. And a lot of the boys were playing cards. They were playing poker, and betting heavy. And they were swearing a lot. And some of them were talking about girls. But I noticed there was one boy who didn't join the rest. He was sitting off by himself. I went over and introduced myself to Joe Santilli. I asked if he was scared, and he said sure, he was scared. The other guys told Joe to come and join them playing cards and talking about girls, but Joe said no. He did not tell them why, but he did tell me. He said 'Father, I don't want to go in to the beach tomorrow with a sin on my soul, or an impure thought.' Well, boys, Joe Santilli went in the next day, in the first wave to hit the beach. He took a bullet through the heart. *But, boys: he died in the State of Grace.*"

Father Dolan gave a lurid retreat. This was a sort of debased Fulton Sheen variety of Catholic anecdote and dramaturgy; it was the Catholic equivalent of rural revivalist dementia and snake-handling rhetoric. Father Dolan was especially riveted by the way that Christ's flesh was flayed and stripped during the Scourging at the Pillar. Father Dolan could advance through the Sorrowful Mysteries with a panting, unwholesome attention to detail. The general method of his retreat sermons was to induce a feeling of shame by detailing all the bloodily physical suffering that Christ endured in order to redeem us. We must strive to be worthy of such pain and sacrifice.

Father Dolan painted a gaudy picture of it. But he was, after all, speaking to boys of the twentieth century—we were ignorant, but we knew enough of the general horrors of the world to wonder (after the Holocaust, after Stalin) whether the sheer sufferings of Christ were that exceptional. We did not wonder about it impiously. We merely thought that perhaps Father Dolan had not played his strongest card.

Perhaps the most effective rhetorical image I heard from a Jesuit arose spontaneously one afternoon in class. A scholastic, filling in for a religion teacher, blurted out this luminous fantasy of temptation:

"One night during my juniorate, a group of us were driving back to Woodstock [the seminary of the Jesuits' Province of Maryland] along a winding two-lane road. We came around a corner in the dark, and suddenly our headlights flashed onto a car parked beside the road, and sitting on the hood of the car, with her legs up and her skirt pulled back, there was a girl reclining and waving for us to stop. We only saw her for an instant in the headlights. The devil wanted us to stop. But we all told the one who was driving, *"Step on it, go by! Leave her!"*

I wondered in later years if that scholastic made it to ordination.

8·Two Divorces

My father divorced my mother. I divorced the Catholic Church. The two events were related, though not simultaneous.

It was during my sophomore year that my parents' marriage at last broke apart. It had become a war. Hughie and I lay upstairs in bed on the third floor, with pillows pressed over our heads, trying to sleep, trying not to hear. There were four young children in the house (two baby girls, Cathleen and Christina, two boys, Pat and Mike). The children never cried. They never said a word.

After months of it, I woke one morning and my mother was gone. My father told me gently, at seven in the morning, in the cool, dim dining room of the house, that they were getting separated. She was moving out.

Thus my father and I began a kind of collaboration. I moved down from my room on the third floor. I took over the room that had been my mother's study—somewhat guiltily took it over. The big, rather ugly house on Newark Street acquired a certain serenity. It was the peace of aftermath.

I remember my father from those years as a man of enormous grace and virtue. He was just forty. His hair was turning gray at the temples. In a way, my mother's departure simplified his role. He had always done the Saturday grocery shopping, for example. He usually had along a couple of children, who acted as his runners. Up and down the aisles of the Giant Food store (Newark Street and Wisconsin Avenue) he made his way with brimming carts. He was a thorough and profligate shopper. He went into a fugue state of efficiency and gluttonous impulse.

My father was fond of eating, and it made him peaceful, I think, to walk down aisles stuffed with food and pluck down at whim whatever he wanted from the shelves. With so many children to feed, he filled five or six shopping carts before he arrived at the checkout counter. (I remember that during the Korean War, another shopper saw him checking out his groceries and muttered loudly, "Hoarder!")

Besides the gallons of milk and orange juice, the cereals and eggs and other fuels for his children, my father liked exotic items—things from the gourmet counter, macadamia nuts, Danish cheeses.

We both knew the store, its vast layout. While he stayed with the main cart, the headquarters vessel, I would venture out on foraging missions. I would raid for sugar, coffee, peanut butter and ketchup at one sweep, and then round to meet him at the dairy cases, where he would be taking on carton after carton of milk. Then he would rumble slowly off toward Bread, while I darted up another aisle for Salt.

It was a military provisioning, but also a form of domestic Zen. We had an old Ford station wagon. When its wooden side panels started to rot away, my father replaced them with a patchwork of aluminum sheets. It looked like it belonged to a Georgia dirt farmer. But it worked. At the supermarket, we would load the station wagon's rear deck with a dozen bags of groceries or more and head home in a quiet triumph. There, with the smaller children crowded around, the boys rooting in the bags for their favorite things (jars of fresh fruit cocktail lasted only ten minutes), we would unpack the weekly abundance and distribute all the items where they belonged in cabinets and bins. It gave the world a domestic order that we did not take for granted.

My father cooked well. Like shopping, cooking put him into a kind of trance of well-being. It seemed to relax him profoundly. My mother had always been an excellent cook, sometimes extravagantly fancy. She was very good at it, very French, hectically intense in the kitchen. Sometimes her productions turned into disasters of blackened pots and charred meats and curdled sauces.

My father approached the kitchen with a puttering serenity. Nothing flapped him. He timed meats in the oven by a casual glance at their crusts, he arranged the outcome of half a dozen dishes with some weird offhanded internal gift to make everything emerge at just about the same time, hot and simple.

His most complex production was eggs Benedict. He made the best hollandaise sauce that I have ever tasted. But it pretty much wrecked the kitchen every time he made it. The process (which, unlike the roast beef sort of Sunday dinner, was pursued with unusual concentration and intensity) left the stove and kitchen table strewn with eggshells and messy pots, which he scattered everywhere in a chaos of creativity.

Many years later, he taught me to make the sauce. I told him I remembered the wreck he made of the kitchen whenever he did hollandaise when I was a child. He arched his eyebrows. "My boy," he said, "I think your memory likes to indulge in caricature."

And, of course, it does. A child's imagination is essentially a myth-maker and caricaturist, and memory preserves the myths and caricatures even as the child advances toward middle age.

With my mother gone, we fell into a routine of defensive, obsessive normality. The boys, Pat and Mike, got themselves off to grammar school with that peculiar autonomy that children in large families often develop. They dressed themselves, made their own breakfasts. I cannot recall that either of them ever asked where their mother had gone. Or when she would be coming back. It was not that they did not wonder, but that even they understood the undeclared law, the injunction in the air, against talking about her. It was as if talking about her would open the door again, and all the rage would pour out again, all of the swarming black bats.

The legal-separation agreement was extraordinarily hard on my mother. In the beginning, her visits to the children were strictly limited—an hour a week. She could not take them away from the house, but must visit them there. It was an ugly arrangement. She suffered deeply.

It was I who became the officer on watch when my mother came to visit. I met her at the front door at the designated hour of the late afternoon. She came like a supplicant. Playing the major domo of these excruciating reunions, I coaxed my mother into the living room—her living room—a strangely elongated room that would be rather dim in the late afternoon light.

In innocuous small talk, no diplomat can equal a child caught in the middle. Starting with those visits by my mother, I became a genius of conversational navigation, making my way across shallows and rapids, always steering for open water. Like a guide with some desperate extra sense, I detected danger at an almost impossible distance, and learned to point my vulnerable, incendiary mother so subtly and effortlessly downwind that she barely noticed.

My mother would perch on the edge of the sofa in an agony of nerves, like a woman in a doctor's office awaiting some awful verdict about her breast. Then I would bring in the children, two at a time.

"How is school, Patty?" she would ask. Pat would manage a shy, noncommittal shrug. A tempest of tears. Then: "Mikey? Mikey, what are you playing now?" Mike would look confused and desperate. I would hover behind the couch, my face composed in a mask of professional normality, like an amiable shrink in the day-room of maniacs, and encourage cheerful interaction.

During her visits my father would stay in the kitchen or upstairs in the hall, just within earshot—pacing with an angry and anxious face. When she left, he would rush into the living room like air into a vacuum and stand, looking around, as if to see if anything was missing, if anything had gotten burned, or broken.

When my mother and I left the house she would be in a bitter, nihilistic mood that concealed, all the same, a certain relief. It would be just five, the start of the rush hour. The air was darkening as all the civil servants filled the streets of Washington and started home.

My mother and I one evening took a cab downtown to a German restaurant she liked. She sat in the cab muttering, "Oh, God! Oh, God!" But her despair had exhausted itself. A new light came into her face, a hint of recklessness. We arrived at the restaurant. As she got out of the cab, two sailors walking up the street stopped and gave her for an instant a thorough and appreciative carnal eye. They paid no attention to me. I looked at my mother and saw that she was giving them back that reckless eye of her own—a look with a flounce and swagger in it, a slightly rolling Marlene Dietrich look.

The Jesuits for a time had thought that I might become a priest. A Jesuit. Eventually they seemed to hope only that I would go to a Catholic college. But they did not suffer any spiritual crisis over my case. I was a convert who had come late to the faith, and under peculiar circumstances.

My falling away was regrettable, but not the sort of tragedy and scandal that it might have been for a cradle Catholic. If anything, a priest might have privately told himself, Well, what would you expect?

The Jesuits knew that they had less authority over me than they would need to call me back. My family was not Catholic—not really—the mother who had brought the children into the Church in the first place was evidently in some trouble and had gone away.

The Jesuits were right. I had fallen more and more under my father's sway. He regarded my Catholicism kindly. He even came to the father-son communion breakfasts that Gonzaga held every year. He listened with his light irony to the speakers that we hired for such events: the pigeon-breasted silver-haired Knights of Columbus Hibernians, heroic breakfast orators, descendants of Robert Emmett, the tellers of nun jokes. My father had a kind of supernatural patience for such events.

I had drifted off slowly. I stopped going to confession on Thursday afternoon with the other boys. I stopped taking communion at the Friday-morning mass. The other students rose in their pews and filed down the center aisle to the ornate communion rail. I sat in my place, defiant and almost alone, and waited for the others to come shambling back from the rail, each boy surreptitiously working the wafer off the roof of his mouth with his tongue, his hands half clasped in front of him, just above the groin, as if to conceal the organ that most got him into trouble: the occasion of his confessions on Thursday afternoon.

The Jesuits noticed that I was no longer receiving the sacraments. They looked at me with a saddened but also hurt and silently hostile gaze. I caught one young scholastic regarding me as we filed out of church one Friday morning. He shook his head: I was a fool.

I saw that look, years later, on the face of a priest who came to visit me in New York Hospital before my bypass operation. When I came to the hospital, my wife filled out the forms. Under "Religion," she listed me as Roman Catholic. The priest came to call at my bedside the night before my operation. He was a man in his fifties, with a smooth white face that looked as if it had been talced. His silver hair was crew-cut. A baby's white bottom with grizzle on it.

I was surprised to see him. "Father," I said, "I have not been a practicing Catholic for nearly eighteen years."

He leaned suddenly forward in his chair, as if to say, Well, time to get down to business, then!

I leaned back in my bed, away from the priest's insistent face. Body English. I would not start up again, not with the Church again, not now. No foxhole conversions, among other things.

"This is a serious operation," the priest said. "You must think of your soul."

I said, "No, thank you, Father." Then he gave me the same look that the Jesuit had given me at Gonzaga, shook his head and left the hospital room.

My mother in years past had wanted me to go to Notre Dame. The priest in charge of such advice, Father Magee, tried to steer me toward Holy Cross, Boston College and other Jesuit schools. He included Wheeling College, in West Virginia.

I applied only to Harvard. Harvard was my defiance of the Jesuits. To apply only to Harvard was foolhardy, a bridge-burning stunt. I was showing off. My application amounted to a formal declaration of apostasy. Harvard was a school where a young Catholic would go to lose his faith. Defying the Catholic Church gave me a certain amount of bravado, an energetic nerve.

No one at Gonzaga tried to talk me out of this folly. The Jesuits were impressed by intellectual quality. And so, they were ambivalent about Harvard. It was, in a small way, the old Jesuit conflict between faith and worldly excellence.

The end of my faith did not seem especially dramatic. Maybe

what happened was that the principle of my father in me overcame the principle of my mother. My mother's religion represented magic, and dark, unreliable, violent worlds. It was miraculously theatrical, populated with saints and devils. It was passionate and sometimes frightening. My mother's element was as thick as blood. My father stood for sanity, a certain airiness, a deftness of spirit, a nimble heart, tolerant and ironic. An agnostic, out of Protestant soil.

I sat one spring morning in religion class at Gonzaga in my last year. The subject of the class was vocations to the priesthood. There were not many future priests, I thought, among the boys in that room. The Jesuit scholastic who was our teacher seemed actually to hate us, and he paced up and down the aisles between the desks with a restless animal energy. He reviewed the conditions for a vocation. He banged his Baltimore Catechism against the heel of his hand as he paced. His black cassock swept among us in a sort of virtuous rage, bearing down. He was a heavy smoker. I could see that he needed a cigarette. It had been a long morning for him.

The headmaster's secretary came to interrupt the class to tell me that my father was on the telephone. It was thus a formal occasion, something special. Otherwise I would not have been called out of class. I shot out of the room as if someone had died. I almost believed that someone had. My father was waiting on the phone.

"Well," he said, "you made it. You're in. Neil MacNeil just called me, and you're in Harvard." Neil MacNeil was a journalist, the Harvard alumnus who had interviewed me in Washington for the admissions committee.

That was my emancipation from Gonzaga, from the Jesuits, from the Catholic Church.

I returned to class, to the discussion of Vocations and the Priesthood. But I was now transformed, invulnerable. I was saved. No seminary doors would be closing upon me. I was free of the murmuring dusks of penitance in confession booths, of that thick incense in the air of the upper church, of crucifixes, saints, scapulars, and all of the working-class, acned boys with their pegged pants and their mouth-breathing.

The Jesuits in their black robes, like crows, now would approach in the halls and then they would veer away and avert their gaze, as if I had died to them, like a son who has married outside the faith, the tribe. They no longer existed to me, either. We were dead to each other.

I floated through the spring. I was now apart from my classmates. They would be going to Notre Dame or Holy Cross or Seton Hall or Boston College or Wheeling or Loyola. Or into the Navy. I had become again a curiosity in their midst, just visiting, and not entirely to be trusted.

Or, to some, I became a source of envy and even of admiration. I went beer-drinking with them sometimes. We went to a bar out Wisconsin Avenue whose walls were lined with Frank Sinatra record albums. The jukebox played Sinatra all afternoon and evening, and we drank frosted schooners of beer. We talked about girls, and college, and getting away from the Jesuits. We talked about all these things outside of the context of sin. At last. We felt an immense liberation. There seemed now no accounting to be done, no more of that baleful arithmetic of venial and mortal sins, that ledger-keeping, that moral litigation, that airless, clammy guiltiness. Sin would always rise, and we would always feel helpless to prevent it. The erection in the middle of mass was as inevitable as the terror we felt that it would come: our terror conjured it up, in fact. Now at the end of it, we swaggered, to be so delivered, as if from the penitentiary.

Classes with the Jesuits became a chore that I attended to with a kind of offhanded contempt. I managed to pass through the final exams without serious damage to my class standing. I graduated one hot night in late spring, sitting on the stage in the auditorium where I had suffered through dozens of elocution lessons and contests. My father sat in the audience for one last event of Catholic oratory. The headmaster, Father McHale, handed me my diploma with a sort of elegantly sardonic nod. Which I returned.

That summer I went back to Danville. I rented a room this time in the house of an old couple. The husband was the janitor in the local high school. He watched baseball games at night in his small living room, with no light on except the flickering black-and-white television set. He sat in a little easy chair in his undershirt. I spent many evenings with him like that, but I think we hardly exchanged one hundred words all summer.

It was easier for me to get away from Danville now. My father had bought me a car during my last year at Gonzaga—a 1951 Pontiac coupé. It overheated on the upgrade, and rarely had the power to get me up over 60 miles per hour. I drove home to Washington every Friday night through the Pennsylvania and Maryland back roads. The car had no radio. I amused myself by declaiming poetry at the top of my lungs. I would do all of "The Hollow Men," a number that I had recited once in a Gonzaga elocution contest. I could pull out the stops. I gesticulated with one hand, the other on the steering wheel, tearing down the country two-lanes toward home, by turns screaming and sibilantly whispering:

WE ARE THE HOLLOW MEN! We are the stuffed men. Leaning together, head piece filled with sssssstraw. ALAS! our dried voices, when we WHISSSSSPER together, are quiet and meaningless, as wind in dry grasssss . . . OR RATS' feet over broken glass . . . in our . . . dry cellar!

I liked Yeats's "There was a green branch hung with many a bell/ When her own people ruled this tragic Eire . . ." I always did that after "The Hollow Men." For fun, I would do Vachel Lindsay's *Congo:* "Boomlay, boomlay, boomlay, Boom!"

But if I had come to loathe Gonzaga, I could not be utterly happy with Harvard either; it was not my world, not my father's world either. I arrived at Harvard Yard in early September 1958. I was assigned to Holworthy Hall. For roommates, I found that Harvard had assigned me the son of a Protestant pastor from Alabama, and a kid from Montana. The boy from Montana was sardonically lost. I missed my father in ways I could not explain.

The rooms were crowded. I drew the top bunk in a tiny room with the Protestant's son. The room always smelled of socks that needed to be washed.

My desk stood against a wall in the living room. The Harvard Student Agencies supplied an ink blotter for the desk that was covered with advertising for the Harvard Coop and the Gold Coast Valeteria and the Brattle Theater. There was an ad for the Tremont

Temple. It said: "Worship God in an air-conditioned sanctuary!"

We ate all our meals at the freshman union. I was intimidated by some of the exotics in the class. There was an extravagant young European who looked like a gypsy of noble birth. He wore a gold earring.

The student employment office found me a job working in the Winthrop House dining hall. I stood in the cafeteria serving line and dished out lima beans and mashed potatoes at dinnertime to the Winthrop House students.

Phillip, another student who worked in the serving line, was in my freshman gen. ed. writing class. Phillip loved Schopenhauer. He had read him with a fierce sense of revelation. I was repelled by him, and so we fought about Schopenhauer as we dished out the vegetables. Admirable Harvard.

"He knows the way life is," Phillip would say. Life was painful, and so on.

"No," I would say, "he knows nothing. Life is not like that at all." I was terrified that it might be.

The Aga Khan lived in Winthrop House. He came through the food line for dinner sometimes. He was a tall, swarthily handsome student prince with an entourage. He carried his round plastic tray, divided into compartments for the various courses. I served him mashed potatoes one night. I ladled out a fat glop. I gave the spoon a smart flick of my wrist so that the potatoes traveled their last inch in midair and landed with a small splat on the Aga Khan's tray. The effect was lost to everyone but me. The Aga Khan was deep in conversation with the young man behind him in the line, who wore an ascot. The Aga Khan looked back at his companion. He did not look at me. The two of them passed down the line toward the salad. There I was in the servant class, giving mashed potatoes to a dynast. Not even an American. My father would be serving up words to Rockefeller.

I detested Harvard then. I had to leave. I felt physically repelled by the place.

The proctor of our entry at Holworthy Hall was an earnest law student. He gave a party in his rooms to welcome us to the hall. He bought a keg of beer for the occasion. He greeted us with a little speech, and he then invited us to help ourselves to the beer.

"I will trust you with it, gentlemen," he told us. "You know your limit." We were deeply touched.

Three hours later, at least half of us were retchingly drunk. We staggered up and down the stairs of the entryway at Holworthy. We had to dump one boy under a cold shower with all his clothes on.

On Columbus Day I sought out a relative of my stepmother's, Dr. Gaylord Coon, who was the chief psychiatrist for the Harvard health services. I found him in an upstairs office in one of those charming houses on Mount Auburn Street that used to serve as little offices for the university.

"Doctor," I said, "I have to go." It was the same as telling a Jesuit that I did not have the vocation.

When I was much older, I returned to the Church. I did so very gingerly, first peering in for a long moment, letting my eyes adjust to the lights and shadows of the place. I knew that it had changed, but I had no feeling for what it had become.

Gradually, I saw that it was a sweeter and softer place than it had been. The anger had gone out of it, that dark punitive vibration, the Pauline scowl. The Church was more habitable now, more human. Perhaps it was also that the anger had departed from me as well.

The old black mystery was gone, too. I regretted that, for a while. I missed the Latin, the elaborate, enameled ritual, the high rhetoric and hieratic pageantry. The sixties seemed to have left their mark of fatuity upon the institution. The mass that I remembered from my youth ended with the magnificent *Ita, missa est.* Now I heard a priest one Sunday morning finish off his performance by saying "The mass is ended. Have a nice day." I saw another priest, a TV priest, saying mass in vestments adorned with a happy sunburst design and the words "Here comes the Son." I wished then to sign up for the heresy of the retrograde, those Catholics who had begun staging Latin masses in defiance of Rome.

But I came to see that perhaps the change was just as well. The departure of the densely brocaded mysteries, it may be, allowed one to confront more simply the real mysteries of things.

I came to see that the Church was not the Father turned into an architecture of eternity, not an inflexible outward form, but was a medium through which the soul might aspire. I saw that struggling toward God was a process, an active and not a passive enterprise.

I went back to the Church in part for the sake of my son Jamie. In any case, I no longer sought authority there, the comfort of its domination, the principle of the father. The Church now seemed a smaller thing, more on equal terms with the world. The Church had grown a little confused, like everyone, I thought. The confusion diminished the Church, but was in some ways endearing.

My father came to Jamie's first communion. It was on a bright spring morning in May, in the Church of St. Thomas More, just down the street from Jamie's school. There was none of the rigid ceremony that once attended the first communion. Jamie and his classmates crowded around the priest on the altar in a sweetly disorderly way, and they helped him along, and grinned out at their parents in the congregation.

I sat in the pew in a crowd of parents, the fathers beaming and taking pictures. At the consecration, we all knelt. Kneeling, my hands folded in front of me, I turned my head and glanced across at my father. He did not kneel, he sat, and on his face I saw that expression of remote and faintly amused irony that I had seen almost thirty years before in a church on Pennsylvania Avenue on a rainy Sunday when my mother returned from the communion rail looking like the Madonna.

9·Breaking Away

My mother called me from Chicago in 1969. She blurted, "Eric died."

I told her how sorry I was, and meant it. I walked down the hall to the international department of *Time* magazine, and found the London *Times* obituary. Eric Dorman Smith, it said. I called back and read the obituary to my mother, and she cried softly. She had not seen him in years, but her past with him came back to her.

I met Eric in the summer of 1961. My friend Wayne Nichols from Harvard was going to London on a student flight. My father agreed to give me $500 for a summer in Europe. In those days, it was almost enough.

I wanted to break away. I had worked for newspapers every summer since I was sixteen. Going away to Harvard had been the first real venture out of my father's world, and into one where he did not belong. He sensed that. That may have been partly why I sought out Eric O'Gowan. Independence seemed to demand an exercise of treachery: an odd logic, but one deeply embedded in the family.

It was also curiosity. When my mother learned I was going to Ireland, she gave me Eric's telephone number in County Cavan. I called him from a telephone booth on O'Connell Street in Dublin, across the way from the Post Office of the 1916 uprising.

Under the circumstances, Eric was remarkably polite, but slightly flustered and guarded. He asked me to call again the next day. I did, from Cork. He invited me to come to Cavan for a visit. He gave me directions. He lived in an eighteenth-century manor house in Coote Hill in County Cavan. It was called Bellamont.

My mother's friend Eric was a mystery to me, an exotic. He was retired from the British army. He had been General Eric Dorman Smith, graduate of Sandhurst, veteran of two world wars, and other things that I learned about only slowly. His brother, Sir Reginald Dorman Smith, was governor of Burma during the war, and before that, Chamberlain's minister of agriculture. Eric had changed his name, from Dorman Smith, to O'Gowan, which, he told me, meant "son of the smith" in Irish. The change seemed odd. His father, I gathered, had been a prominent landowner in Ireland, and a farmer. Anglo-Irish, surely. Eric seemed to want to be utterly Irish; his genes seemed very English.

He met me in Coote Hill when I got off the bus. I was scruffy from days on the road. I carried a knapsack. Eric examined me gaily and kindly, and pronounced me to be like my mother. I thought that I was more like my father.

Eric was certainly nothing like my father. He was very British and as thin as Fred Astaire, and he carried himself with a dated and debonair distinction. His eyes were bright and dancingly alive. His thin face was framed by reddish-graying curls. We went across the road to his Anglia and drove to Bellamont.

The house, like Eric, was a splendid specimen of aristocratic certitude. It was an ancestral red brick mansion in a forest. The house was draftily elegant. I was to sleep in a guest bedroom on the second floor. A servant girl mortified me by taking my filthy clothes out of my knapsack and returning them washed and folded the first afternoon.

On the piano downstairs in a sort of ballroom stood a silver-framed portrait of Ernest Hemingway. It was inscribed: "*To Poppelthwaite, after many years. Hem.*" Eric's nickname for Hemingway was Chink. Eric had fought in the Battle of the Somme. He told me that once he was on patrol and had to walk across a sunken road that was carpeted with corpses. He had to walk across the bodies to get to the other side: *upon* the bodies, his boot on their backs and shoulders and guts.

Eric was sitting in a café in Milan in 1918 when the war ended.

By chance, the man at the next table was Ernest Hemingway. "We both said the same thing at the same time," Eric told me. "We said, 'So we've got to go on living.' That made us friends. We went out and got drunk together." Hemingway put Eric into some of his stories. Eric was the young British officer in *Men Without Women* who shot the Germans as they crossed the bridge.

I stayed at Bellamont for ten days. Eric got up every morning at six to run. He said he had run that way every morning all his life. Once in North Africa he almost got captured by the Germans while he was out on his morning run. Wearing gum boots, he ran six miles every day, up and down hills, along the trails through the forest surrounding the manor house. I got up with him every morning. We listened to the news report on the BBC and drank tea, and then went out into the light rain and ran.

One morning we passed a pair of wild swans that were sliding on the misted lake. I was filled with W. B. Yeats then. And huffing and puffing, I repeated a few lines from "The Wild Swans at Coole":

> *But now they drift on the still water,*
> *Mysterious, beautiful;*
> *Among what rushes will they build,*
> *By what lake's edge or pool*
> *Delight men's eyes when I awake some day*
> *To find that they have flown away?*

Eric glanced at me and said crisply, "Quite."

I discovered that he disliked Yeats. He dismissed Yeats as an Anglo-Irishman with only a shallow knowledge and understanding of the Irish. He thought that "Easter, 1916," for example ("All changed, changed utterly:/ A terrible beauty is born") was merely Yeats's rather silly discovery that deeds have consequences, that history is real.

Still, Eric was gracious. My third morning at Bellamont, he arranged an expedition for us. We drove up to County Sligo, to Yeats country. We passed through several counties. When we met a man on the road, he would salute us. Eric pointed out that each county had a distinctive salute. One could recognize a man on the road by his gesture of greeting. In Cavan, as I recall, a man gave a short sharp downward jerk of the head. Or it may have been a very Irish little flick of the right forefinger outward from just above the right eyebrow. I forget. Eric demonstrated the salute of each county as we passed through. Ireland seemed to give him an enormous pleasure of authenticity.

Eric was generous about Yeats. If I had a misinformed enthusiasm for Yeats, he would indulge it. He pointed out the Yeatsian scenery. There was bare Ben Bulben's head, like a whale's brow looking out toward the North Atlantic. We stopped at Drumcliff churchyard, where Yeats is buried.

The cemetery was divided into Protestant and Catholic sections. On the Protestant side the graves were neatly tended, the grass cut, the stones arranged in orderly rows, all upstanding and rectilinear. Yeats's limestone marker was exactly as prescribed:

> No marble, no conventional phrase:
> On limestone quarried near the spot
> By his command these words are cut:
>
> > *Cast a cold eye*
> > *On life, on death.*
> > *Horseman, pass by!*

I loved the epitaph, and it was several years before it occurred to me to wonder if it had any meaning at all. I decided that it did not: that it was Yeats in his high, grand, enigmatic manner.

Across the fence line in the Catholic burial ground, all was chaos. The gravestones were centuries older: they were worn and tumbledown. They stood at all angles to one another, and the weeds grew thickly over most of them. We wandered for a while in the Catholic section. Eric seemed to enjoy it. He gave the Catholics a reverence he did not show to the Protestants.

"So many centuries of Catholics have been buried here, you know," he said to me, "that they are all piled one on top of the other."

I picked up a piece of what I thought was white stone, as if to give it an archaeological inspection. Eric looked at me and said with kind amusement, " 'Alas, poor Yorick . . .' "

I saw that I was holding, of course, the shard of a skull, and laid it quickly down again, embarrassed and shocked. We continued through the mess of Catholic mortality.

I gathered that in the process of becoming an Irishman, Eric had become a pious Catholic as well. He seemed like a Jew of the Diaspora who now had become utterly Jewish, utterly Israeli, de-assimilated. Eric had been thoroughly absorbed into English culture. His wife, Eve, seemed to be British. His Irishness seemed such a thorough repudiation of all of that that I wondered later if there was something unhinged in him.

In the late morning we gathered for a drink in the room behind Eric's study. A fire burned in the fireplace. Eric and Eve and Eve's mother drank Scotch, neat. I drank a bottle of stout. Eve's mother had been a suffragette and a Fabian socialist. She recalled George Bernard Shaw coming to her father's house and holding her on his knee. She lost five brothers in World War I. One of them was a rancher in western Canada. When the news of the war came, he hiked for twelve days and nights to take the boat to England. He enlisted. He was shipped to France and he died within ten hours of arriving at the front.

Eric's mother-in-law lived on Jersey. She had come to Cavan for a visit. "In Ireland," she said, not entirely charmed, "every day seems like Sunday."

We talked about Catholicism. I mentioned Francis Thompson. With Eric's encouragement, I found myself reciting "The Hound of Heaven," in a self-conscious rush: "I fled Him, down the nights and down the days;/ I fled Him, down the arches of the years;/ I fled Him, down the labyrinthine ways/ Of my own mind; and in the mist of tears/ I hid from Him . . ."

On Sunday, we went to mass at a Sacred Heart brothers' novitiate several miles away. Eve and Eric and I were the only laymen at the mass. The chapel was spare. The priests greeted Eric with soft, elaborate deference. His was clearly an aristocratic form of Irish Catholicism.

The white-frocked novices sat in front of us, facing the plain stone altar. I watched the backs of their heads, which were barbered in a close, country way. The novices were sheepishly quiet and docile, and moved through the gestures of the mass with a sort of low, shuffling compliance. The priest was an American. He stood with his back to us, of course, through most of the mass. It was a high mass, and the priest's delivery was surprisingly operatic, Italian. I did not take communion.

I spent mornings at Bellamont working with Eric in his study. He wrote articles for military journals. He wrote letters to the *Times* of London. He worked with pen and ink at a large table that was covered with a litter of correspondence and newspapers.

One morning Eric looked up and asked me if I knew that Churchill had been related to an Iroquois woman. He suddenly burst into gales of laughter. I learned later that Eric hated Churchill and won a lawsuit for something that Churchill wrote in his memoirs about the North African campaign.

I sat in a corner of the study and read and made my own notes. Eric lent me books on archaeology and almost mystical Celtic history. He had me reading *The White Goddess*, and *The Races of Europe* by Carleton S. Coon. He had developed theories about the Quetzalcoatl legend in Mexico. Quetzalcoatl was clearly an Irishman, Eric said. The Spaniards found him depicted as fair and blue-eyed. He was the messiah whom the Indians awaited. And a red-haired "viracocha" had gone to the Easter Islands from Peru. *Vir-coch* was Indo-European, Eric said with an air of Eureka!, for "red-haired." Old Irish: *fir-coc*. Irishmen had colonized the world a hundred times while other civilizations slept like tubers under the earth in February.

I sat at Eric's knee in all of this. He told me I must read *The Alexandria Quartet*, which I suppose he liked for its North African atmosphere.

We talked about Hemingway. Eric remembered literary discussions in Hemingway's mill house in Paris in the twenties. He remembered when, at the christening of Hemingway's first son in Paris, Gertrude Stein turned to him and said, "Chink, what *is* the Apostle's Creed?" He talked about hiking trips in the Pyrenees with John Dos Passos. Dos Passos was night-blind, and when dusk came on, Eric had to lead him down the mountain trail like a seeing-eye dog.

Eric was a soldier, like my great-grandfather, whom I also adopted as something of a hero. They were knights.

I took the boat-train back to London. I found Wayne Nichols one morning in a cheap hotel near Russell Square. He was dislocated and weirdly terrified. He had just awakened from a dream in which Hitler had been chasing him with truckloads of SS troopers and dogs. Wayne was a long way from Kansas City.

We went to Copenhagen. Wayne bought a Volvo there, and we drove south, through Germany, to Paris. The morning we arrived, I bought a *Herald Tribune* from a vendor outside American Express. The headline said that Ernest Hemingway had died of a gunshot wound in Ketchum, Idaho.

I was ashamed of myself for my trip to Ireland. But that summer I wanted to get away from my father, away from newspapers, away from his world. I wanted to be something different. I suppose I missed him too. In one of my notebooks I wrote in southern France: "HM's disgusting habit of wolfing down peanut butter with a spoon, straight from the jar. Of wolfing down milk straight from the bottle and sticking the bottle back in the refrigerator." Then I wrote: "No, wrong, you idiot!"

Wayne Nichols and I and another friend from Harvard, Jack Nordby, drove south from Paris to Pamplona. We meant it, I suppose, as an homage to Hemingway. We arrived in time for the last day and night of San Fermin, the festival of *The Sun Also Rises*.

There were no tickets for the last bullfights. We slept for a couple of hours in a field outside Pamplona, and then drove in to celebrate the end of the fiesta.

My father, I suppose, liked Hemingway well enough. He may have been ironic about Hemingway's fame and about the quality of fraud that Hemingway acquired in his later career. My mother worshiped Hemingway. I think she exchanged a letter or two with him through Eric. I had read all of Hemingway's books by the time I was fourteen. I spent a certain amount of my adolescence imagining that I was Nick Adams. I loved the mountains in West Virginia and the Shenandoah Valley, where Hughie and I hiked a great deal when we were growing up. When I was moving through that landscape, I almost always described it to myself in the way that Hemingway would have described it.

That night, we wandered through Pamplona, from bar to bar. We joined the sea of drunks wearing red neckerchiefs. Spaniards bought us *vino tinto* in all the bars, one peseta a glass. One of them demands endlessly in Spanish that I write to him from New York. I do not understand. He despairs, and ricochets out of the bar, into the street, drunkenly obsessed with the idea of finding an American to write to him.

I watch a Spanish boy of sixteen or so, small and very drunk, careering around the loud, bright bar. He imitates a charging bull, hunched down, holding a straight-backed chair in front of him whose finials represent the horns. Another boy is matador, using his shirt as a cape. Men shout *"Eh! Eh! Toro!"* I turn back to the bar. A French girl, very beautiful, dressed in a gold blouse and gold trousers, is standing surrounded by men. She is flushed and wildly alive. She shimmers. I long to join the men around her, to reach my arm in among them and seize the girl and lead her away. But I do not. Robert Cohn at the party. I turn back to my friends. They have vanished. I realize I am very drunk.

I lurch out into the street. The street is almost empty, for a moment. The crowds ebb and flow through the town this last night of fiesta. Down toward the corner now, for an instant, I see the boy who was playing the bull. He veers from the dark side of the street, still hunched over, charging a matador who is imaginary now. Suddenly the boy charges against the opposite wall: the bright side. He charges into a long iron spike that sticks out from the wall. He takes the spike directly in the eye.

Now he pitches sideways, back, and reels and falls to his knees, and clutches his face, and on the sidewalk not far away from him, I see his perfect eyeball, detached, surprised, staring up at me.

It has been as silent as a hallucination. The boy says nothing. Then he screams. And blood rushes between the fingers he clutches to his face. Men come exploding out of the bar, indignant and drunk and delighted to investigate, ready for anything. I run for several blocks in a dead panic, like a fish going screaming away to try to get off the line.

We slept outdoors most of the time in Spain. On a deserted beach near Valencia we would wake in our sleeping bags and spend the morning dozing, reading. A Spanish police plane would swoop in low over the beach, looking for smugglers. As Eric suggested, I was reading *The Alexandria Quartet.* Then I would get out my notebook and start working out the plot of a play.

It was to be called *Foucheval.* It was about a sort of megalomaniac sculptor. The character was modeled on Korczak Ziolkowski. Korczak had been a friend of my father's for years. In the early fifties my father wrote an article for the *Saturday Evening Post* about Korczak and his grandiose project: carving an immense statue of Chief Crazy Horse out of a mountain in the Black Hills of South Dakota. Korczak, a bearded, patriarchal character, had been working at the statue for twenty or twenty-five years. He worked with jackhammers and dynamite. But he was only getting started. The outline of the chief was barely discernible in the shape of the mountain.

My brother Hughie worked for Korczak one summer in the mid-fifties, hauling dynamite up the mountain on his back, planting the charges, enduring Korczak's autocratic whims. Hughie hated Korczak, regarded him as an empty showman and a fraud.

I came back from Europe to my father's house. He lived in Yonkers then. He had not yet moved across the line into the opulence of Bronxville.

I hated America. I was shocked by it. My father met me at the airport. He saw me get off the plane with my beard and knapsack. "Well," he said. "Didn't miss a cliché, did you?"

We drove through sprawling urban mess, toward Yonkers. The United States seemed dirty, with a depressing, crass, shallow filth about it.

My interval in Europe was over. My father's house seemed squalid to me, after Bellamont. It was full of children. My father and stepmother had a new baby. Dirty diapers soaked in the toilet bowls. The house smelled of diaper pails waiting for the diaper service to come. In the morning, my father would get into his Mercury station wagon and drive down the Saw Mill River Parkway to Manhattan, to Nelson Rockefeller's office.

I stayed at my father's house, suddenly motionless, going no farther than the living room in the late afternoon. I became fascinated by a pair of golden roses that stood on the mantelpiece, roses that my father had bought at Tiffany as Christmas gifts for my stepmother. They seemed shimmeringly vulgar and decadent and sinister.

Sometimes I would go out into the street and play catch with Patrick. We used a hardball. We burned the ball back and forth with a killer velocity. We did it silently, throwing each ball as if to murder, as if to bore a hole through the other's glove. We kept at it for hours, until the late-summer light began to fade. The Good Humor man would come jingling down Rockland Avenue and stop to sell ice cream sticks. By then Patrick and I could barely see the hardball screaming out of the dusk to make its shock on the palm. When at last we went inside, my glove-hand palm would be swollen and red. Patrick and I never said anything about the fact that we had been trying to kill each other.

From the notes I made in Europe, I wrote *Foucheval* in a night and a day. I sat in a small upstairs bedroom smoking endless cigarettes. The play was written in urgent and angry mock-metaphysical verse. Korczak became a version of my father in the work, although I did not recognize him in that extravagant character.

The conceit of the play was that the immense statue was a creative labor amounting to an effort at transubstantiation: the stone would overwhelm life, become life. It was about the transformation of the Chief, about flesh become art and son become man. The structure of the play was something like that of the Catholic mass. The dialogue was full of liturgical imagery and language.

The sculptor was a kind of lunatic priest, an all-powerful and ultimately all-destructive autocrat, with certain characteristics of God. He was a highly elaborate and clumsily imagined fantasy of my father, of the idea of the Father and the Father's magic. The sculptor, inventing the Chief, re-creating the Chief in a mountainous work of art, meant to give his ego the prestige of eternity. It came out badly. He was an aggrandizement of my father combined with an assassination of him. A setup.

The mad artist of the play was downstairs in the kitchen as I wrote it. My father was concocting baby formula. He was measuring out his powders and potions and pouring them into steaming bottles. I sat upstairs banging on a typewriter, attributing great powers to him, wishing great powers for him, fearing great powers in him. All the while, my father went abstractedly about his business as a father.

When I returned to Harvard that fall, I contrived to have the play produced in Dunster House. Jack Nordby made a handsome woodcut for a poster, which we plastered around Harvard Square to advertise the production.

I had to play the part of Foucheval myself. I enlisted friends to take the other parts and set up the lights and erect the stage in the Dunster House dining hall. The *Harvard Crimson* sent a reviewer on opening night. After the performance we had a party for the cast. Then we drove over to the *Crimson* office on Plympton Street in the middle of the night, and Jack Nordby went in alone, with great tottering dignity, to ask if he might read the review. He was gone a long time. He finally emerged, loyally incensed, waving a copy of the review. It was a small masterpiece, perfectly just, of dismissal and incredulity. After summarizing the plot, the reviewer said in effect: All of this has something to do, if you can believe it, with the Roman Catholic mass and the doctrine of transubstantiation.

A friend who was an English tutor promised, half drunk, to write an outraged letter to the *Crimson* destroying the reviewer. He never did. It was difficult to go through with the other performances. Friends packed the house, however. Three of them always showed up a little drunk and sat in the first row and, out of loyalty, laughed loudly at all the wrong places during the performance.

Foucheval shared the Dunster House stage that week with another play, *The Rain Never Falls*. *Foucheval* was hermetically private nonsense. *The Rain Never Falls* was an earnestly public play. It was written by Fred Gardner, a grimly intelligent leftist who later in the sixties did work in the anti-war movement. Fred was full of Brecht and socialism. His play took place in a bomb shelter after a nuclear attack: the American family inside, the neighbors banging on the door, begging to get in, the crisis of conscience, etc.

Both plays were oppressively serious. The difference between the two was the difference between the private conscience and the public conscience. My father had taught me, or I thought he had taught me, that the private spiritual life (if he acknowledged such a thing) could only end badly in public places. That, in its way, was the message of poor *Foucheval*: that the religious-artistic imagination has fanatical tendencies in the real world. Obsessions are totalitarian. Artistic visions, realized too grandly, are nightmares for everyone who gets in the way. I suspect that in my grandiose sculptor I put something of Nelson Rockefeller as well as of my father. Rockefeller was overwhelming in something of the same way, and autocratic. I sensed, too, only vaguely, that there was an element of casually loony hubris in Rockefeller's ambitions.

Mine was the last class at Harvard, or the next-to-last, that was essentially nonpolitical, instinctively nonpolitical. The real sixties had not really begun. We graduated in June of 1963. It was not until November that John Kennedy was killed.

So the strains of passionate, vivid self-importance that overwhelmed the decade were not detectable yet. Timothy Leary was still on the Harvard faculty, working with psilocybin, still within the respectable academic limits. There was one weird pioneer in Dunster House, called Snakeskin, who took drugs of a new and different kind. He seemed to eat alone in the dining hall most of the time, as defiant and sullen as a religious zealot awaiting his moment. Even marijuana was still comparatively rare around Cambridge.

I went to buy cigarettes one night at the Cahaly brothers' grocery store on Mount Auburn Street. When I stepped outside Cahaly's, I heard a sound coming from the blank storefront of the Club Mount Auburn next door. It was the purest flowing crystal sound—infinitely younger and clearer than any sound she made when she became famous. Joan Baez was an adolescent, just in from California. I never saw her that night; she meant nothing to me except as a voice of impossibly sweet clarity coming through a blank door.

I listen to Joan Baez now, more than twenty years later. She became an anthem singer. I have put on Baez records on Christmas afternoon and laid on my back, distantly saddened, singing "We Shall Overcome"—singing along. But her singing in those later years might as well have been Ethel Merman, compared to that night on Mount Auburn Street.

The street had its politics. One night in early December I walked along Mount Auburn Street in a soft snowfall. The snow made the evening silent and picturesque. There was no traffic. Harvard was softening into a nineteenth-century postcard scene.

As I came past the final clubs on Mount Auburn, I saw that there were several chartered buses pulled up outside Lowell House. They were idling their engines, the black diesel fumes blasting out into the falling snow. A few dozen undergraduates stood in huddles on the walk near the buses, waiting to board. They had picket signs stacked with their luggage, their knapsacks. They were members of SANE. The buses were bound for Washington. The Committee for a Sane Nuclear Policy was doing its lonely business, as peculiar as bird watchers.

Across Mount Auburn Street, opposite Lowell House, I saw the doors of the Lampoon castle open. Out into the gently falling snow strolled a dozen undergraduates wearing dinner jackets. Black tie. They carried champagne glasses in their hands, and bottles of champagne. They formed themselves into a loose, choral semicircle on the stone porch of the Lampoon castle. The light from the castle door behind them poured out and backlighted them. They raised their champagne glasses in the falling snow, and sang. They serenaded the SANE people:

> *Where have all the flowers gone?*
> *Long time passing.*
> *Where have all the flowers gone?*
> *Long time ago.*
> *When will they ever learn?*
> *When will they ever learn?*

The SANE people glared back across Mount Auburn Street.

The Lampoon people finished their song and saluted with their glasses in the snow and then silently drained them, and turned and disappeared inside, closing off the light as they closed the door.

I was mysteriously thrilled.

My father came up to Cambridge to see *Foucheval* on its closing night. It must have seemed to him a lurid and somehow unwholesome version of those nights he spent in auditoriums when I was at Gonzaga. He and my stepmother loyally appeared and listened to me compete in elocution and oratorical contests: "I Speak for Democracy," for example, a contest in which I advanced to the regional finals. One night in an auditorium of a Catholic college in Baltimore, my father listened as I and six other finalists enlarged endlessly upon the saintliness of Pope Pius XII. My father endured such evenings with a grace that now amazes me.

He came to Harvard for my play, but I think that he did it with less good will than he had felt in the days of the American Legion halls. We were now more strangers than we had ever been to each other. I felt his presence in the audience, and I had the intelligence to be embarrassed by my ranting on the stage. But the embarrassment made me rant even more defiantly. I chewed the furniture. I hurled collegiate metaphysics around like a chimp in a cage. My father applauded dutifully, and caught the last shuttle back to New York.

10·Going Back

I graduated from Harvard in the spring of 1963, and went down to live for a time at my father's house in Yonkers, just north of New York City.

My father had moved there when I was a freshman, the year that he went to work for Nelson Rockefeller. The house, at 6 Rockland Avenue, was a white, wooden three-story place of conventional middle-aged American design. It sat on the top of an astonishingly steep hill. The backyard, a kind of scruffily terraced garden, fell away abruptly, at a 60-degree angle. My brothers and sisters almost never used the yard—it was nearly vertical, and overgrown. At the bottom of it was a two-car garage, its roof at a level far below the house. My sisters confined themselves to the little concrete space at the top of the hill, a bleak apron where they skipped rope on summer evenings. They chanted, "Red hot, red hot, pepper's in the pot!" and waited for the Good Humor man.

The house was filled with children. While I was in college my stepmother had given birth, in rapid succession, to my half brother, Davison, born in 1962, and my half sister, Carolyn, born some twelve months later. And there were, besides, my stepbrothers Buzzy and Happy, my brothers Patrick and Michael, my sisters Cathleen and Christina. The children ranged in age from infancy to mid-adolescence.

When I left Harvard, I had no plans about what to do with the rest of my life. I thought for a time of going to graduate school and becoming, eventually, a college English teacher. I had planned to study in Ireland on a Fulbright grant, but the project, something on Yeats, was turned down. (I imagined that the academic bureaucrats had a rubber stamp with which to reject those thousands of Yeats projects tumbling in from college seniors who were looking for a ticket to Ireland).

My tutor from Harvard was leaving to become a professor of English at the University of Denver and offered me a graduate fellowship there, to teach and study for a master's degree in English. One afternoon I went to ask my father's advice. We spoke in the darkened downstairs hall. Should I take the fellowship in Denver or should I look for another job in journalism and continue at his trade?

My father made his effort at impassivity. He rattled the change in his trousers pocket. He brought into play the Morrows' instinctive sense of fairness—a way of adjusting the eyes to a nice glow of courtesy. He did his best to look impartial. The effort made him uncomfortable.

I think that my father both mistrusted and envied universities and academics. The idea of my becoming an English teacher horrified him a little, but he did not wish to say so.

We had drifted apart during the years when I was at Harvard. When I was younger, at Gonzaga, he and I had collaborated at things, had been exceptionally close, brought together by his struggles, by my mother's absence.

I had been the best man at his wedding to his second wife. There were these patterns. I came eventually to feel that I had some odd vocation that involved ushering my parents toward other lovers. I retroactively collaborated with my mother on O'Gowan. I idolized her second husband, Robert McCormick. I stood up with my father at the altar of a church in Alexandria when my mother's successor came down the aisle.

My father was ill on the way to his second wedding. He had a violent reaction to an antitetanus shot derived from horse serum. I had to drive the station wagon down from Washington to Alexandria while he sat in the front seat beside me, writhing and moaning in pain. I felt, once again, like a kind of faithful servant to the emotional life of his generation.

It was a peculiar participation in their lives, a participation too intimate. The son became confidant, older brother, or else a young butler of versatility and tact.

But now he was long settled into his new marriage and a new career with Nelson Rockefeller, of whom I knew little, and I had become something of a stranger to him. I had gone off to Harvard, to a world he did not know, and come back with a magna and a Phi Beta Kappa key and a beard and a collection of odd friends. They would blow into town in the middle of the night from Cambridge or Kansas City and carouse for a while and sleep on the living-room floor and leave. They would arrive like a pack of amiable neighborhood dogs, come to call and have a frisk with one of their pals, me.

My father was an elegantly forbearing man, but when he thought of this, it must have irritated him. He was starting another family. He had ten children now, including two babies and six boys and girls still in school. He did not need a grown son camping in his study and bringing home his overgrown friends—young men acquiring all of the bad habits of manhood, without its manners or responsibilities.

Travis Williams, for example, came to visit for a few days. Travis had been a friend since we were freshmen together in Matthews Hall in Harvard Yard. He was a tall, very funny and very intelligent character from Durham, North Carolina. His father was a barber, and Travis came to Harvard on a handsome scholarship. His family was exceptionally strong and cohesive, with a determination that I have sometimes noticed among other North Carolina blacks. Travis rode all the way into Harvard on that discipline, but then in some sense rebelled against it. At any rate, Travis could be a heroic drinker—something that his God-fearing parents, I think, did not know. Once during my senior year at Harvard, Travis, standing on a sidewalk outside, heaved an empty quart beer bottle through the fifth-floor window of my room at Dunster House. He wanted to get my attention, to invite me to join him at Cronin's for a beer. He didn't want to walk up those flights of stairs.

Travis had an easy way with children, and charmed my younger brothers and sisters. I am not sure he entirely charmed my father, not always. One morning my father walked downstairs a little after dawn and found Travis passed out on the living-room rug, the coffee table overturned, an empty bottle of bourbon beside him.

I might have left Yonkers sooner if my father had advised me to take the fellowship at Denver. But he grimaced at the thought and suggested that before I did that, perhaps I would like to talk to some of his friends in newspapers, magazines and television.

I sent a résumé to his friend Theodore H. White, and White kindly steered me to other friends. I began making my way around the network of media pals. I rode into Manhattan every morning with my father, sluicing down the Henry Hudson Parkway, my father mowing away at his chin with the Remington electric razor. He would park in one of Nelson Rockefeller's spaces in the Rockefeller Center garage, and then walk up to the town house at 22 West Fifty-fifth Street, where Rockefeller kept his New York offices.

I would set off around the office buildings of the corporate media. I spent the days sitting in outer offices among the potted plants, across the room from the puttering secretaries.

After a number of interviews with people like Charles Collingwood, it began to occur to me that the visits were purely ceremonial, a matter of dealing a courtesy to my father. It did not occur to anyone to actually hire me.

Finally I realized that my father was powerless to help me further and that it was somewhat degrading to go on expecting his help. I wrote to the city editor at the Washington *Star*, where I had worked before, during my leave of absence from Harvard. He offered me a job on the dictation bank, with a promise to become a reporter-trainee in a few months. I said goodbye to my father and stepmother and brothers and sisters and moved to Washington.

I had no place to stay. The Sunday afternoon that I arrived in Washington, I dropped by the old house in Cleveland Park. The house belonged to the Andersons by then. When I returned to Washington from Harvard, I knocked on their door, and Bud Anderson came padding out with his great bassett's sad eyes and saw me, and called back into the house with an air of slow wonder, "Why, it's Lanny!" They took me in. I rented my old room from them.

Bud worked for the Defense Department. His wife, Laura, was a sharp Capitol Hill lobbyist from Georgia.

The Andersons had brought up two black south Georgia girls to live in the house and clean and baby-sit. They lived in a bedroom at the back of the house. They were seventeen-year-old twins, very black and very country. They were small girls, with sweet but wary dispositions, and they moved almost noiselessly through the house, darting shadows.

It was odd to live as an adult and stranger in the Cleveland Park house. The girls made my bed. My old room was a guest room now. I walked through the house in a minutely gingerly and deferential way, knowing that I no longer had claims there. When the Andersons had company (which was rare), I managed to vanish. I slipped through the front door and up the stairs to my room and read.

When I was a child I had a trick of vanishing. I could spend hours being invisible, being nothing. I could contrive to pass entirely through the house without ever being visible. There was an upstairs porch that was used as a storage room, and I could disappear into it, could find places to slip between mattresses, under couches.

I hated living as a guest in the house. It was like an interminable game of being invisible. Still, it had been the strategy of my life with my parents.

One Saturday night Bud and I sat up especially late. Laura was away on a business trip.

I woke the next morning to hear the black girls screaming. It was broad daylight. The girls were screaming that the house was on fire.

I rushed out into the upstairs hall and there found Bud in his pajamas. He stood by the closed door to the third-floor stairs. He thought that his son Brandon was asleep upstairs, and he stood howling. I opened the door. A wall of heat and smoke slammed out. I shut the door and reeled back.

One of the black girls rushed up the steps and said that the boy had spent the night at a friend's house. But the dog was up there, a dachshund. I opened the door. I had an idea of rescuing the dachshund. The wall of smoke was even thicker now.

Bud and I retreated downstairs. We called the fire department. We went out onto the front lawn. We looked up and saw that flames were licking out of the third-floor windows: bright yellow flames, almost smokeless, flames frank and crackling and brisk. It was a slaughtering, crisp fire, and it was taking down the house as efficiently as a lumberjack.

Bud took a look and bolted back inside. He emerged with a bottle of Scotch in his fist. He stood on the front lawn in his pajamas and then, like King Lear, he began bellowing, "Burn, you son of a bitch! Burn! Take everything I have!" He waved the bottle of Scotch at the flames and then drank from it.

The fire department arrived a moment later. The firemen led Bud aside and saved most of the house. They poured ten thousand gallons of water into the place. They left the house blackened and dripping and profoundly soaked.

By late afternoon Bud's wife had arrived home. She took charge. The Andersons found a temporary apartment nearby.

The Andersons took what they needed from their house and left. I drifted around Georgetown. The hours passed and I let them go by without thinking where I would spend the night. Finally I came back to Newark Street and stood in front of the burned house.

Then I went inside.

The house dripped with firemen's water, and it smelled overpoweringly of fire. The wood upstairs was blackened or black-margined, and the charcoal was almost shiny.

So I slept in the house. I wandered upstairs to find a room that might be dry enough for sleeping. The house was soggy and bombed out. I found the driest mattress in the room that the girls occupied, and I lay down on it.

I was exhausted and needed to sleep. The house was utterly dark, but there was a moon. The fire had burned out part of the ceiling, and I could see the sky through the holes.

All night, the burned house ticked. The house made ticking

noises, noises black and alive. I listened to them in the way that I once listened to my parents screaming at each other in the middle of the night in that house. The joists and rafters rearranged themselves after the fire. The house was a different house entirely, and yet it seemed to be similarly haunted.

Now all my clothing smelled densely of smoke. When I came to work at the *Star* the morning after the fire, Carl Bernstein sidled up to me to bum a Marlboro. It was his way of greeting me in those days, an amiable gesture which he did rather jauntily. He was even a little formal about it. He would speak a cockney formula in a Maryland accent, hunching his shoulders slightly and inclining his head a bit: "Hey, Morrow! Give us a butt!" It was a running joke, but Carl had a sense of honor about it. Once or twice during the year I stayed at the *Star*, Carl showed up in the morning with a carton of Marlboros, which he presented to me with the same air of mock ceremony.

On the morning after the fire, Carl approached me, got as far as "Hey, Morrow!" and then reeled backward from the reeking smell of smoke. I told him about the fire.

Years later, in the spring of 1974, I came down to Washington to stay at Carl's apartment in the Adams-Morgan section while I was working on a free-lance article. Carl had become a celebrity of Watergate then, in partnership with Bob Woodward of the Washington *Post*. He had begun seeing Nora Ephron. I arrived in late afternoon. Carl was not home. I spent an hour discussing with Nora the question of how many oysters I could eat at a sitting. I reported that I had once consumed eighteen in an afternoon at the Union Oyster House in Boston. I saw that at that moment Nora decided I was not a serious man. She had just returned from a magazine assignment that involved food research. She had eaten something like five dozen oysters at a sitting.

Carl arrived from the Washington *Post*. We went to a restaurant called the Dancing Crab, out on Wisconsin Avenue. Carl asked about my father, and solicited a story.

I told him what my father had told me. Richard Nixon's people had called my father. It was Nixon's friend Bob Abplanalp, I think, who made the contact. Would my father come to Key Biscayne to see Nixon and discuss taking a job with the Administration, a Cabinet-level post? My father said he would come to Key Biscayne, but could not take any such job.

Abplanalp sent a private jet for my father. He flew to Florida. He was taken in a limousine to Nixon's house in Key Biscayne. Then, something strange: Nixon and Bebe Rebozo walked up and down the beach outside. My father sat in Nixon's study with Abplanalp and Alexander Haig. The television was on—the New York Jets against the Miami Dolphins. Between plays, Abplanalp and Haig tried to persuade my father to accept a job as Nixon's chief of public relations. My father was to come in and manage the entire Watergate act and make everything seem normal again.

I sometimes wondered what it was about my father that made Nixon and his people think that my father could repair the damage of Watergate. My father was a man of character, they knew, and skill. That is no doubt why my father told them he could not accept the job. His cause—or client, anyway—was Nelson Rockefeller, not Richard Nixon. And Nixon's cause was probably lost already, anyhow. It would have been out of character for my father to join that uniquely unsavory cast that had grown up around Nixon—Ziegler and Haldeman and Ehrlichman and Dean and the rest. My father did offer some advice, though: "Why don't you simply have the President go up to the Hill one day, unannounced, and tell the Ervin committee he understands that they have some questions they'd like to ask? And have him answer everything. It would disarm them."

They put my father in a cab, and he flew back to New York on a commercial airliner.

I told that story to Carl and Nora. Nora was determined to get something more important. While we banged away at a bushel of crabs on butcher's paper at the Dancing Crab, she went to work on Carl about the identity of Deep Throat. She worked all through the evening, using her charm and shrewdness and wit. He would not tell her. Not that night, anyway.

The galley proofs of *All the President's Men* had arrived by messenger that afternoon from the publisher in New York. We went back to Carl's apartment and sat up all night reading the book, the three of us passing the galley sheets around in wads.

The year that I got out of Harvard, Carl and I worked the dictation bank at the *Star*. The newsroom was on the third floor of the new *Star* building in Southeast Washington, not far from the Capitol. The *Star* was an afternoon newspaper, with a series of editions running off the presses all day. Reporters often had to call in their stories, dictating them to us on deadline. We were hired to be fast, accurate typists capable of making our fingers work under pressure.

There were four or five of us on duty during the day. We sat at a bank of typewriters arrayed just opposite the newsroom telephone operator. When we were not taking stories from reporters over the phone we wrote obituaries, or composed small filler items for the paper from press releases.

I think that in a sense I went into the newspaper business after Harvard as a gesture of reconciliation with my father. I returned to the same job at the *Star* that I had held before I went to Cambridge. I went back to his business.

My father had broken me into the trade years before. When I was in junior high school I was the editor of the school paper. My father helped me compose an editorial on the wisdom of having regular dental checkups. The editorial line that my father advised was the mature and responsible thought that taking care of the teeth sensibly today will save much pain and distress later on. I wrote it just that way. The odd thing was that both my parents had a kind of hillbilly carelessness about doctors and dentists. I had my teeth checked by a dentist only once or twice when I was a child.

When I took a year off between Gonzaga and Harvard, and lived at my father's house, I worked at the *Star*. My father helped me then as well. I apprenticed myself again to his world.

I answered a classified ad and got a job as a copyboy. At that time the *Star* was still published at its old building in downtown Washington, an ancient place from another century. It looked like the building in which young Citizen Kane began his publishing career, except that now another half-century of dirt lay upon it.

Everything there—floors, desks, elevators, walls, windows, every-thing—was encrusted. The newsroom was dramatically filthy. Generations of thick, cheap, two-sided carbon paper had left deep blue-black smudges on desks and typewriters and tables and floors. I would shower for thirty minutes when I got home from work there.

It was once again a world of my father's, as the Senate had been. He understood it perfectly, and laughed at its stories. I told him one night about Earl Heap, for example. Heap was the copy editor of the *Star*. He sat in the slot of the horseshoe-shaped copy desk, and presided over the men who wrote the headlines and copyread the stories in the final editorial stage before they were sent up to the composing room to be set in type. Heap was a character out of the nineteenth century. He had a raw, strong, autocratic face and dictatorial manners. He wore suspenders. He loved to intim-idate his copyreaders, to insult them, growling sarcastic pedantries around the rim of the desk. His copyreaders tended to be defeated men, fearful of losing this one last chance, and bitter that it was just that, the end of the professional line. They tended to be middle-aged. Some, I thought I detected, were reformed alcoholics, with that singed look about them as if a fire had burned through their skulls and left them a little blackened around the eyes.

There was one character though, who was on his way up—perhaps. He was a foppish young man in his late twenties. He wore three-piece suits to work, a white handkerchief always folded jauntily in the jacket's breast pocket. Heap especially loathed the man. Heap rode him relentlessly, but the fop took it with a cheerful obliviousness. One day the fop came to work with a briefcase—an outlandish article that no newspaperman would ever carry in those days. It was a stylish case, somewhat smaller than most, a rectan-gular box covered with good leather. The other copyreaders sensed blood in the water. They began some oafish kidding: "What's in the box, Sam? Huh?" The man in the three-piece suit sat imper-turbably at his station on the rim of the desk. They kept on, "What's in the case, Sam?" Earl Heap looked up. "Ah," he said. "That would be his duelling pistols."

When Heap at last rose from his chair after deadline, he walked with a certain swagger, a stiffness that derived no doubt from spending so many hours at his post, but which, in him, seemed more the result of a two days' ride with Jeb Stuart.

I liked Heap, although he terrified me whenever I was sent back to be his copyboy. In that job, I had to stand just behind him, next to the pneumatic tubes that ran to the composing room and elsewhere in the operation—the photoengravers, the picture editor and so on. I had to know which copy went to which departments.

The pneumatic tubes were powerful and omnivorous. They kept up a fierce, whooshing intake. The flow of copy from Heap's out-tray was also fierce: he expected it to be kept clean, the copy firing off instantly to the right destination. One morning on the 9 A.M. deadline I was stuffing the pneumatic-tube cartridges with captions and stories, and abruptly my necktie went flying up a tube and got stuck there. I was so terrified that Heap would turn around just then and see me struggling to pull my tie out of the sucking tube that, without hesitation, I grabbed a pair of scissors and cut off the necktie and let it rush up and away, liberated.

The day I went to work for the *Star* in late 1958, during my leave of absence from Harvard, I joined the Newspaper Guild. It had been my father's union years before at the Philadelphia *Inquirer*. I remembered a story he told about how he and some of the other reporters had banded together to prevent the guild local from being taken over by Communists in the late thirties.

I was delighted, and astonished, when the Guild called a strike only a week or two after I reported for work.

I did not understand the issues, but I fell into the spirit of the thing. The weather that week was bitter, the temperature around 5 or 10 degrees. I took up duties on the picket line in a spirit of adventure. We walked for hours, passing out broadsides about the strike to passers-by, and retreating after our shifts to a bar called the Chicken Hut across the street. The Chicken Hut was the *Star*'s hangout. It served schooners of beer in frosted mugs. The strike was a bracing party for me. It had its rituals and its camaraderies and an air of virtue that I did not think to question.

Once the wife of one of the owners of the paper emerged from the *Star* building, and in all innocence I sought to give her a leaflet explaining why we were striking. The woman was a stately middle-aged dreadnought, and as I offered her the union's screed, she muttered *"Fool!"* and steamed across the picket line to her waiting car.

I did not know if the strike accomplished anything or nothing. It was settled after some days, and we all went back into that Dickensian warren and started putting out the newspaper again. I was still a stranger and could not tell if anything had changed.

The *Star* was owned by the Noyes family and the Kauffman family. I admired the paper in some ways, although that was often difficult. Its genes were essentially Republican, and its instincts provincial. The ownership of the paper had a certain boneheaded smugness that was infuriating: what Dickens called Podsnappery. But the quality could occasionally be endearing. Once on a viciously cold morning one of the owners encountered a reporter on the street outside the building. The reporter was not wearing an overcoat. He clutched his suit jacket to his chest as he hurried along. The owner rushed the man into the lobby of the building and asked with great concern why the reporter was walking around in such cold without his coat.

The reporter, a wonderful writer with a couple of ex-wives and a taste for gin, replied angrily, "Because you don't pay me enough to afford an overcoat!"

The owner, all concern, said, "Come to my office at three o'clock this afternoon."

The reporter, in freshened hope, came around to the owner's office. He was ushered inside. There the owner, a fat, pink man with bottle-bottom glasses that made his eyes look like fish in an aquarium, formally presented to the reporter a used tweed overcoat that had obviously come from the back of the owner's hall closet.

That was the essence of the *Star*, I thought. It was sometimes a sweet place, but the people who made the decisions about it seemed to have misplaced themselves in time somewhere. Something there was inherently damaged, even though one might wish to root for the *Star* over the morning Washington *Post*. Years later Time Inc.

bought the *Star* and tried to make it run. It failed. I kept wishing that someone in the company had consulted me about it. I might have warned someone off.

Not long after the strike, the *Star* moved to its new building at Second Street and Virginia Avenue, off in the wilds on the margins of Capitol Hill. It was touching to me that the *Star*'s owners had decided to proceed into the twentieth century. Their architectural idea of the century looked like a dreary new factory in an industrial park. But it was infinitely cleaner than what the *Star* had left behind.

One night I was working as the night dictationist—listening to the police radio, taking the crank calls to the city desk. Haynes Johnson was the night city editor.

The night side on an afternoon paper is a kind of out-of-body experience—a muffled, echoing state a little like a dream. In fact, it mimics the dream state in a way, as many night shifts do, because they occur when so many other normal daytime routines and functions are sleeping.

Haynes and I talked. The police radio amplifier that sat on the city desk kept up its flat-voiced constabulary dramas. We both knew how to listen to them in some lesser part of the brain. We knew the dispatcher's codes. If we heard, say, "Cruiser 26"—heard the words in the midst of our own conversation, or our own thoughts—then we would stop the conversation or the thought, quite abruptly, and turn an ear to the amplifier and attend the drama.

Any cruiser between 25 and 30 meant the homicide squad. Hearing a homicide squad cruiser summoned meant the report of a murder. Next the task was to listen for the address. Black neighborhood or white neighborhood? A homicide cruiser going to a black neighborhood meant that someone had gotten knifed or shot, or maybe no one had, but at any rate, it was not terribly important, the players in the drama probably all being black. But if the homicide cruiser was directed to Georgetown, or Cleveland Park, or Foxhall Road, or somesuch, then the victim would be white, and we would leap from our chairs and go to work.

So we listened with a racially educated ear. This night we heard a bizarre report. A bear had gotten loose, no one knew from where. It was sighted in the outer fringes of Southeast Washington.

I had no car. My father agreed, in the middle of the night, to drive down from Cleveland Park to get me and drive me out to chase the bear. I spent the rest of the night chasing the bear, talking to cops. We never found him. My father waited for me, leaning against his car. I got my first front-page story out of the effort, though without a byline.

So I went off to Harvard and came back to the *Star*. I eventually became a reporter. I moved into a town house with two other, older reporters. Once my father and stepmother came down to visit. They stopped at our house, on Capitol Hill, for half an hour. My stepmother could not wait to leave; there was some Republican dinner to go to. My father looked acutely uncomfortable.

But he came another time, alone, and took me to the Press Club. When we arrived in the lobby, one of the copyreaders from the *Star*, an old newsman from my father's early days in Washington, recognized him, and then recognized me.

The man said, "Well, Hugh, you must be very proud of your boy. We think a lot of him over at the *Star*."

My father smiled, and I took enormous pleasure in the pleasure that he got from it.

These days, I take my father to the Harvard Club in New York, and it is a transaction, the roles changed, that is very much like going to the Press Club with my father as a child. But the man who signs the check is different.

Except for those visits, I did not see my father when I was in Washington. Once during some riots in Harlem in the summer of 1964 I came up and spent the weekend with him in Yonkers and wandered around Harlem to do a story for the *Star*. I walked down one Harlem side street in the middle of the riot, in the middle of the night, and a fifteen-year-old kid leaned down from a fire escape and asked with a kind of hostile incredulity, "Hey, man—you Bobby Kennedy?"

After a year in Washington, I showed my father my newspaper clippings, stories I had done for the *Star*. He gave them to his friend Shirley Clurman, and she gave them to her husband, Dick Clurman, who was then *Time* magazine's chief of correspondents. He invited me to come to New York and talk.

Time gave me a job as a writer, doing the People section. I moved into a building on West Eighty-fifth Street that was populated by homosexuals and pimps. Some of them were oddly protective of me. They decided, I came to understand, that I was dangerously innocent. One night I locked myself out of my apartment, on the fifth floor, and I went to the apartment above and asked the pimp who lived there if I could climb down the fire escape. He let me do it, but followed me down with a brotherly "Watch yourself, now!"

11 · Michael

My father picked me up in his blue Mercedes. He drove the car with a serene, expansive, proprietary air. He always settled behind the wheel with a profound satisfaction, with the sigh of a man easing himself into his tub. The Mercedes put him into a trance of well-being, an altered state. It armored him.

When I walked out of my apartment building on East Ninety-second Street, I found my father waiting for me. He sat behind the wheel with his portable electric shaver in his hand, mowing away at his whiskers. Seeing me, he flipped a master switch on the dashboard and all four of the door-lock buttons on the doors popped up simultaneously to the "open" position: a Germanically disciplined display from the Mercedes, I thought. I put my bag on the floor in the back and got in front.

My father liked to travel heavy. When he went on a trip, he loaded up the Mercedes with gadgets and supplies until it began to look like a George Price cartoon in *The New Yorker*. Like a nomadic desert seigneur, he wanted to be surrounded by his domestic effects, even when he was on the road. He switched off the electric razor to say hello, then mowed away again at his face as he eased the car down toward the light at Second Avenue. He had his traveling no-slop coffee mug on the console between the two front seats. Spread open on the back seat was the briefcase that served as his traveling medicine chest and Dopp kit, with bottles of antacids ajumble with pens and aspirin bottles and portable mouth sprays, hairbrushes, and in an insulated Pepsi bag with a Freezit in it, the insulin for his diabetes.

We got on the FDR Drive at Ninety-sixth Street and looped over the shoulder of Manhattan by the Harlem River Drive and on up to the George Washington Bridge. It was a crisp, blue day in January. I looked north up the river, past the Palisades. The trees were bare. It had snowed lightly during the night. The countryside was a flecked white, like chocolate-chip ice cream.

We were happy to be starting off. We both have always found driving a wondrously suspended state, the car almost an engine for meditation. It was a sweet rolling immunity from the outside world. Conversations in that state could be pursued driftingly, with a pause of long miles between thoughts. The body links itself to the machine and works it with the strange concentration of habit: steers it, drives it, brakes it almost abstractly. The hands and feet work calmly away like the crew belowdecks, and the eyes make their automatic highway calculations but also drift over the landscape, taking in the world—while the soul makes its own excursions over place and time. It is an old phenomenon of travel: the principle of physical motion jostles loose the spirit and sends it on its own adventures, for which the actual trip serves only as the first stage, the launching pretext.

We rolled south through Fort Lee, New Jersey. My father sorted us all but unconsciously through the dense tangles of traffic options, of lanes and off-ramps, merges and shunts, and we took a ticket from the toll machine and headed down the turnpike, across the marshy wasteland of northern New Jersey.

I associated my father with cars. I did not normally like to ride in a car with anyone but me driving: if forced to ride as a passenger, I would watch the road nervously and sometimes press my feet onto the floor, feeling for the brake. But I never did that when my father drove.

Driving was one of the masculine ceremonies which my father performed, with an exact and even elegant sort of style. It was hard to tell that now, with the Mercedes: the car had automatic gears. That meant my father could not display his uniquely fluid motion in shifting: the odd, deft follow-through in his throw of the gear lever, the arm engaging the gear and then releasing the stick and sweeping on out in the air a little, along the line of the stroke, as if the gears and car would go truer if the shift were thus so smoothly done: a perfectly fluid and almost slow-motion style, athletic, balletic. The follow-through looked a little like his motion with a pool stick: the stroke made vectors, abstract lines of force in the air. It was a strange sort of self-absorbed performance. His gear-throw was so tuned and timed to the pitch of the engine that he could run a straight-stick car far more glidingly up to 60 than any automatic gears could. The coffee might lean back in its cup in such an acceleration, but it would never slosh.

The Mercedes had a stick on the floor. But it merely slid forward and back to the automatic-gear settings: a sort of falsie. My father held the stick in his hand as he accelerated, as if he were working his way through the gearbox, but in actuality, it was all the Kraut-work under the hood that did my father's ballet, while the cylinders, running on diesel oil, made their distinctively busy clicking noises.

My father swooped the Mercedes out of the turnpike tollgate and held the gas pedal on the floor until the car hit 80, and then he eased it off to a purr at 75. He was the sort of speeder who with the help of his sharp distance vision could spot a cop almost always in time to decelerate smoothly into the legal range, brushing his brakes lightly, never stomping in that panicked abruptness that announces guilt.

We rode companionably. I was hitching a ride with him to Washington. He was going down to interview some old colleagues for a Nelson Rockefeller archive. It was a year and a half since Nelson died. My father was filling out his service before retiring. Great black loose-leaf notebooks full of interview transcripts were accumulating in his office on the fifty-sixth floor of the RCA Building in New York. He was talking to everyone who had known Nelson during all of those years in public life. My father would be ushered into the office or den of some aging subaltern or aging upstate pol or ally or sycophant who'd been through the campaigns with Nelson. My father, old friends with most of them from the wars, would set up his Sony tape recorder, with its hand microphone on a small plastic stand, pointed toward the subject, and the two would fall into a sort of official reverie for a couple of hours.

At the Joyce Kilmer Service Area (they named all the turnpike gas station–and–Howard Johnson stops for more or less distinguished citizens of New Jersey), we stopped for coffee. I went into the souvenir shop and found there a little model of the Liberty Bell for Jamie, who was five then. My father picked up the bell and shook it once, loudly, smiling at me with a look of amused paternal horror on his face. "Just how long have you been a parent, my boy?" he asked. "You have a thing or two to learn about self-preservation."

My father was odd about children. Of course, he had ten of them, but I was never sure that he liked them. Or just how he liked them. He loved them as infants, surely, and as small children. He performed the offices of fatherhood with a tenderness that was surprising.

He filled the offices of a father so superbly in many ways that I was sometimes startled by the sardonic side of him that seemed to find children insufferable (W. C. Fields again—dogs and children) and even obscurely dangerous. They seemed sometimes to have done him a concealed injury, to have stolen something from him, something they may have taken without knowing the wound they were inflicting.

One day in the late seventies we were talking with great raillery about a neighbor we'd had in Washington. He was a tiny, frantic man who worked for the Central Intelligence Agency and took tranquilizers.

"Neil came shambling across the street one day looking very upset," my father began. "You remember what a little shit their son was? Cranston? Well, Master Cranston had done something unspeakable and poor Neil was outraged and stuttering, and he said piteously, 'Hugh, Hugh! What do you do with children like that? What do you *do*?' And I looked at him"—here my father curled his lip and gave his odd gangster snarl—"and I said, '*Survive the bastards!*'"

. . .

Survive the bastards. My father had nursed Mike for months in Memorial Hospital in New York. He had slept in a beach chair beside Mike's bed for weeks at a time, watching Mike shrink down to his irreducible seventeen-year-old bone and then, at last, vanish.

Every January about this time, I would drive up to Gate of Heaven Cemetery. Always it seemed to have just snowed, and I would do the same rage-ridden little dance, looking for that marker that lay flat upon the ground. Where's Mike, goddammit? "I think he's just about here," my wife would say. "No, no, he's closer to the son of a bitch with the Italian palace . . . Here, maybe?" Scrape, scrape. I'd sweep my foot sideways, dragging away the snow, searching. We should have brought a shovel. We should find a forked stick that is sensitive to bodies and will dip just when it passes over Mike's. Dowsing for Mike.

That day in the funeral home in Bronxville the bronze casket was on display in what looked like a solemn little ballroom—all the family and the school kids Mike knew sat around the walls on folding chairs like grieving wallflowers. I walked over to the casket and got down on the velvet-cushioned kneeler there and crossed myself (the eyes of all of the wallflowers fixed on me now with a low, solemn curiosity) and I stared point-blank at the metal. The casket was closed. Mike at the end looked like a remote caricature of himself. I tried to bore through the metal with my eyes. I tried to X-ray it. I tried to see, to imagine, Mike within. Then I felt myself to be within, and I abruptly suffocated and screamed and beat on the soft silken quilted lid that they'd laid down on top of him. Then with a sharp mental recoil, I extricated myself and went back to looking for Mike in there. I tried to imagine just that instant when life went out of him, like escaping gas, like a bubble, and it therefore became all right to zip him into a plastic bag and take him (he was so light, wax on sticks) and lay him in a metal box and under the earth.

When I went to Gate of Heaven, I stared through the stone and into the ground, and through the metal and down into the body. I wondered if Mike had deteriorated, if he was merely bone now. Or what? What does happen in a modern casket? How long does it take? I could not stop myself with this. I went on until the tears burned up through my throat and shot out of my eyes.

I dream of Mike sometimes now. I dream that he is my son: he had the same sweet, funny intelligence that Jamie has. I dream that Mike is ill, that they have found the cancer on the outside of his lung, but they have treated it, and it is going to be all right, and they are bringing him home from the hospital. There was a dream about a biplane. My father was bringing Mike home from the hospital in a ragged and fragile biplane, and Mike was terrified. He did not want to go up in the plane. He thought that he would crash, that he would be killed. But my father obliviously started the engine, and with a bland smile, taxied and took off, with Mike in the rear seat, terrified, looking down at me as the plane raced along, begging me to stop it. But I could not.

I was on a plane when Mike died. I was in the sky between New York and Chicago. When I arrived at the Chicago airport I heard my name called on the loudspeaker. They gave me a message, a number to call in New York. I stood at a bank of pay phones at O'Hare and called. My father, standing at the pay phone in Memorial Hospital, in the small waiting room down the hall from Mike's room, told me, "Well, it's all over. Mike's gone."

I stood at the bank of pay phones and cried. A group of teen-aged girls walked by, giggling, and I imagined that they were laughing at me, that they had seen me crying and thought it was funny. I smashed my fist against the telephone and stared at them with a wild hatred. They thought I was trying to break into the telephone for the money. They gave me a queer, alarmed look for an instant and then turned to giggling again: not leaving, but standing there and watching me, from a safe distance.

I got back onto a plane and headed for New York. I buried myself in Bruce Jay Friedman's stories, *Far from the City of Class*. All the way back to La Guardia I sat blubbering and laughing out loud simultaneously. I can still practically recite the Friedman stories from memory. Hanky and the Boss, New Yorkers exiled to a Kansas cow college, dreaming Runyonesque dreams of Lindy's and cherry cheese cake. I've invested the stories with a weird hilarious bereavement.

Now, as we rode south in the Mercedes, I turned to my father. We were in northern Maryland by this time.

"I still think a lot about Mike sometimes," I said.

"Yeah," my father answered. "So do I." He thought for a moment. "You know, tomorrow it will be eleven years." It had not occurred to me.

"You remember how he used to drive?" I asked.

"Mike was a good driver," my father said, as if he were passing a distant, impartial judgment on a matter of minor curiosity. Then his eyes filled with tears. I said nothing for a long time. I wondered if I should have brought up the subject.

Mike shared my father's idiot delight in cars. During one period of the sixties, the round driveway at my father's house in Bronxville looked like a used-car lot. The inventory included a new Volkswagen bus, a Triumph convertible, a Volkswagen Beetle, a Dodge Dart, a Ford station wagon. There was also an old wreck of a 1954 Mercedes sedan that I had brought up from Washington. My father was irresistibly drawn to the car. I gave it to him to cover some money I owed him. Ill as it was, he spent hundreds of dollars to have it rehabilitated. He had it painted black, and he had the tattered cloth inside replaced by new white vinyl. It became Mike's car as soon as Mike was old enough to drive. Mike drove it like a beautifully coordinated maniac. He'd inherited my father's ear for the pitch of an engine.

Mike had a gift for music. He could pick up any instrument and play it. Mainly, he played guitar and trumpet. My father in those days had a handyman, named Julius, who lived in a room in the basement in Bronxville and more or less took care of the place. Periodically Julius disappeared on a binge that might last days, or weeks. Then he would come back looking contrite, and my father would take him in again. No one ever asked him where he was during those absences. Only once did he volunteer some information: he told me that he woke up on a table to hear two doctors casually discussing his death, talking about him as if he were already gone. Julius said he tried to see, to speak, to tell them he was alive, but he could not. He told the story with a gasping hilarity, dipping his body from the waist as if he were an Orthodox Jew at the

Wailing Wall. *"But I ain't dead!"* he shrieked with his high laugh, showing me. Finally the doctors noticed something and said, "Well, I'll be damned."

Julius played the guitar. He and Mike would sit for hours in Julius' room picking at songs, Leadbelly dirges and whoops, mostly. I heard them sometimes from the kitchen above, the two of them laughing and whanging chords, then raising their voices in great wailing solemn hilarity, the song being emotionally wrung for all it was worth, in their eye-rolling, whoopingly mournful, burlesquing hot times—blues from the slave quarters in Bronxville.

Mike and I both loved Julius. Julius and I got drunk a few times together. I would buy a quart of 100-proof Old Grand-Dad, which was Julius' preference, and we would drink boilermakers all afternoon. Julius would solemnly tell me about his boyhood in North Carolina, the stepfather that he had hated. That stepfather once even took Julius' girl friend from him. "Stand back, boy, and watch how it's done," the man said. And the girl just went with the older man. Julius was so ashamed that that night he rolled up his things in a blanket and went out of the back window and walked across country for miles until he came to a road. Then he hitched a ride on a mule-drawn wagon and found his way east toward Winston-Salem.

Julius loved women, but he thought they were unreliable and possibly dangerous. For a time while I was living at my father's house in Bronxville, I owned an elegant 1951 Bentley sedan that I'd bought for $1,800. It was a beautiful car, with infirmities that I discovered later. I added it to my father's accumulation in Bronxville. The car was a great silver-gray British boat with a majestic, dowager way of getting around. Julius fell in love with it. He and I would sometimes drink Old Grand-Dad and then pile into the Bentley. He would climb into the back, with its luxurious cushions and its walnut paneling and vanity mirrors, and I would ceremoniously chauffeur him over to New Rochelle. We would pick up his girl friend and bring her back to the house in a state of shock and shrieking mirth and sometimes she would stay down there with Julius for a couple of days.

Julius loved Mike. Mike was a form of sunlight. I think of him in terms of bright, clear air. He had blond hair and blue eyes and a quick, mobile face. He was open and remarkably funny, with a mimic's gift. He memorized the cast album of *Beyond the Fringe* and flounced around spouting its routines.

Once when he was in the hospital for one of the cancer operations, my wife and I came to see him. We brought him a helium-filled balloon that we'd picked up at the Central Park Zoo on the way. We tied the balloon to the end of his bed. His roommate, an old man with large stricken eyes, became angry about the balloon and complained to the nurses. A cancer ward was no place for balloons. It was not a circus, not a circus, not a birthday party. On the contrary.

Mike sighed, a little embarrassed. He was still ambulatory then. He got out of bed and walked us down the hall to the elevators, pushing his IV pole along beside him. Suddenly he started doing his Jewish-mother routine. Doleful and kvetching: "I've enjoyed your little visit. Go now, enjoy yourselves! Don't worry about me! Listen, I like eating this way [pointing to the IV]. It's delicious. If they offered me food right now, if they offered me maybe a steak, some French fries, would I take it? Don't be ridiculous. Go! You're going to a restaurant maybe? You're going to eat *traif*? French fries? Shellfish? What? You should stay with me and have IV. Listen, it's kosher, the IV. Don't laugh—a little cream cheese on it . . ." He cheered us thus all the way to the elevator. We said goodbye to Mike, laughing, and left him there. When we came back the next day, the balloon at the end of his bed was gone.

Mike's cancer was discovered during the summer of 1966, when he was fifteen. It had been working on him for some time. He had been throwing up a lot, but he did it privately, it took a while for anyone to notice. The X-rays showed one of those malign shadows on the outside of his lung, the size, as they said, of a grapefruit. (They always compare tumors to fruits and vegetables, or to tennis and golf balls—bright round things that go into the body and turn black). It was mesothelioma, a comparatively rare cancer that is almost invariably fatal. They operated immediately and said, as they always do, for the record, for comfort, that they had "gotten it all."

But in the next two years, there were three more metastases. The family quickly picked up the jargon of that doomed business: metastasis, remission, chemo, and so on. Mike went in and out of Memorial—for operations, for radiation, for chemotherapy. Toward the end, my father managed to take Mike down to Little Dix Bay, the Rockefeller resort in the Virgin Islands, to lie on the beach in the sun.

Remembering now as we drove toward Washington, my father said, "Mike was very brave. Although of course that is a pathetic thing to be proud of." His mind had been wandering over the same subject as mine. It had occurred to me how difficult it must have been for my father to watch Mike being brave about dying. But he also admitted that Mike's stoicism had helped to make his own, my father's, task bearable. "I mean," my father said with a shudder, "I used to see a fifteen-year-old girl running down the corridor in the hospital screaming, 'Why me? Why me?'"

The question was never discussed with Mike, as far as I know. Not by my father, not by me. My father camped in his room, lived there. The sheer acceptance with which father and son collaborated to make what they could of the son's inevitable end brought to the awful business some consolation, and a certain sad stillness and clarity.

Mike listened to a shortwave radio that my father bought him, a Zenith Transatlantic. He liked to twiddle the dials, pulling in crackles and muzzes of voices from everywhere in the world. He liked to listen to the pilots and control towers at La Guardia and Kennedy airports. He would follow the approaching planes as the tower talked them in.

Toward the end, in early January, my father had his income taxes to do. He brought in his IRS forms and his financial records. He spread them on the floor, on Mike's bed—a chaos of canceled checks, Exxon receipts, telephone bills, and of course all of Mike's medical bills, his huge expenses, huge deductions. He would mutter over the forms and calculate, scratching figures on scrap paper, scanning the bills, looking for this or that, peering through the big clumsy horn-rimmed reading glasses that rode down on his nose. Then he would look up at Mike—Mikey, he called him—and ask if he wanted anything. Mike would often not answer—he would be off in the shallow daze of his painkillers, sleeping a little. My father might then turn down the lights and arrange himself on his lawn chair and go into a shallow sleep himself: The two of them sleeping lightly under these white blankets of bills and tax forms.

The last time I saw Mike was on the night before he died. He was in such pain that if I merely laid my hand on the foot of the bedframe, he would instantly, involuntarily writhe. I could not comprehend a body so sensitive, so without defenses, the nerves utterly raw, without padding. Seeing his pain, I drew back my hand as if from an electrical shock.

Mike lay uncovered in bed. His bones had almost no flesh to live on anymore. His skin had been burned black on his back and sides by the radiation treatments. He asked me to hold the pan for him while he urinated. I did so, and he made a weak sprinkling that fell onto the stainless-steel pan with a small, hard splatter. The room was almost dark, a small room near the nurses' station. I stayed through the early evening, until eight or eight-thirty.

But then I could not stand to stay in the room any longer. I had to go, to get up and leave, to get out. A repulsion or fear seized me and lifted me out of the chair.

I felt his death coming. I was afraid of it. I did not want to stay for it. I did not know what it was, what it meant.

Mike was heavily drugged. He was drifting in and out of sleep. His face and skull looked now as if all of the life had been eaten out of them. I told him I was going. I made the sort of noises of normality that one makes when leaving a dinner party early: "Well, got to get up early in the morning, got to fly to Chicago, got to get going, see you soon . . ."

Mike muttered at me and vaguely waved, as if saying, "That's okay." A nurse saw me doing it and gave me a hard, contemptuous look. I backed out of Mike's room, fast, making my parting noises all the way out, fumbling into my overcoat. I left him there alone. I knew that I would never see him again. I bolted for the elevator. The last thing of him that I saw was his bare left leg like a matchstick in the dim light.

. . .

It was a haunted year, a year of catastrophes. There came to seem to me a violent interchange between the public and private. Great public disasters had their immediate private equivalents, as if death were in the air, and it was catching.

The Tet offensive began in Vietnam as Mike lay dying. One night in late March, Travis Williams and I sat in an apartment in Greenwich Village and watched Lyndon Johnson on television as he withdrew from the presidential campaign. Travis rose out of his chair and did a little whooping dance. I did not believe it. I was having trouble absorbing developments in 1968.

Then Martin Luther King, Jr., was shot. I was having dinner at a Chinese restaurant on Fifty-second Street that night. I was with the national editor of *Time*, Michael Demarest, and a couple of other writers. When we went to dinner, we had heard only the report that King had been wounded. We came back to the office and found that he was dead.

After Mike, I no longer had any thought of immortality. Or I should not. I suppose that in a way I thought, or sensed, that Mike's death immunized the rest of us. His death was such an outrage against nature that nothing of the kind would happen again, not for a long time.

And then Travis Williams died. First there was the death of the public black, then the death of the private black. Travis was twenty-eight. He had a weakness of the blood vessels, congenital, I gathered, and he drank too much. He had high blood pressure.

Travis had gone to work for *Life* magazine as a reporter. One night when *Life* was closing an issue, late one night when they were having drinks at the office and trimming and fitting the magazine, Travis abruptly went down like a tree.

A blood vessel had burst in his brain. They took him to St. Vincent's Hospital, in the Village.

When I came to see Travis the next day, he was conscious, and very frightened. He did not want to move his head, lest his blood slosh in his cranium and spill his life away.

Travis was jaunty enough, given his immobility, his stiff, gingerly way of lying on the bed. I thought he looked as if he were about to be buried at sea, as if he were already lying on the pallet held by a couple of sailors, and when they tilted it down, he would squirt off the foot of the bed and splash into his death. But he managed a joke or two.

I gave Travis the *New Republic* and *Commentary* and *Time* and *Life* and *Newsweek*. We talked for a few moments.

I met his doctor on a stairwell and asked what his prognosis was. I was shocked that she seemed skeptical he would survive. She wig-wagged her hand, palm downward. Maybe. Maybe not.

I thought of what Travis had done for Mike as Mike lay dying. They had been extraordinarily close. Travis came to Memorial Hospital often. Sometimes when I arrived there in the afternoon, I would find the two in deep consultation and would feel like an intruder.

Travis talked to Mike about death, simply and directly, when the rest of us were sleepwalking around the possibility. The possibility. The probability. The inevitability.

Travis talked to Mike about dying and about what he had missed, and even about sex. Mike died a virgin, and I think the fact—not the technical fact, but the entire thing, the immense absence, the terrible incompleteness of his experience contained in that one circumstance—may have troubled him more than anything else. Because it meant that he died without having become a man, without having lived, in that fundamental sense.

Mike's funeral was held in a Catholic church in Bronxville—a requiem mass with a gruffly neutral eulogy by a local priest, a eulogy that was long on God and short on Mike. Travis came. He should have sat with me and the rest of the family, but I thought my stepmother would object to one of my Harvard friends joining the inner circle of mourning, and so Travis sat toward the back of the church.

Then we buried Mike at Gate of Heaven. And a few months later I flew down to Durham on a DC-6 bucking in the stormy air, and took a taxi to another church, and helped to bury Travis.

12·Chasing Victorio

I have become urban light cavalry. A parody of my great-grandfather Colonel Albert. I ride a bicycle everywhere in the city, a Panasonic five-speed.

I ride off among the hurtling taxicabs and the commuter buses that blast down Fifth Avenue, swirling behind them their black excretory diesel clouds. I go into Central Park at Seventy-ninth Street, just south of the Metropolitan Museum. I know all the trails through the park.

Coming home in the early evening through the center of the park, I ride along Library Walk, where the Puerto Rican dope dealers do their trade down the way from the statues of Shakespeare and Sir Walter Scott. One dealer knows me now by sight. He expects me, almost. I think I would disappoint him if I did not come rolling down Library Walk between the rows of broken benches and overhanging trees—churning along in my blue blazer, with the club tie flying over my shoulder.

I approach. He detaches himself from the whispering conspiracy of his friends beside the bench—the group watchful and huddle-shouldered, like wolves in colloquy. My dealer walks out toward me with an air of surreptitious greeting. It is now a satire of the furtive: He holds his closed right hand down next to his hip and gazes at me, and as I draw near he opens his hand and rotates the palm toward me to disclose three joints—the bright white little torpedoes in his brown hand. And in a low, cooing voice he calls to me, "Smo-o-o-o-o-ke! Smo-o-o-o-o-oke!"

My dealer does this every day. And when I shoot past, heading north, he snarfles back to his friends, watching me over his shoulder, with a low coyote crackle. The cavalry rides on.

When I discovered my great-grandfather Colonel Albert Morrow, I seized upon him. I made a myth of him. It eventually occurred to me that I wished to make him an idealized version of my father, somewhat like the sculptor Korzak carving Chief Crazy Horse in the rocks of the Black Hills.

One early fall I flew down to West Texas to find Fort Concho, the post in San Angelo where the colonel served for a time. When I returned to New York I told my father about it. We were walking to have lunch at the Harvard Club. We stood on the corner of Sixth Avenue and Forty-eighth Street, waiting for the light to change. When I told my father I'd been in West Texas and found the barracks where his grandfather had lived in the fort that he had commanded, my father looked at me, surprised, and asked in his satirical tone, "What are you trying to do, make a hero out of the old lush?"

There. Again. That strange old antagonism, that snarl.

I discovered that, oddly, my father knew very little about Colonel Albert, knew less than I did. He mispronounced the name of the fort in Texas. He called it Fort Concha. The past, for both of my parents, seemed an oddly forbidden region, a shadow to be waved away or else derided quickly, dismissed. My parents were superstitious about the past. If I meant to turn my great-grandfather into an equestrian statue, a cavalry myth, Indian fighter and frontier hero, my father would curl his lip: a psychic reflex.

Yet the more I told my father about Colonel Albert, the more I read him passages from cavalry histories that mentioned the man and his deeds, which were historically minor but nonetheless impressive, the more interested my father's eyes became. They filled with a look almost of wonder, and I could see his mind drifting back a long distance, trying to square this hero's tale now with his memories of what his own father had told him.

The colonel was an Indian fighter. He was John Wayne in *Fort Apache*. He fought up and down the American plains for twenty years after the Civil War. His troopers actually called him Old Iron

Ass: he could stay in the saddle so long, for days, for weeks, in rain and snow, soldiering, battering across the empty American landscape. Scouring off Comanches and Apaches and Utes and Mescaleros. He had pursuit. I admired that. He had a relentlessness, an endurance. An exemplar of the father side.

I took a pride in him—in the physical force of his character (as I imagined it) and of his work. He carried weapons and commanded soldiers, and I thought that people respected him and feared him, even. I liked to think that there was no subservience in him. I liked the nineteenth-century, American, horseback business of his life. It seemed a man's business: including the killing. I would put him up against Nelson any day, I thought. But Nelson was a bit of a killer, too. He had that hard American capacity in his eye.

Albert Morrow had been born in Adams County, Illinois, but when he was still an infant, his father, Hugh Morrow, moved the family east—reverse commuting, traveling against the flow of westward pioneers—by Conestoga wagon, to Hatboro, Pennsylvania. Hugh Morrow was a schoolteacher. The Illinois where Abraham Lincoln was then practicing law may have been too little civilization for him. He opened a boys' academy in Hatboro. He taught Greek and Latin and mathematics.

The Civil War arrived. Albert, nineteen years old, went to Philadelphia (where I was born eighty years later) and joined the 17th Pennsylvania Volunteers. In deference to his classical education, the army made him a sergeant.

He fought the Peninsula campaign under McClellan, was commissioned second lieutenant, and took a saber cut in the head at Old Church, twenty miles from Richmond. He was captured and held at Richmond, then came back to the Union lines in a prisoner exchange.

He fought at Antietam and Chancellorsville (captured again, released again). He made the rank of temporary colonel at age twenty-one. He suffered two more wounds at Trevillian Station, pursuing Robert E. Lee as aide-de-camp to General John Buford. In 1864, he was back fighting Jeb Stuart under Philip Sheridan, this time in a brigade commanded by George Armstrong Custer. He rode against Jubal Early in the Appomattox campaign. He took a bullet in the right hip at Dinwiddie Court House, and the slug stayed there for the rest of his life, a long misery in all his later years in the saddle. He was breveted colonel "for conspicuous gallantry in action" during the third day of the Wilderness and Dinwiddie Court House battles.

I found an obituary notice in the *Army-Navy Journal*, January 27, 1911:

Albert P. Morrow, Colonel, U.S.A. (retired) died January 20th, 1911, aged 69, at his home in Gainesville, Florida, from a complication of diseases resulting from wounds, hardships and exposures due to an active military life during the Civil War and Indian Wars on the Western frontiers. His remains were laid to rest in Arlington Cemetery, Virginia, Monday, January 23rd, with full military honors. Colonel Morrow was of a very gentle, loving disposition, and had the esteem and respect of all who served under him. His coolness and gallantry in action under the most trying circumstances was an inspiration to his fellow officers and men, and his military record is one that his comrades and family may well be proud of. Colonel Morrow was a member of the Loyal Legion Grand Army of the Republic and other societies. He was a communicant of the Episcopal Church, Gainesville, Florida.

"A gentle, loving disposition." So the killer, I thought, had the other side as well. There was that strain of sweetness in him too. It was at curious odds with the warrior's trade. The sweetness made him more interesting to me. It was a trait of my father's as well: the antagonism and the sweetness mixed—all of these complex compounds of character.

If my great-grandfather had not gone to command black cavalry, he would have died with Custer at Little Bighorn. He would have stayed in the Seventh Cavalry, serving under that plumed and jaunty narcissist. The Sioux would have slaughtered him with all the others, and Albert Morrow would have attained a somewhat higher subsequent historical shine. Maybe not. Custer's ego dominated the stage in that great American death scene. Albert would have been merely another bluebelly corpse.

After the war Albert went home to Hatboro, Pennsylvania. But there were no jobs there. Besides, like the others who fought that war—all wars—he found home a sudden anticlimax, insufficient, too abruptly peaceful. After one Pennsylvania winter at home, Albert wrote to Secretary of War Edwin Stanton and asked for his commission back. Phil Sheridan wrote a letter of recommendation for him. The regular army took him back, but only as a captain now. Albert protested, briefly. Then he discovered that Custer himself had been recommissioned only as a captain, so he accepted this affront to his twenty-four-year-old dignity. The Army put him in the Seventh Cavalry, which he joined in winter quarters at Fort Hays, Kansas.

Then there came an offer of promotion to major, and a $500 pay raise. The Army needed officers for the Ninth Cavalry, a new regiment of black troopers being sent west to police the plains. Albert Morrow accepted. He went down to Brownsville, Texas, in 1867, to soldier with the niggers. That is the way his brother officers would put it; they did not think much of the proposition: commanding ex-slaves, illiterate, new from the plantations of the Deep South where they were recruited. They were sent out to do frontier scutwork. The whites in Texas, citizens of the late Confederacy, watched with contempt when the black cavalry rode in wearing blue uniforms. The Texans may have been even more contemptuous of the white officers commanding the blacks.

I admired my great-grandfather. He commanded men, led them into battle, kept them going over long marches. Once in 1874, in the Red River Wars, Major Morrow took three companies of his black Ninth Cavalry out of Fort Sill, Oklahoma, and chased Comancheros up to the Pease River in bitter winter rain and snow, and he turned back only after fifty-four of his sixty mules had frozen to death. If he was a man of "gentle and loving disposition," he was also capable of long endurances.

But I was also attracted by the touch of failure and the stoicism in his life. There passed through the details of it an undercurrent theme of humiliation. I liked him better for that. It was not a triumphant life, really, but a representative Morrow life, though done with occasionally glamorous military effects.

Signing on to command the blacks in the Ninth Cavalry estranged him from some other officers in the Army. There was something second-class about his career, they thought. Something of the contempt they felt about blacks fell upon the white officers who commanded blacks. The smell of the slave quarters would cling to him. When I visited San Angelo, in 1980, I mentioned rather proudly that my grandfather had served there. The Texans in the room gave me a look of faint distaste.

Albert Morrow's career proceeded through a certain murk of bad luck and haplessness. It was often his medium. I wondered why he was captured and wounded so often during the Civil War. His life was not charmed. Not doomed, but not blazingly right, either. The trajectory of it was always complicated, deflected a little. There was a sidelong lucklessness in it, an element of unsuccess that I found moving and even admirable, in a saddening way. There was something charmingly mortal in it.

Things did go wrong. In early April of 1870, Major Morrow left Fort Quitman with ninety-one men of the Ninth Cavalry and rode upriver to El Paso. He hired Mexican guides and then marched due east into the Conudas Mountains of South Texas. He was hunting Mescalero Apaches. He hoped to surprise them in their fastness.

Instead, a private in I Company named John Johnson somehow set fire to the dry grass. Immense clouds of smoke rose. Every Indian in the Southwest must have seen it and watched Morrow's progress with a detached, almost abstract interest, even with amusement. It must have been an undignified ride for Albert, like traversing a ballroom floor with a rip in his trousers.

Still, Great-Grandfather bore on with that stoicism, or stolidity, that I liked. He plunged into the Guadalupe Range with his black troopers. They searched the canyons systematically, like policemen going through a house after a crime opening and closing doors, checking the closets. The cavalry found not Indians, but all the supplies that they had left behind in fleeing.

But the pattern of haplessness had set in. Great-Grandfather wrote in his report:

> The guides knew nothing of the country we were now in but . . . again took up the trail, and after marching four or five hours found myself back in the camp of the night before. [He had circled back upon himself.]

Our guides, although the best in the country, were completely lost and baffled by the multiplicity of trails running in every direction crossing and retracing. They finally succeeded in finding a trail leading down what appeared an impassable ravine, the horses and pack had to be lifted down over the rocks. One or two fell into crevices and could not be extricated. Toward evening, we came across a rancheria of 75 lodges which the Indians abandoned at our approach leaving a large amount of mezcal bread, about a hundred gallons of an intoxicating beverage brewed from the maguey and other commissary supplies, a great number of hides, robes, dressed and green skins, baskets, ojos, and all sorts of utensils and furniture pertaining to an Indian village.

By now the men were in miserable condition. They had lost so many horses that half the command was dismounted. Their boots were falling apart; many were barefoot. Still, Great-Grandfather kept on. He marched southwest, past the Sierra Diablo, and headed for Rattlesnake Spring. His advance party surprised a group of Mescaleros, who ran away. They left behind their lodges and twenty-two horses for Major Morrow.

Finally, after fifty-three days in the Guadalupes and a march of a thousand miles, Great-Grandfather led his men back to Fort Quitman.

Those were the Red River Wars. In the midst of them, in 1873, Great-Grandfather was on a three weeks' patrol out of Fort McKavett. He rode back into the fort on August 7, and found his wife in labor. The next morning Ella Mollen Morrow gave birth to my grandfather, Hugh Morrow.

My great-grandmother was a woman of some force. She was born in Cleveland. Her sister married Captain George Purlington, my great-grandfather's friend and fellow officer in the Ninth Cavalry. Ella Mollen came west to Fort Concho in 1869, when she was seventeen years old. It was an adventure outside civilization. She wrote in her diary about the last leg of the trip:

We left San Antonio by ambulance—and a very comfortable one it was. My brother-in-law having had it well lined with blankets, with seats which lay flat at night and made a good bed for our six-day overland trip. We traveled over sun-dried plains for miles and miles to see nothing but the road winding before us like a great snake as though there was no end to it. Each day we would travel 25 to 30 miles if possible to make the "water hole." We had an escort of 12 cavalry men in addition to our colored cook "John Myers" and my maid. On account of the horses, we had to reach water. I confess after the second day out, my ardor dampened considerably. The ambulance ride overland and camping out commenced to lose its romance, and a feeling of home sickness began to steal over me . . . By this time, I had decided I had gotten into a terrible country.

But she stayed. In the early spring of 1870, Major Morrow met Ella Mollen and began courting her. They were married a year later. Major Morrow wanted to take his bride to Europe for six months, but the Army refused his request for leave. They were married at Fort Quitman. They walked out of the post chapel under the crossed swords of the honor guard. Then they climbed into a wagon and set off for the place in the countryside, five miles away, that they had chosen for a honeymoon. All the way out, their cavalry escort fired rifles in the air—the Army equivalent of throwing rice. They honeymooned among the rattlesnakes and chiggers.

I liked Ella Mollen. She soldiered. She slept under the Comanche Moon. She was the only woman in the posts of Texas who rode in the steeplechase with the officers. She knew how to use a rifle and a .44 Colt.

One day in 1875 she was alone in her quarters at Fort Clark when a white man came climbing in through the back window. She screamed at him. She threatened him. He kept coming. My great-grandmother shot him between the eyes with her Army .44. Under the circumstances, no trial was held, or deemed necessary.

In 1876 the Ninth Cavalry, the black "Buffalo Soldiers," as the Indians called them, moved west to Fort Bayard, New Mexico. Geronimo was loose. My great-grandfather's task for the next two years became a Mescalero Apache warrior named Victorio.

My great-grandfather chased Victorio and his war parties for months through the mountains of southern New Mexico. Javert and Jean Valjean. Ahab and the whale. He never caught him. Victorio kept vanishing into Mexico and turning up somewhere else.

Victorio was a renegade from the reservation. He killed whites up and down the countryside. It is difficult not to take his side now. Victorio was a Stone Age chieftain dodging my great-grandfather's bullets in the last dusk before his people's extinction.

My great-grandfather pursued Victorio with his stoic force. Major Morrow rode mile after mile through those mountains while the horses dropped. His men ran out of rations. Their uniforms were tattered, their ammunition exhausted.

They caught Victorio time after time, exchanged fire with him and his band, then broke off. Victorio would dematerialize, into the mountains. My great-grandfather would pick up his dead and wounded. He would march down out of the mountains, to someplace like Ojo Caliente, and refit and rest and water his men, and then start off on the trail again.

Once in a place called Alamo Canyon, Great-Grandfather overtook a small party of Victorio's warriors. Morrow's men killed three of the Mescaleros and captured twenty of their animals. But Victorio was gone.

Victorio went west, across the Rio Grande and into the Mogollon Mountains. He killed sheepherders and miners—any white men he met. Major Morrow marched after him, by way of White Sands, into the San Andres Mountains. He watered his troopers at San Agustin Spring and then turned west to the Rio Grande. He sighted Victorio again. But the horses were so broken down, he could not chase him when he saw him. He gave up and struggled back to Ojo Caliente.

Weeks later, Great-Grandfather was back after Victorio, this time near the head of the Palomas River, a tributary of the Rio Grande. Major Morrow pushed his horses and men until he caught up with the Apache's rear guard. He killed three of them and wounded several more. He chased the main force to the Mexican border. But orders from Washington now forbade him to cross, even in hot pursuit. He and his Buffalo Soldiers pulled up at the river. They watched in a rage as Victorio rode away to the south.

Six days later, Great-Grandfather did a thing that I have found haunting. He caught a group of Apaches making its way into Mexico. His troopers killed two of them and wounded three others. One of the dead Indians was Victorio's son.

Major Morrow and his men knew only that they were firing at Mescaleros. They could not have known that one was Victorio's son. And had they known, they would, if anything, only have aimed their rifles more carefully, lest they miss such a prize.

I read the details of Colonel Albert's life in a family record that was prepared by the colonel's namesake, my cousin Albert, who is a painstaking family historian. The archive, a pile of fifty-two Xeroxed typewritten pages, came to me from Uncle Chris.

I read in this family record the almost offhanded sentences about Victorio's son. The incident reverberated distantly in my mind. I held Cousin Bert's archive in my hand one night in New York City and read it for the first time. I reread it. I saw Victorio's son shot off his horse into the dirt that day next to the Rio Grande, and saw the blue-uniformed cavalry riding up to the body slowly, and my great-grandfather coming up behind them on his horse, with his hard, triumphant eye, and saw the body turned in the dust by a soldier's boot. I wondered if he recognized immediately the trophy he had shot.

I felt I had witnessed a disturbing sacrifice. The father side and the son side fought for my sympathies. The sins of the father destroyed the son. The killing had a quality of ritual in it. It seemed to enact some deeper business.

The long campaign against Victorio had all but dismounted the Ninth Cavalry. My great-grandfather was so exhausted that he had to be carried back to Fort Bayard. It was now June 12, 1880.

Colonel Edward Hatch, who commanded the Ninth Cavalry, reported to the Assistant Adjutant General in Fort Leavenworth:

Major Morrow's command shows that the work performed by these troops is most arduous, horses worn down to mere shadows, men without boots, shoes and clothing. That the loss of the horses may be understood when following the Indians in the Black Range, the horses were without anything to eat for five days, except what they nibbled from pinon pines . . . Major Morrow has over-exerted himself to such an extent as to produce a dangerous hemorrhage. Long night marches have been made on foot by the troops in their efforts to surprise the Indian camps. Morrow deserves great credit for the persistency with which he has kept up the pursuit, and without the foot Indians' constant vigilance, must have fallen into ambushes resulting in the destruction of his command.

My great-grandfather rested. The Army let him go back to civilization. It sent him to Paris in the fall of 1880 to watch the maneuvers of the French army. But somehow he managed to arrive too late. He stayed in France for a few months; then he came back to live in Washington and serve as aide-de-camp to General Sherman.

But he returned to the frontier. The Army made him a lieutenant colonel and gave him a post in Arizona, Fort Huachuca. Being back seems to have depressed him. An officer at the fort, Major A. K. Arnold, reported to the Adjutant General of the Army that "he, Lieutenant Colonel Albert P. Morrow, Sixth Regiment, U.S. Cavalry, being on duty as commanding officer of the post of Fort Huachuca, A.T., was found drunk on said duty."

Not once, but a least four times: June 30, August 2, August 5 and August 22. He was court-martialed in November. The court suspended his rank and command for one year and put him on half pay and sent him to the bottom of the list of lieutenant colonels.

Great-Grandfather, I suppose, survived the humiliation with the stoicism he displayed in the saddle. He returned to duty. He fought against Geronimo in the summer of 1886. He was given other commands—Fort Stanton, New Mexico, and then Fort Union. In 1891 he became a colonel and took over the Third Cavalry, stationed in Fort McIntosh, Texas.

When I learned about the colonel's court-martial for drinking, I felt a sort of falling sense of shame for him. It was not really necessary, I suppose. I might have been thinking of my father swaying at the top of the stairs with a glass in his hand one afternoon years ago on Mount Pleasant Street in Washington. He had been drinking while trying to write, a mistake he did not normally make, and when I came home from school with my friend Robert, my father was himself, so to speak, drunk on duty. I was overtaken by the eerie sense one always has with the intoxicated, that they have become someone else. That should be no surprise. After all, it is to become someone else, temporarily, that they drink in the first place. That surely was the case with Colonel Albert.

My father's brothers and sisters drink sometimes as a form of communion. I rather like them when they drink.

One of my cousins was married on a lovely October Saturday afternoon in Baltimore. The reception was a handsome, decorous business in a nineteenth-century mansion that is now a private club. All my father's brothers and sisters were there, all eight of Dr. Morrow's children. When the reception was over, Uncle Rowland, the father of the groom, said, "Come by the house."

His house is a small mansion in the Guilford section of Baltimore, a beautiful house surrounded by trees in an expanse of grass.

When all of the brothers and sisters arrived at the house, they were several drinks along and started to loosen. We got a little drunk together. The process had a primitive, Scots-Irish tribal quality. I saw that we were all melting toward one another in a ceremony that was both bacchic and rather sweet.

The deeper levels of this ceremony were not accessible to my younger cousins. Hughie and I understood it, though not as profoundly as the aunts and uncles. It was a communion of memory, of grandmother and grandfather, of the Depression and World War II, of marriages and children, the business of the tribe.

The Morrow faces, those familiar features, fell meltingly together. We all became one another. We recognized one another in the most primitive way. I thought that we found in this communion, for a while, a peculiar tribal peacefulness.

13·Coronaries

In my imagination, my father and Nelson Rockefeller and I formed a complex triangular arrangement. It changed over time. In my hallucinations of it, things that happened to one of us in one year illuminated or shadowed things that happened to the others at other times. It even seemed to me, sometimes, to involve matters of life and death.

There was Kansas City in 1976, for example. I had a heart attack there. A crushing pain in the center of my chest, and a piece of my heart died, an area the size of a fifty-cent piece. I remembered everything that happened there, at that moment in August 1976, when, two and a half years later, I learned what happened to Nelson Rockefeller's heart in a town house on West Fifty-fourth Street. His damage was larger than a fifty-cent piece. It was larger than everything he had.

Rockefeller had gone to the convention in Kansas City in 1976 to attend the ceremony of his own political extinction. Gerald Ford was dropping him. Rockefeller had become Ford's Vice President, by appointment, after Richard Nixon's resignation. But Rockefeller seemed a political liability in the 1976 campaign. He was too moderate, Ford thought, too Eastern. At that late date it may have been wrong to think of him as unconservative. At any rate, he had too much complicated history. That somewhat wild-hair heartland wing of the Republican Party, the one with the light of zeal in its eye, must be appeased. Ronald Reagan had come in from the primaries with a dangerously good chance of taking the nomination away from the sitting President (sitting but of course unelected, and therefore more vulnerable than he might otherwise have been). Ford would have to run with a more conservative character on his ticket. He had chosen Robert Dole of Kansas, a Senator with a sardonic, menacing wit.

So Rockefeller came to Kansas City mainly as a good sport, the way an old girl friend comes to the wedding and ruefully throws rice. He would smile publicly through his demise as a public figure. He would be philosophical. Once when Flaubert was feeling disconsolate, Turgenev sent him a note telling him he ought to cheer up: "After all, you are Flaubert." Nelson Rockefeller had the consolation of being Nelson Rockefeller. His relationship with American politics had always been somehow an unequal mating anyway, morganatic. He had always been slumming in the trade of electoral politics. He was surely too good, or at any rate too rich, for a business in which any clerk or servant was entitled to reject a Rockefeller in the voting booth. He was surely too baronial, possessed too much the dignities of birth, to go out at regular intervals among the serfs and waitresses and eat their pizzas and knishes and meatball heroes and clutch their hands and give them all those teeth, that energy, those disconnected whoops of ebullience—"Hiya! . . . Hiya! . . . Beautiful! . . . Marvelous! . . . Yer terrific! . . . Swell!"—as he waded through their sweating, jostling life.

Rockefeller enjoyed the messy, human business of campaigning. Or at any rate, it suited his purposes to seem to enjoy it. Of course, it would be fatal to the ambitions of any politician if he visibly recoiled from the populace that he was obliged to court. But Rockefeller, being a Rockefeller, had to make a deeper plunge into the crowd. Part of his political charm derived from that effect: the multimillionaire as a regular guy—"Rocky." In his biography of Theodore Roosevelt, Edmund Morris records a story. Roosevelt stands in line for hours on the afternoon of his inauguration, greeting thousands of well-wishers who file through the White House. Roosevelt grins that carnivorous, slightly lunatic grin of his, and takes their hands in his hands and squeezes them. But when this warm Jacksonian effusion is ended, Roosevelt walks upstairs and carefully, thoroughly, obsessively washes and rewashes his hands.

I sometimes thought that Nelson Rockefeller must have done that. If so, it must have been a psychologically complicated transaction for him to have been rejected for national office so many times. Who washed his hands of whom? *And by what right?*

For years when I was a child, my father and mother went to political conventions. They relished them. I grew up with the impression that a political convention was a splendidly rich ceremony of democratic life, filled with color and characters and suspense: a wonderful power brawl, fought in public and therefore uniquely and lovably American: innocent. A convention was an event, a party—a treat.

The first time I atttended one, in Chicago in 1968, I was a national affairs writer for *Time*. I stood on Michigan Avenue in front of the Hilton and watched the demonstrators surging up against the massed walls of Chicago cops. The air was thick with tear gas and with the stink bombs that the Yippies detonated.

I watched all this with Winston Churchill, who was covering the event for a London paper. We stood behind the police lines, and thus being rather bizarrely detached from the action, we managed to chat for ten minutes as if at a cocktail party.

Churchill was a sleek and ironic and strangely exhilarated man. He was a young, handsome version of his grandfather. He enjoyed the jolt he could give Americans by introducing himself: "Hullo, I'm Winston Churchill." They would peer at him and see the genes and be lost for an instant in wonder and time-traveling recognition and confusion.

The convention—or rather, everything that happened in Chicago around the convention—was political theater, street theater, far different from the festive whoop and bunting that Americans expected of conventions. It was a public brawl. But it was not what my parents had in mind when they rhapsodized about conventions. Maybe Chicago in 1968 spoiled me for subsequent conventions. Chicago was a rawer form of democracy—democracy with clubs.

The Chicago cops in the line outside the Hilton were a heavy, brutal presence. Jean Genet was covering the convention. He loved the huge cops and their leather and billy clubs. They radiated an animal heat. Their faces looked like sides of beef. I watched the blood pressure rise within them, a blood-outrage held by the thinnest membrane. But it was not their blood that got spilled.

There seemed something obscurely Oedipal in the transaction there. The children in their bright paramilitary rags and football helmets screamed and taunted the cops the way an eight-year-old goes to work on his father until the floodgates of anger open up and the retaliation comes. The demonstrators thrust their faces, filled with hate, into the cops' faces, nose to nose, and screamed "Pig!" and "Nazi!," or chanted "Hey, hey, L.B.J., How many kids did you kill today?" and "Fuck you, L.B.J." There was a nasty, buried aspect, too, of class hostility and condescension in the encounter. The demonstrators were the middle class, come from Berkeley and Harvard and Yale and the University of Wisconsin. The cops would have grown up in the Chicago immigrant neighborhoods, Poles and Irishmen and Italians. The demonstrators made clear their contempt for the cops, not only for the role they were playing there, but for who they were, and where they had not gone to school.

I was torn in my sympathies. I was against the war and the draft. But something in me was with the cops, some father side of me. I thought they should not have to endure the taunts of the privileged. The son in me, however, resonated perfectly with the anger of the demonstrators.

The great beefy fathers charged. They swung their clubs. Blood flowed.

I was astonished by the sound that a police club makes when it strikes the human skull. The head (with its armor of bone and nimbus of hair and personality and life) is abruptly vulnerable: just a big piece of fruit with a bashable rind. The club makes a sickening, meaningful *thunk* upon it, and you hear the mortality inside, the perishable brain: thought and memory and spirit, all just a wet pulp in a shell. The club hits the human head and sounds a bass note roughly in the same ominous range as the noise that a clod of earth makes when it falls onto a wooden coffin. The air on Michigan Avenue was heavy with those low, blunt notes.

Winston Churchill and I fell back, flourishing our press credentials, authentically scared. I lost Churchill and dodged inside a glass side door to the Hilton. A huge Chicago cop followed me in, club clutched at a killer angle, his body in a crouch, ready to swing. Over his shoulder, through the glass doors, I could see the tumbling, clubbing seethe of the battle, the uniforms earnestly at work upon everything not in uniform. The cops' mouths grimly closed. The civilians' mouths all open, screaming, cursing, or soundlessly agape.

I yelled "Press!" at the cop advancing on me. He hesitated an instant. Then an expression almost of disappointment crossed his face. I was an animal that was not in season. Someone might see him. He straightened up and grabbed me by the shoulder and hurled me into the lobby, and then waded back into the street, smelling blood.

Chicago 1968 was not a typical convention, of course. What happened in the streets was more vivid and meaningful than what occurred in the convention hall. Or so it seemed at the time. There was blood on the moon, and Hubert Humphrey had not understood it. He wanted the old style back, the happy-days-are-here-again good times: the Politics of Joy, as he called it. Live television, meanwhile, had at last collided with its proper object, a political spectacle worthy of the medium's possibilities. Vietnam had arrived in the middle of America.

I attended five other conventions after that. I came to detest them. Conventions depressed me. With their staging and multimillion-dollar television coverage, conventions seemed to me items of Americana that had become sad and bogus. One might admire the democratic process proclaimed, or intended, but still find the drama a sort of travesty. The faces of the delegates looked wrong to me— either merely empty or else charged with an irrelevant zealotry. The pageant came to seem to me forlorn in a very American way.

Whatever enthusiasm Nelson Rockefeller and my father may have had for conventions in the past (and they had much, for they were the arenas of Nelson's desires), they could not have brought anything but truculent ruefulness and resignation to Kansas City in 1976.

My father and stepmother checked into the Crown Center with the Rockefellers. I did not see them. My hotel was downtown: a threadbare place that surely never would have been full without a national political convention in town. I came to the convention as a writer for *Time*, but I avoided the Kemper arena as much as I professionally could. I looked up old Kansas City friends—Wayne Nichols' brother Jay and their parents. I went to lunch with them at the Country Club Plaza.

During some sessions of the convention I sat in the press gallery with other people from *Time* and watched the milling soup of delegates. Sometimes Rockefeller sat with the New York delegation. With my binoculars, I picked him out, the cynosure. I detected that he was behaving with the odd sort of noisy fuck-you nihilism of a Mafia don saving face: a provincial potentate, aced out, but lording it a little now with his retinue in full view of the party that had turned him down so many times in so many conventions just like this. I thought of the scenes in *For Whom the Bell Tolls* when Pablo, paunchy and cunning and losing authority over his band in the cave, tries to cover his retreat with bravado. That was Rockefeller among the New York delegates: something askew in his character, gaiety and menace and loss all loose in his countenance.

I eased my binoculars over the New York delegation, a degree to the left. My father's face swam into my round picture. He wore his intelligent, attentive-courtier's face. He was working, attending Nelson, but perhaps not with the urgent sense of consequence that he had brought to earlier conventions. What the hell. The outcome here was known. If Nelson wanted to cut loose a little, let him. Still, my father's head was cocked toward Rockefeller. He was obviously trying to hear everything that Rockefeller said, through the usual boom and stir of convention noise.

It was his long practice, his professional habit. When he listened to Nelson talking in public, my father always inclined his head at just that angle. I could see his brain at work. He intercepted every word and weighed it and X-rayed it. He checked Nelson's words for concealed dangers. It was his job to frisk Nelson's sentences. And if one of them went too far, if one of them looked suspicious and started to get away in the crowd of other sentences, my father would leap to retrieve it and disarm it before it could do his man any damage. He would deflect, rephrase, offer the quick correction. It was his work. Nelson needed some supervision.

I was proud, in a curious way, to see him there. I handed the binoculars back to the researcher from whom I had borrowed them. I asked *Time*'s chief of correspondents, Murray Gart, for a floor pass. (Credentials were limited, and we had to trade them off.) I told him I wanted to go out and speak to my father, who was an old friend of Gart's. Gart, too, had once worked for Rockefeller.

I pushed through the rent-a-guard security checkpoints and out onto the convention floor. Through the loudspeaker boomed interminable procedural business—something to do with the party platform. The delegates were arrayed in a thousand attitudes of boredom. They wore the expressions of travelers caught in an airline terminal that has been shut down by a blizzard. They did crossword puzzles. They sat heavily in their folding chairs, faces glazed, their plastic red-white-and-blue boaters perched at angles, their hams akimbo in their doubleknit trousers.

I found my father as he was leaving the convention floor, trailing behind Nelson Rockefeller. I am not certain that my father even knew that I was in Kansas City.

We had been drifting away from each other for years. Since I became a father a terror of mine has been that I would drift away from my two sons. I have feared the almost accidental falling off. I have feared the sudden misunderstanding, something stupid and final.

My father and I simply went into a silence, which endured for several years.

Now he looked at me suddenly, there on the convention floor among the jostling Republican delegates and the television floor reporters, each with his following gang of camera-bearers. My father looked at me as if some remarkable coincidence had just occurred, as if some unknowable impulse of fate had deposited the two of us just here, in Kansas City, in the same place at the same time. "Well, I'll be damned!"

We leaned our heads together and cupped our hands and shouted greetings into each other's ears, "Where are you staying? . . . When you get here? . . . Got to run!"

Saying that, my father held out his hand to me, and we shook, like two professionals after a chance encounter. Then he turned and pushed away through the surge, following Nelson. The TV lights beamed off his bald spot. The crowd carried him away and closed behind him.

After that, I saw my father only at a distance for the rest of the convention. He would sweep in and out of the hall with Nelson, and I would watch them from the press gallery.

I had been assigned to write *Time*'s cover story that week. I found it impossible, for some reason, to get my journalistic bearings. The night of the balloting for the presidential nominee, the Reagan people packed the galleries and screamed in an endless tribal point-counterpoint across the convention hall, "*Viva! . . . Ole!*" The Reagan supporters brought in blaring noisemakers, like nasal klaxons, and filled the air of the hall with the sound—an angry, insect sound, as of giant bees or locusts. The Californians felt their own presence and possibilities, and their noise had an overbearing defiance about it.

I listened to the sound of ascendant Reaganism for a little while, and then fled from the hall. The convention had an orchestration about it that seemed to me tinny and pointless and inauthentic. The air seemed filled with stupidity and fraud.

The night of acceptance speeches, Thursday night, I stayed in my hotel room and watched on television. I ordered a room-service steak and ate it in the tiny room, with my nose six inches from the black-and-white screen, and listened to Gerald Ford's acceptance speech.

I got up at five in the morning. I walked to a room in the Muehl-bach Hotel that *Time* had rented for writers to use. I sat down at six in front of a folding hotel buffet table with a Royal desk model typewriter on it. I spread out my notes and the files that *Time* correspondents had been sending on the convention. I stacked three packs of Marlboros and my Zippo lighter next to the typewriter, and began writing.

The work was painful. It took all day. I could not strike the note, the tone I wanted. I detested the convention. I had no feeling for Ford or Reagan. They seemed foreigners to me. They might as well have been Italians making deals in the Chamber of Deputies. The process through which they struggled, the stratagems, the deals, the ideological frictions, all seemed peculiarly futile.

The air in the hotel room in the Muehlbach turned blue with my tobacco smoke. Through the afternoon my pages of manuscript accumulated. By five o'clock I had pieced together a cover story. I pencil-edited. I gathered up the story and began walking from the hotel to the Kansas City Civic Center, where *Time* had its convention headquarters.

I walked across a broad avenue which, in its abstracted and unpeopled spaciousness, reminded me of Washington. I lit another cigarette. I was working on my third pack of the day. I inhaled. I immediately began to feel a burning in my chest. I felt the blood drain from my face. My hands began to sweat. My breath grew short.

I threw away the cigarette. When I arrived at the Civic Center, I turned in the story to the national editor. *Time* had staked out an area on the mezzanine of the center. Other magazines and newspapers and television networks had curtained off areas for their headquarters. The center was like a large factory, turning out information and opinion and interpretation, the air filled with the soft, distant clacking noises (typewriters, teletypes) of journalists working. I sat for an hour or so in the *Time* area. I talked with the writers and researchers gathered there. My chest still burned slightly. I walked into an outer corridor and found a men's room, and went inside and stared at my face for a long time in the mirror.

The face was very much afraid. The skin had turned the color of a sidewalk. An alarming mottled gray. My hands still sweated.

The editor asked me to make a few revisions on the story. We went out to a stairwell to discuss them, away from the noise. Henry Grunwald, the managing editor, joined us, and made suggestions. I went to a typewriter and prepared to revise.

As always when I sat down to a typewriter, my right hand

reached over to slap the cigarette pocket on my left chest. I pulled a Marlboro from the pack with two fingers, without extracting the pack from my pocket. I lit it with a match.

What I inhaled was pure pain. The cloud of smoke descending to my lungs became at once a hot crushing black rock plunging into me. Then the pain began to squeeze like a black hand reaching from within and clutching the chestbone.

I never lost consciousness. I walked to a leather couch in a cool, dark corner and lay down, face down, holding my chest and writhing slowly, trying to writhe out the pain.

Dick Duncan, then the deputy chief of correspondents, saw me, and grew concerned. He talked to Murray Gart about me. Murray's reflexes were decisive. He and Judith Shapiro, who handled the administrative work of the Nation section, led me outside to a hired car and took me to St. Mary's Hospital.

The emergency room was empty. The young doctor and nurse on duty seemed both curious and grateful for the business. They lay me down on a bed in a room with a sort of dormitory quality about it. The doctor squeezed a cold gel onto my chest and sides and ankles. He wired me up to an electrocardiograph. I watched the monitor screen. Across it, monotonously, danced the playful beep of my life. The endless repetition of the bouncing course seemed sinister to me. The jagged, rhythmic, bounding picture had to be repeated, over and over, so that we would know, instantly, that when it was not repeated just like that, death was out there in the woods again, close-by.

Murray and Judith sat for hours in the waiting room. The pain had passed now. I felt better. Finally, the nurse and an orderly moved me upstairs to intensive care. They put me in a bed next to that of an old man. Cancer, I saw at once. All night, his throat emitted ugly noises, terminal *kaaak*s, death gurgles. Only once, when I arrived, did he turn and regard me for an instant. His eyes were filled with a wild woe of death: hectic, imprisoned eyes in a face gone utterly gaunt. The man looked like the old cancer patient in Mike's room in Memorial Hospital seven years before, the one who objected so bitterly when my wife and I brought a balloon for

Mike from Central Park. Here, in Kansas City, the man measured me for a second with his eyes, and then he instantly withdrew into his own mortal business, and never looked at me again.

In the morning the day doctors came. I was supposed to be on a plane halfway back to New York. The doctors read my enzyme tests. (When some of the heart dies in a heart attack, the dead tissue releases enzymes into the bloodstream. That is how the doctors know if a heart attack has occurred. The more enzymes, the more damage to the heart.)

A doctor with an air of joviality concealing something else came to my room, smiling and studying reports that he held at an angle away from me, like cards he was proud of and eager to play. He looked at me with a secret, satisfied smile.

"Well, you've had one," he announced. The heart attack had been moderate. It had killed a small part of my heart, he thought, and he held up his right hand to make the A-OK signal, forefinger making a circle with the thumb, in order to show me just about what I had lost. On the left anterior wall. The term meant nothing to me. The doctor wanted to know exactly what I had felt when the attack first came.

"It was a burning at first, in the center of my chest," I said gesturing. "And then a crushing kind of constriction, as if . . ."

The doctor looked almost happy. He insisted on giving me the simile. "It was as if," he said, "an elephant had stood on your chest. Right? An elephant standing right in the middle of your chest!"

I thought that was the wrong comparison. No, that wasn't right at all. No, I started to say, it was more like a vise on the inside going to work. It was as if my chest were imploding. I could not breathe and . . . But he waved me off amiably and insisted, "No. It was like an elephant standing in the middle of your chest."

Then, with ceremony, he drew from his white starched doctor's hospital coat a tiny brown bottle of nitroglycerine. He presented it to me, arm thrust out, little finger extended, bottle clutched between thumb and forefinger, as if the nitro were a gemstone or a communion wafer.

"This must never leave you," he said dramatically. "You must always keep this with you. You must tie a string around your finger and keep it there to remind you to carry this all the time. And if you have a pain in your chest, you take one of these and place it under your tongue like this. [He demonstrated.] Then you wait for the little headache to arrive. It should come almost instantly. And then your pain should stop."

I thought the doctor was a fool, though not necessarily about nitro. I have carried a little bottle of it everywhere with me ever since. I have never had to open the bottle. I replace it every few months with a fresh one. I carry it always: a kind of superstition, a rabbit's foot.

I moved to a large private room. They told me later it was called the Bishop's Room because a Roman Catholic bishop of Kansas City once used it periodically when he wanted a kind of vacation. He would check into the hospital and settle into the room and invite his cronies to come and drink bourbon and play poker through the night.

I took everything in through a daze of Valium, a dandelion haze. The pills were a dandelion yellow, and did send me off into chemical meadows. I have never lain more utterly still than I did on the bed in the Bishop's Room. At first I felt a peculiar serenity. I think that I enjoyed the stir I had created. Illness always seems to be a deeply childish transaction. One goes back. Perhaps because one is so helpless.

Then on the afternoon of the second day after the attack I felt something in my chest: the black hand beginning to tighten on the bone again. I seized the nurse's call button. She came instantly. She told me to take one of the pellets of nitroglycerine, and told me to place it under my tongue. Immediately, the action of the pill, dilating vessels, gave me a sharp pain in the temple. The nurse said to wait three to five minutes and then, if the pain in my chest persisted, to take another.

The clutch in my chest remained. I took another pill. Again the sharp pain in the forehead. I rang for the nurse. When I told her I had taken two nitros and the pain in my chest remained, she looked at me in a curious, knowing, solemn way, as if to say, "Well, then, you are going to die."

It was a professional look. The objectivity of it chilled me. I saw her calculations of my mortality precisely. She was adding me up, as matter-of-factly as the girl at the checkout counter. She turned and went away.

Now the serenity vanished. It had been peculiarly infantile. I had not grasped the event. I had almost enjoyed it, as if it had been a kind of dangerous prank. One night when I was twenty years old in Paris, I got drunk with Wayne Nichols and Jack Nordby and we took an elevator up to the highest tourist deck of the Eiffel Tower. We decided that was not high enough. We climbed out over the railings and proceeded to scale to the top of the tower, woozily exuberant, hand-over-hand, up the girders. Paris looked splendid from that dangerous height, and we practically swooned and swung in the air admiring it: like drunken chimps, like King Kong. We were still more or less drunk when we got back down. No one had caught us at the stunt or stopped us. We remembered it as lovely, risky fun.

Now my heart attack no longer seemed to be merely a risky novelty. I got serious about it. I felt a deep terror. I thought I was going to die.

I was also angry. A treachery had been committed. Abruptly the body, the companion of one's life (the one that had gone up the Eiffel Tower so easily that night), the old abused and familiar flesh, the crony one inhabits, turned into a psychopathic stranger.

I lay for hours at night in Kansas City and listened to my heart. I covered its every move. I felt that I had been locked in a cell with a convicted murderer. I stayed awake, my senses as clear as an animal's. The body became as terrifying as a house in the woods in the middle of the night, far from help. The house is dark. The phone line has been cut and there are sounds downstairs. Someone is down there, moving around. One lies and listens and hears everything: the sighs of the refrigerator, the ticking in the pipes, the sounds the bones make, the dark busy syncopated flood-rush of the heart. The spirit goes dark with a sense of betrayal.

Being so abruptly at the mercy of impulsive, lethal things that dwell inside the chest, the mind becomes as superstitious as a savage. It is bad luck to lie with one's legs crossed at the ankle; the blood might not be able to flow through the obstruction. It is bad luck to lie on one's left side. It is bad luck to think of certain things. I rinsed my mind the way that I had once done in the lower church of St. Aloysius Gonzaga. It was an attitude of prayer. I concentrated upon it, upon keeping my mind in a state of blinded whiteness, upon keeping it clear and still and empty.

The soul, inside its alienated body, lies upon the white sheets in blinking vulnerability. A broken wingbone grounds the bird. It waits for the worst, vibrating slightly, but tense and motionless.

Then the drugs arrive in the nerves. And time, the medium through which they move, like mists, will itself soothe the terrors. When an hour has passed, and the Valium has dazed away the worst vibrations, and the chest has not attacked again, a sort of hospital half-sleep sets in: the surreal doze the body may allow itself (by some complex negotiation) even when it is in danger. The thing goes on autopilot for a little while, and the mind slips below and dozes, with its clothes on. *Wake me if anything suspicious . . .*

With longer experience, I discovered that the pains in my chest were not always real. The more I feared the onset of them, the more likely I was to conjure them up. The pains were not actual. They were not the signals that the heart muscle was deprived of oxygen; they were phantoms, like the killers we imagine to be skulking downstairs in the middle of the night. The pains that would not respond to nitro were like that. Anxiety can tighten the chest and shorten the breath and cause the palms to sweat in crude simulation of cardiac symptoms.

For many months, it was difficult for me to distinguish the two. The phantoms can be disabling, too, in their way. They are dybbuks. They arrive at inconvenient moments. They come suddenly, like old intimate enemies who turn up unexpectedly and make a scene. They have a talent for interruption, for intrusion.

Once, in the winter after my heart attack, I was shopping with Jamie in Gimbels. The phantoms came, and the fist closed around the chestbone. I felt overtaken by an annihilating fear that was, at the same time, very close to rage. The air flecked red. My palms sweated. I plunged a hand into my trouser pocket and fingered my tiny bottle of nitroglycerine.

Jamie wandered on in front of me in his happy pre-Christmas agitation, almost reeling with the sensory overload of the toy department. My rage departed. The fear remained. I clutched a counter that was covered with stuffed animals, and dizzily held it for a moment. Then I took deep breaths and went lurching on after Jamie.

The phantom attacks did their worst physical damage, I suppose, to my shirts and sweaters. When an attack of this kind arrived, my right hand went instantly to the center of my chest, to my solar plexus. I rubbed it, hard, with my fingers, in a nervous circular motion, as if by massaging the skin and bone over the heart, I might encourage the heart itself. I was trying to reach in and get to the muscle, the animal, and touch it and comfort it and make it safe. These moments left my skin red and raw. Soon my shirts had a worn, dirty oval of cloth, like the heel of an old sock, just over the center of the chest. The wool of my sweaters was all pilled and worn just there.

A couple of years after Kansas City, I met a friend who had recently had a heart attack. When I saw him, he was just coming off a tennis court. He smiled and waved with his right hand. And then the hand went down involuntarily to the center of his chest and rubbed it, hard, exactly there, and when the hand came away, I saw a dirty oval in the middle of his alligator shirt. I came to regard the oval as a secret sign, a badge. I have never seen anyone except a veteran of a heart attack make that hard chest-rubbing gesture. It has some kinship to the smudge of ashes that one sees on the foreheads of people in the street on Ash Wednesday. Members of the tribe.

My father left Kansas City the morning after my heart attack, without knowing about it. (Nor did I know that my stepmother had also collapsed in Kansas City. It was the start of her terminal struggle with cancer. She flew back to New York loaded with Percodan from the White House physician.) My father called from New York when he heard about my heart attack. He offered to fly back out to see me. I thanked him and said there really was no need. The next day a basket of flowers arrived with a card from

Nelson Rockefeller and his wife. I assumed that my father had arranged that.

Having a heart attack seems the sort of thing that a father does, not what is expected of a son. I felt that some role reversal had occurred. The process felt somewhat like other times when I had almost become their parent. It is possible that I felt a strange competitive pride about the usurpation I had committed. I had usurped one of the ceremonies of fatherhood. A heart attack, after all, is a man's estate, a rite of passage, a way of looking death in the eye: a little like going off to war.

My father had never been sick. His diabetes was a chronic nuisance—serious enough, of course, but not, in his case, a sudden killer. I thought, childishly, that he enjoyed an immunity from sickness that amounted almost to a form of grace. It was a privilege of his, a dispensation—like his intelligence, like his good looks. He had his boyhood's country constitution. I do not think he even took aspirin more than a dozen times in his life.

No one in the family had ever died—until Mike. I grew up with the impression that death and sickness were something that happened to others, not to us. So even my heart attack seemed, in some sidelong way, an act of supercession. I wondered if my father thought it strange that his sons were either dying (Mike) or wandering around for a time in death's neighborhood (me).

I wondered how my heart attack, Mike's illness, may have reverberated in my father—the children falling by the wayside while the father goes on. "The cowards never started," Kit Carson said, "and the weak died on the way." Oedipus thwarted by Darwin.

Did Mike and I make my father feel invulnerable? Or did the mortal vulnerability of the children make the father feel that much older, that much closer to his own death? It seemed almost a crime against nature for the father to survive so vigorously while his sons were clogging and infarcting, or else dying in a riot of cancerous cells.

I thought of the day that Richard Nixon came to lunch in one of the private dining rooms at the Time & Life Building. It was in 1967. Nixon was still some months away from the Republican nomination the following summer. But he had been quietly and methodically campaigning for it for years, speaking to any Republican group that would invite him, accumulating friends and IOUs. It was hard, lonely work. (It is possible, I suppose, that Nixon was never *not* lonely.)

When he came to lunch in 1967 with fifteen or twenty writers and editors at *Time*, he was just at the end of that long labor out in the wilderness. He was just coming up on the outskirts of national power again. He could see it in the distance.

Nixon spent two hours with us in the private dining room. He was pleasant and comfortable and shrewd. He analyzed the coming 1968 campaign with calm intellligence resting on a bed of fatalism. If Rockefeller goes this way, he said, and if Romney goes this way, and if Scranton wins the Pennsylvania primary, then such and such will happen. He carried in his mind the most intricate, intimate political map of the United States, and he was at home in every corner of it.

What I found disconcerting was his detachment. He talked about himself in the third person. He called himself "Nixon." "I think that Nixon will probably . . ." This sort of political analysis was for him, I saw, a sort of out-of-body experience. He was able to disconnect himself from himself and float up above political America like the Goodyear blimp over the Super Bowl, and make his calculations as if that Nixon down there were someone else altogether. It occurred to me later that it was this dissociative talent, this self-estranging peculiarity, that eventually turned Nixon into his own Iago.

When the lunch was over, we rose from the table. I joined the rest in shaking hands with Nixon and thanking him and making small talk. He said to me, "Hugh's son? Oh, Lord! When they start introducing me to the full-grown sons, I know I'm getting old."

My father had the spectacle of his sons not only full grown but even dying, or cracking up with middle-aged disasters like heart attacks. Did pieces of him sag and die when these things happened? Was there even a kind of Dorian Gray effect at work? Did he pay for his good health with the illness of his sons?

I thought such perverse things. My father seemed to me to inhabit, for all his burdens, a special state of grace. I thought that he had the resplendence of the lucky about him, the cloudless eye of his immunity.

I stayed in the Bishop's Room in Kansas City for ten days. I remember each of those days now with an odd, light clarity. If I sometimes felt afraid and vulnerable, there were other moments of a strange peace, and of a bizarre sort of immunity. I plunged for a time into a deep acceptance. The mind is a tricky bargainer. If I did not protest, the danger would pass. I would be a good boy. Hospitals bring such regressions. The patient is lying in a nursery, and the food is brought and the sheets are changed, and one is trundled from place to place in a wheelchair, or, flat on one's back, on a gurney. I was not much more independent than a baby who travels in a carriage and gets put to bed for a nap.

The hospital, of course, is also a sinister parody of a nursery. The patients are fully grown and soiled and damaged. There is something perverse and corrupt in their helplessness. They have become the time-lapse wreckage of the creatures that are lying a few floors away in the hospital, newborn and perfect and unused, before the clots and the black cells arrive.

Still, the illusion flickered there. The doctor takes care of everything. The doctor comes with a father's authority, and the father's magic powers to repair. He is better than the father, really: he will not lose his magic. The patient is hopeful, submissive, suppliant to that power.

I did not miss my father. There is no reason I should have. I was a thirty-six-year-old man, married, with a child and a career, and a life long removed from my father's orbit. Our relationship for years had been difficult. His second wife and I did not get along well. I did not see my father for months at a time. But when my brothers and sisters and I got together sometimes for long dinners at Italian restaurants, the conversation would eventually come around to our father. And I was always startled to learn how similar we all were—daughters as well as sons—in our feelings about him, feelings of longing and grievance all entangled with one another. I saw that, but I was working my own channels; my father was a submerged obstacle, sensed but not seen, except when the tide was very low.

But now everything contracted to a smaller world. The hospital had its tasks and routines, its rhythms. Taking a shower and shaving were an accomplishment.

I arranged for a friend to bring a typewriter. The nurses looked at it suspiciously when they brought my pills. The doctor warned against using it for more than a few minutes at a time. I wrote jocular, manful letters to friends and editors, kidding about my heart attack. I wrote more honest diary notes to myself. They were jittery notes: *Timor mortis conturbat me.*

They were oddly minute and precise in their details, as if I were trying to steady myself by fixing the exact scene, the exact place and time:

The nurse (the older one who wishes she had been an actress) just came and took my blood pressure, chatting as she squeezed the collar tight. 110/85. Fine. It is a clear bright blue Kansas day outside. Half an hour ago, my chest began to tighten, and I had five minutes of panic. I did not call the nurse. I thought about a nitroglycerine, but from one second to the next, I thought I would wait a little, and then the tightness passed. I am afraid of dying, afraid almost constantly. I am terrified that the thing that attacked me in the first place will come back, that it is still there in my chest, in the dark. The orderlies here behave with a strange, reverent kind of friendliness. I did not know why until I discovered that they think I am the editor in chief of *Time*. The night that Murray Gart and Judith Shapiro signed me into the hospital, they said that I was the editor of *Time*. Or anyway, the confusion originated then. So I get these peculiar touches of service. One of the nurses came in and asked me for an autograph yesterday. I was baffled. Does the editor of *Time* rank as a movie star when he comes to Kansas City? I have typed too long. I have to rest for a while. When I work on this machine, I can feel something in my chest begin to object. I have to lie down. I need something to read. I am very frightened now.

But another time in the Bishop's Room I went sailing off into this:

We spend all our lives yearning for completeness. I began to see the shadows of a sinister sort of completeness for myself (death), and those

shadows make me think we must not want our completenesses pre-
maturely. Or must not be too happy when they arrive. Our passions
are always incomplete. It is incompleteness that gives them energy. It
is true of emotions, true of molecules. One derives energy only from
yearnings of one kind or another. Completeness is a stasis. I think of
my father sometimes in these terms. I wonder why I feel—Hughie and
I both feel—this strange longing for him. Emulation ripening into
narcissism. The yearning for the father is old business. It should have
been long since settled. Why does it persist, and why this sense of
incompleteness? Something missing earlier on, and ever afterward sought.

But surely it is simple. I have for years suffered a peculiarly
intense anxiety when sitting down to write. I have been amazed
by some other writers who do it effortlessly, who sit down to a
typewriter as if to, say, a sewing machine or a lathe. They simply
do the thing.

To me, writing involves a deep agitation. It thrums the most
intimate membranes of the self. For some years I could not write
until I had worked myself into a state of near-panic. I had to wait
for the pressure gauge to go red-lining up into the desperate range,
my blood pressure rising with it. Surely the strain of all that helped
to bring on the heart attack.

Both my parents were writers. I suppose (a dreary revelation)
writing was an aggression against them, and therefore something I
feared. Anyway, I think I sensed I must not exceed either of them
at their trade, for that success would be dangerous. In a way, both
of my parents regarded their children as rivals, as competitive brothers and sisters. The odd antagonism that my father felt about children, even his own, must have been a matter of the oldest, the
prize and apple of his mother's eye, discovering the inconvenience
of having seven younger brothers and sisters.

One night I thought suddenly of Katharine Bryan and her proph-
ecy. Katharine Bryan was my mother's friend. She was a rich and
elegant woman. Eventually she married John O'Hara and went to
live with him in Princeton. She made him sliced chicken sandwiches
in the middle of the night while he was writing. She would joke
about being a twenty-four-hour maid for John O'Hara, the buried
part of the joke being that this Irishman with the big ears and the

bruises of grievance against old money that did not want him in its universities and clubs was having an heiress wait on him in the middle of the night—like some tyrant bullying his wife in a dirt-floor cottage in Galway. America had made O'Hara a duke at last, and given him a waitress from the Social Register.

O'Hara died in 1970. Katharine stayed on in Princeton. Then one rainy night she went to a dinner party, and as she drove home, her Mercedes skidded and crashed, and she was killed.

I loved Katharine Bryan. She seemed to me a handsome and raffish woman. She had a drawling whiskey voice. She and my mother became friends when we lived near her estate in Bucks County. I was three or four years old then.

Over the years, Katharine and my family seemed symbiotic. When we lived in Georgetown, she bought a house directly across R Street from ours. When we moved to N Street, again she bought a house just across from ours.

She had a daughter and two sons who were slightly older than Hughie and I. Katharine would pass along to us her boys' expensive tweed jackets from Rogers Peet and Saks and Chipp and Brooks Brothers. They never quite fit me, but they were wonderful jackets, tough tweeds that lasted for years. They made me look like a prep-school boy. I impersonated a prep-school boy. Those jackets gave me both a wistful comfort and a covert sense of shame. One of Katharine's boys, Courty, became a novelist, C. D. B. Bryan. When I see the photographs of him on his dust jackets, I always inspect the tweed jacket. He still wears great jackets. I wonder what will become of them when he has outgrown them. But he is not my size any longer. He passed my 38 regular many years ago and grew to a higher altitude.

When we lived on R Street, I walked Katharine's dogs for her every afternoon in Rock Creek Park. I called for them after school. Katharine had an English butler and a French maid. The French maid brought the dogs, a boxer and a mixed-breed collie—sweet romping dogs. And I would spend an hour or more wandering with them in Montrose Park, behind Dumbarton Oaks.

One afternoon in 1950, Katharine Bryan read my palm. It was a party trick of hers—the heiress as gypsy. She took my ten-year-old hand in her hands and studied its lines. I was flattered and mystified that she thought there was enough to be seen in my palm to be taken seriously. She looked for a little while, and said, "When you are halfway through your life, you will be very sick."

My mother frowned across the living room and warned Katharine off that line of fortunetelling. She thought it would frighten me. Then she said to me, "It's just a party trick, sweetie."

In Kansas City twenty-six years later, I remembered that day. I was a little more impressed than I should have been by Katharine's prediction. I am superstitious. Newspaper horoscopes, with their wisps of plausibility *("How the hell did they know that?")* can make me minutely anxious. Eventually I learned to take comfort from Katharine's prediction. I concentrated on the second half of it, the implicit: if the serious illness was to occur halfway through my life, then there were, to be precise, thirty-six years of it left. That did not seem a bad bargain.

There was no history of heart disease in the family. I did not know what Morrows died of generally, but it was not heart attacks. Old age. Mike's cancer. The bodies of the tribe always seemed unusually healthy.

That somehow squared my own interpretation. I regarded my heart attack not as a natural disorder that was predictable, in character with the medical pattern of the family. It seemed instead to be an unnatural event, a warning and a punishment. Some force was addressing me in the primitive language of retaliation.

After two weeks I started back to New York. I left St. Mary's and walked into sunshine and August heat. As I walked through the glass doors and into the outer brightness, all grass and parking lot and a sense of large, vaguely suburban distances, I was struck by a blast of agoraphobia. I felt the prisoner's or the patient's sudden sense of lostness in the outer world. The orphan's panic. I had been cast out. The withdrawal of hospital routine made the world seem abruptly risky. The doctors had subdued the thing that had attacked me, and now that they were no longer there to guard, it might get loose again.

I flew back to New York. The phantom pains returned. They worked like summer lightning around my chest: distant and ominous and difficult to interpret—a real storm, or just melodramatic effects?

I fled back to the hospital's safety. I went to the emergency room at New York Hospital one Sunday night, clutching the brown manila envelope that contained my medical records from Kansas City. The Puerto Rican orderly managing the emergency room traffic at his central desk waved me off, deflected me, ignored me. He kept me waiting for an hour. The pains in my chest grew more insistent. I raged at the man. He was stoically street-smart, the perfect malevolently oblivious Third World bureaucrat.

I took my collection of Xeroxed EKGs out of the manila envelope and waved them like a passport at the man. He regarded them impassively. He shrugged.

I subsided into an orange rump-molded plastic chair. All of us in the waiting room sat like refugees trying to escape from a Central African coup. We waited, the passive masses, boredom and fear stirring among us. I sat next to an immense black woman who was surrounded by big-eyed, silent children. She reminded me of Leola, but I saw that she was defeated in an urban way that Leola never was. I could not tell why she and her children had come to a hospital. She sat in her chair with a dead, peasant heaviness.

At last my cardiologist, Robert Ascheim, appeared, like the American ambassador sweeping into the waiting room to rescue one of his nationals from some outrageous misunderstanding. He rode his prerogatives in like a carriage. He took over. He hurried me off, privileged and white again at last, to the waiting electro-cardiograph. They wired me up to machines again on which I could watch my bouncing heart on the screen: my dybbuk objectified.

I saw my father next through a gradually thinning haze of anaesthesia. He stared down at me with a look of helpless alarm that he tried to conceal in a wan smile. Hughie told me later that I looked awful. I had been on a heart-lung machine for several hours (the machine was breathing for me and circulating my blood; *look, ma, no hands*). Now, as they wheeled me out of the operating room, there was still a thick round plastic respirator tube stuck down my throat, choking me. The operation had lowered my body temperature: I shivered uncontrollably under several blankets.

They had split my chest like a chicken's. They had used a rotary power saw, something like a jeweler's, to cut through the chest bone. Then they pried back the ribs with a kind of winch. They had stripped a long vein out of the tissue of my inner thigh, taken a length of chitterling from the knee to the groin, and then they had gone fingering into the heart to bypass two arteries.

I was as still as a leg of lamb on the table, and the surgical team bent over me like priests of the occult intently performing intricate witchcraft. They took the engine of my life, the wondrous electric muscle, and held it in their rubber-gloved fingers. And fixed it like a household appliance.

It was a piece of medical genius and a miracle turned into routine plumbing. The blood that once had stopped at obstructions as it approached the heart now flowed through a couple of tubes that were not there before, and the pain eased. Or at least the cardiac pain. For the moment, of course, I felt as if I had been shot in the chest.

I had not seen my father's face since the convention floor in Kansas City. My eyes, emerging from the operating room, from the knockout potions, photographed him through my scrim of semi-consciousness, his face intently peering down at me as he had peered down at me thirty-six years before as I lay in a hospital, that one in Philadelphia. Then he vanished again.

14·The Emergence of Fang

The coronary somehow seems to me—now, at this remove—to have completed a triangulation. At last, in an almost appealing way, there seemed something fatal and fallible about Nelson Rockefeller. Strangely, in some transformation of my relations with my father, I came to identify myself not so much with my father as with Nelson—and with his worst qualities, with his remoteness and calculation and covert brutality.

A man has a side that is the son and a side that is the father. The son side of me detested Nelson Rockefeller. The father side understood him and even approved of him.

The first time I met Rockefeller was when he came to Harvard during my junior year to deliver the Godkin Lectures in Sanders Theater. My father and several others had written the lectures. Dyslectic Nelson plowed through the committee prose like a stag in a deep snowfield, bounding and struggling. I cannot remember a word he said. The lectures were called "The Future of Federalism." The ideas have gone blank in my mind.

I remember that Rockefeller attracted a crowd. He was young and glamorous then. *Life* had paraded his virility on its cover, all teeth and strength and bronze hair. After the first lecture (there were three, on successive evenings), I made my way through the mass of undergraduates outside Memorial Hall, and found my father as he shoved along the sidewalk in Rockefeller's wake. I struggled along beside my father.

I was wearing a beard then, newly grown, a detail that made my father wince. We caught up with Rockefeller in the crowd, and my father introduced me. Rockefeller gave me his power grip and he complimented me on my beard. "My son Michael had one of those," he said. Then he told me, "Your father's terrific." He went plowing off. His jaw moved though the crowd like an icebreaker. He could take a crowd with him like a magnet sweeping iron filings through a sheet of paper. I met my father later that night in the bar of the Hotel Commander in Cambridge. We drank there in the dark until midnight with other Rockefeller staff men. They talked about Rockefeller—"Nelson," or "the Governor," never "Rocky," which was his falsely intimate public nickname—in the knowing, slightly abused way of hirelings, rueful and awed and essentially proud of their connection with the man.

I'd been startled that Rockefeller mentioned his son. The fall before, Michael Rockefeller had vanished on an anthropological expedition in New Guinea. Rockefeller had just separated from his wife and headed off for his eventual marriage to Happy Murphy.

I had followed the story of Michael's disappearance with an abnormal interest. There was my father's connection with Rockefeller, of course, but also something else: the drama of the father searching for his son moved me. I think I was obscurely jealous of Michael Rockefeller. If I disappeared among headhunters, if I drifted out the estuaries among crocodiles, clinging to a jerrycan, crying his name as the riptides took me out to sea—would he cease receding? Would he charter planes and comb the coastline for days, seeking a sign, weeping over the maps, conjuring his lost boy?

I thought of that touching and faintly ludicrous episode during the Civil War when Dr. Oliver Wendell Holmes learned that his son and namesake had been wounded at Antietam. Dr. Holmes set out by train from Boston and searched for days up and down the Maryland countryside for his wounded son, haunting the field hospitals, wandering among the dead and dying, asking everywhere for his boy. At last he found the future Justice Holmes recuperating in a house in Hagerstown. The father's heroic search for his boy was ended. He was overjoyed. And he could not help noticing with some satisfaction that there was a copy of *The Autocrat of the Breakfast-Table* in the parlor.

As father and wounded son rode the train back up to Boston, the son watched with what must have been a complex irony as his father worked hour after hour on an article for the *Atlantic*, to be titled, "My Search for the Captain." The doctor lost no time in converting that fatherly mission into a pageant of his own ego.

Nelson did no such thing, of course. I was impressed by the resources of his stoicism about Michael. He was capable of a matter-of-fact humility that I was forced to admire. He was not Shakespearean about it. Nelson Rockefeller was not really Shakespearean about anything, although his ambition had size. In any case, he took his loss bravely.

Nelson Rockefeller collected art and antique cars with a greedy ardor: passionate American materialism plundering the world for the finer things. I did not understand the art-collecting side of him. He did not seem to me a man of much taste or style. His intellect seemed as boxy and oafish as his suits, as the old Chrysler Imperial limousine he used (the car was the perfect automotive expression of the worst side of the man: powerful, overbearing). He did not have an intellectually playful or adventurous mind. His energy was headlong, his teeth carnivorous.

It was not art he was interested in, I thought, but power: the power of acquisition. Collecting was a form of conquest, I suppose—a species of erotic conquest even. Once, John Kennedy told Harold Macmillan that he would get a headache if he did not have sex with a woman at least once a day. Did Nelson Rockefeller suffer headaches if he did not regularly acquire Picassos, Miròs, Klees? Collecting was a more refined compulsion than satyriasis, I suppose. Rockefeller had some of that as well.

In the summer of 1963, after I graduated from Harvard, I lived at my father's house in Yonkers, waiting to be called by the draft board. One morning, my father rousted me out of bed: "I need you to drive over to Pocantico."

I dressed and poured down a cup of coffee. My father had to drop off a speech at Rockefeller's Westchester County estate in Tarrytown, just up the Hudson. We would need two cars. We would go in caravan, drop off the speech, then drive south to Riverdale, where we would leave the Ford station wagon for someone who was borrowing it for several days. My father drove the Ford. I followed in the rattletrap Peugeot he used as a second car.

We headed up the Saw Mill River Parkway in the bright summer morning, then turned off onto a winding secondary road and drove west toward the Hudson. I followed my father's Ford as it pulled into a side road, through stone and wrought-iron gates, unmarked, up through the trees. We had arrived at Pocantico.

We passed through the Rockefellers' parks and forests. Here, off the public roads, came a sense of kingdom and privacy and magnificent exemption. We pulled up to Kykuit, Nelson's house in the family complex. His father, John D. Rockefeller, Jr., had built it at the beginning of the century. It looked like an ornate and compact and private museum of gray stone. The stone suggested a permanence almost too permanent; an air of the mausoleum clung there.

Yet it was summer. The place was gay with bright striped awnings, and trees and flowers. Beside the house lay the profligate garden of art—a reckless millionaire litter of Henry Moores and Calders and Giacomettis and Noguchis, all strewn across the grass, among the boxwood. I felt the casual and overbearing power of that display, the sheer unanswerable force that commanded so much of the world's artistic imagination to come and lie down upon the grass of one man's lawn. And it was all private—family décor— not the work of institutions or governments but of an individual's whim and will. Such a display belonged to an earlier civilization, to the feudal.

A butler let us into the house. A prince's house, but augustly impersonal and casually intimidating. The effect (Rodin's "Age of Bronze" and a Gilbert Stuart of George Washington set among family mementos) was oddly one of lifelessness. My father passed a copy of his speech to the mute butler, with a word of explanation. Then we withdrew. I felt that I had seen something wonderful and infuriating: an exclusivity so profound that it existed almost out of time. The amber of that summer morning held it forever like a myth.

We drove the two cars down to Riverdale and found an address on a side street there, an expensive modern house, mostly glass. Coretta Scott King met us at the door. My father enjoyed my surprise. Mrs. King had two small children at her skirts. Martin Luther King, Jr., came down a short flight of stairs and shook hands with me, kindly and gravely. My father and I came on a strange, prosaic errand; King was borrowing the Ford station wagon from us for a few days. He was in New York on business; he needed a car and his friend Nelson asked Hugh to take care of it.

There, in that upper-middle-class living room in Riverdale, with its mellow polished floors and potted trees, King and his wife moved with an air of serenity and fatalism that moved me. It seemed to me that they had deep resources. I had no way of knowing in the summer of 1963 how far their resources would carry them, and how much they would be necessary.

King returned the car a day later than expected. He had discovered a long dent on one side and thought that he had done it. So King sent the car first to a body shop in Brooklyn to fix the damage that my father had inflicted before he loaned the car. My father joked for months about his (unintentional) ripoff of the civil rights movement.

That was Rockefeller's world. He collected people as easily and omnivorously as he collected art. He had a reputation for going after the best that he could buy. My father was an acquisition, and I guess that both my father and I were flattered, in a way, that a man who only bought the best should wish to buy my father. And make him a friend as well, of course—up to a point.

The business was never simple. Rockefeller did not merely buy people. His exuberance and charm could take the curse of crassness off the relationship. But when people went to work for him, I came to suspect, Rockefeller never could escape his instinctive (no doubt inherited) habit of behaving as if he owned them.

And yet Nelson Rockefeller gave me a sense of immunity. I felt sometimes that I lived under his protection. My father took on his powers. Once, flying home from Harvard, I shared a cab from La Guardia Airport to Grand Central Station with a soldier on leave. I started to pay the fee on the meter. The cab driver tried to charge us a double fare. I told him, "Listen, my father is special assistant to Governor Rockefeller. I can see to it that you never drive a cab in New York again."

I merely gestured toward the lamp, as if to rub it. The actual genie was not necessary. When a garage mechanic tried to cheat me on a repair bill, I invoked the name of the special assistant to the governor. Once my father asked the state commissioner of motor vehicles to ask his computer whether I was in danger of a suspended license for some parking tickets I had not paid. But my father never actually intervened. It was the vaguely imperial illusion that counted. One was traveling under Nelson Rockefeller's—or my father's— protection. It was like carrying a British passport in the nineteenth century. One went out into the world with a sense of dispensation, of privilege. It was ridiculous to think so, of course. Rockefeller's political domain seemed to me a rather scruffy place—crass and alien, full of low old ceremonies, the encrustations left by wave after wave of immigration and assimilation and corruption. My father once told me how bribes were sometimes delivered to state legislators in Albany. The briber, a lobbyist or somesuch, would get into a poker game with the legislators he meant to influence. The lobbyist would methodically proceed to lose the required amount—$10,000, say—if necessary folding his hand even though he had splendid cards, a full house, four of a kind, whatever. When the lobbyist had thus delivered his bribe, he would drain his glass and push away from the table and put on his jacket and announce with a wink, "Well, boys, it's too rich for *my* blood."

Still, there was a kind of low-grade magic in the way that bureaucracies fell away at my father's touch. Telephone calls produced wonderful effects. Influence was a kind of trick: what splendid penetrations of the obdurate world it made. My father could pass like a force beam through the walls and resistances, and travel to the heart.

Henry Kissinger regarded Rockefeller as a first-rate judge of character principally because Nelson Rockefeller thought so highly of Henry Kissinger. Kissinger could hardly fault the taste of the prince who made him his friend and pre-eminent adviser on foreign policy.

In my sophomore year at Harvard, I called on Kissinger, who was then head of Harvard's Center for International Studies, on Plympton Street in Cambridge. He had a vast network of international connections. He was Nelson's boy by then, but he was not yet famous.

I went to Kissinger because my father suggested it. Kissinger was a friend of his. They were together in the Rockefeller service. Behind his back, my father amiably called Kissinger "der Loudenkrautenboomer." I was about to go to Europe on a summer Harvard Student Association flight. It occurred to my father that Kissinger might call on his connections for me.

I appeared at Kissinger's office promptly at three in the afternoon. Kissinger met me in an anteroom. I still wore that beard; it seemed to irritate him as much as it irritated my father. In those days, a beard was a subversive statement, a declaration of aggressive heterodoxy. I told Kissinger defensively that the beard was for a play I was acting in. What play? *Caligula*, by Camus. A beard for *Caligula*? Really? Modern dress, I explained. Well, not so modern—Edwardian dress, as a matter of fact. It was the truth, but of course Edwardian dress was even more idiotic than modern dress: an Edwardian Caligula. The play and the beard became more ridiculous the further I explained them.

Kissinger sighed. He asked me a few questions about the world, but it was clear that I was a fool, untraveled, unconnected. He handed over to me four letters of introduction he had prepared to friends in Paris, Geneva, Bonn and Rome. I went to Europe that summer, living out of a knapsack, and kept the letters like money in the bank, but never cashed them.

At the time, Henry Kissinger was a bright young Harvard professor in Nelson Rockefeller's livery. When I saw him next, in 1971, he was as famous as Muhammad Ali. Time Inc. held a cocktail party at the Carlton Hotel in Washington. Practically the entire hierarchy of the U.S. government assembled for it. I was there as a writer for *Time*'s Nation section.

I drifted around the ballroom from one star to another, from Edward Kennedy to the Chief Justice of the United States to the highest ranking black in the U.S. Air Force, General Chappie James. I approached Henry Kissinger at one point and introduced myself as Hugh Morrow's son. Kissinger said absently, "Ah, yes, Hughie. No one does the words better than Hughie."

He sounded as if he were giving an endorsement to the pastry chef. I was affronted on my father's behalf. My face reddened and I stared at the rug. President Nixon's Adviser for National Security Affairs wandered away.

The next year, *Time* assigned me to write a "Man of the Year" cover story on Kissinger and Nixon. It was 1972, the year of the Nixon opening to China (and the last good year that Nixon was to enjoy in the White House). The editors of *Time* like to keep their choice of Man of the Year a secret. I went to work on the story in an unventilated hideaway office on the twenty-sixth floor of the Time & Life Building in Rockefeller Center, just down the hall from the *Time* morgue. At two in the morning I sat in that office struggling for breath, writing through the night. I came to associate Kissinger with a terrible airlessness, a feeling of suffocation.

The complex arrangement of Kissinger's mind fascinated me— its clarity and intricacy, its rich textures and powers of association. I was above all arrested, and a little chilled, by the unique and rather un-American way that he was able to manipulate power by the force of his thought and language.

His European urbanity, his sepulchral tones, his crystalline, faceted syntax, all went against a lot of American political traditions. Americans like to believe, almost must believe, in their own powerful innocence in the world. And innocence cannot survive for very long in the drawing rooms of the sharply verbal. American virtue should be expressed in actions, not elaborately articulate words. To hell with words. It's easy to intimidate with words, to falsify. It was not words that cleared the land and built the cities and factories and the American power and greatness. Words were timid and elitist. Words never met a payroll. Words were whores, in a way. They would do anything. Thomas Jefferson was brilliant with words, but that was in another country, in the clear blue air of the Enlightenment. The American prejudice against the overly articulate had much to do with class and power. Jefferson, though a democrat in certain other ways (not always consistent or convincing) was an aristocrat of language. From Jackson on, through Harry Truman and Gary Cooper, Americans mistrusted words and slick ideas.

Here came the phenomenon of Kissinger. Most American public figures cannot think more than a word or a phrase at a time. In fact, they have been subliminally instructed for all of their lives to believe that it is somehow immoral to be excessively articulate. Kissinger thinks not in phrases or sentences or paragraphs, but in whole pages and chapters at a time. He speaks as if the book had already been written—in his mind, or in eternity—and he has merely to read from it. That is one reason he is so un-American. The premise of his thought is that the whole thing has been settled. He remained a European. The best of America believes that nothing is ever finally settled. Kissinger brought to America his nimble survivor's wits, but also a certain sinister fatalism, his death-dealing realpolitik. He brought a kind of knowledge of the world that, when combined chemically with a native American innocence and idealism and ignorance, could produce lethal results.

Americans carry some version of the Gary Cooper model in their minds. Americans need to be sincere, and too many words mean insincerity. The mistrust of words leaped generations. It went from the Gary Cooper model to that sixties ideal of inarticulateness in which words (the property of the older, war-making generation) were betrayers of true feeling and virtue. Words were the vehicles of lies.

Virtue was forever to be found in the inarticulate wilderness. Language meant civilization, things already settled and defined. The inarticulate was a territory out to the West somewhere. It meant the promise, the future, everything that had not been appropriated and nailed down, by aristocrats, by the privileged, by language itself.

I found it hilarious that Henry Kissinger thought of himself as Gary Cooper. He once told the Italian interviewer Oriana Fallaci that he imagined himself as a lone gunman riding into town to settle matters at high noon. His natural weapons were loaded with words, not bullets. He told me, "Nobody does the words better than Hughie," but that was merely a pleasantry, and if one cared to look deeper into a pleasantry, it was a lie, perfectly automatic and perfectly artful. The fact is that nobody did the words better than Henry Kissinger, and English was not even his first language, as it was of course my father's. Something in Kissinger was alien and manipulative, and I mistrusted him precisely because he was so good at it.

Kissinger's moral perspective meshed well with Rockefeller's, I thought. Rockefeller had the sound instinct to campaign as an exuberant democrat, wading through the crowds at Coney Island, accepting knishes, pretending to devour them while the photographer from the *Daily News* recorded the image. But the soul of the man was colder than that. Like Kissinger, he believed in order, authority and the force of his own will. Rockefeller and Kissinger were both imperious men. Both possessed a subtle human instinct— one, in any case, that told them where their advantage lay. But the tenderer impulse was subordinate to a hard streak that could be dangerous, obliterating.

One afternoon in September 1971, my father called me at my office at *Time*. "Would you like to come and talk to Nelson?" he asked.

It was clearly not a social invitation. Two days before, Rockefeller had ordered the state police to storm Attica Prison in upstate New York, where prisoners were holding thirty-nine hostages. In the attack, thirty prisoners and ten hostages were killed. They were all killed by police gunfire.

I walked up Sixth Avenue from the Time & Life Building to 22 West Fifty-fifth Street, the blue-doored town house from which Nelson Rockefeller usually governed the state of New York. Parked outside was Rockefeller's black Imperial, with chauffeur and bodyguard lounging on it. The security man inside the front door, an ex-cop with a cheerful, florid face, recognized me and waved me inside. I found my father in the cozy warren of the town house, which was furnished and staffed as densely as a submarine, and my father led me to Rockefeller.

His office was a strangely tacky room—brightly lighted with overhead fluorescent tubes and furnished with what looked like motel furniture. I had seen the room before. It looked (and may have been consciously designed to look) like the office and conference room of a union local president. There were no imperial effects: a minimalist workroom.

Rockefeller looked tired. His complexion was dead gray. He was appropriately subdued, gracious in a quiet way. We sat at the conference table. Rockefeller said he wanted to tell me anything I wanted to know about what he had done at Attica. He knew that *Time* would be writing a major story on the event (a cover story, as it happened) and he wanted me to relay his point of view to the editors there.

I was uncomfortable performing in front of my father. I felt that my filial piety was at war with my professional instincts. Obscurely, I felt that I must take on some of my father's deference with Rockefeller, even when I wanted to attack him. I tried to ask a hard question: "Governor, you once said there was no substitute for a leader being on the spot to make decisions. Why didn't you go to Attica?"

That question became the most important in the whole affair. But as I asked it, it sounded a little stagy, like a set-up, a parody of a reporter asking a hard question. Rockefeller answered with a chastened virtuosity, with the requisite regretful, manly air, all according to a formula that was somehow written in the air for this occasion. I began to see that I had been drafted to play a small part in a ceremony of post-mortem.

Rockefeller said quietly, "I accepted the responsibility, and I have to accept the responsibility, for what happened there. It is possible a mistake was made, but in a crisis, a leader must . . ."

This was Rockefeller cutting back across his own wake, making apologetic gestures: the remorseful shrug, the burdens of power, the dense complexities of the world. But I knew, and he knew, that the attack on Attica was a fairly faithful expression of his own predilections. The drama did not falsify his character by one centimeter. On the contrary: Attica reflected Nelson Rockefeller's emotional and political approach to the world.

The newspaper stories about Attica often mentioned my father as Rockefeller's spokesman. My father's name was thus attached to the event, on the side of the state. Black radical groups telephoned the house in Bronxville with death threats. My father installed floodlights. For a couple of years after Attica, the house was bathed at night in a harsh white light, like a prison. The police cruised by every half-hour, sliding up the drive very slowly and carefully, in that animal way that police cars have when they sense danger.

Rockefeller dealt generously with my father, with my family. But that aside, he seemed to me a somewhat ominous character.

He had begun his political career with great bounce and promise. He was fresh and full of energy, handsome, rich and liberal, it was thought—a New York aristocrat whose inherited wealth freed him to pursue the public good and gave him a large and generous attitude toward those less fortunate. He had the dash of hereditary nobility, like Roosevelt, that grated upon the middle class, conservative nerves of heartland Republicans, those with grimmer and more punitive hearts. The Goldwater wing booed Rockefeller at the 1964 convention in San Francisco, and he took it with his high-born gaiety. Yet over the years it seemed to me he changed. He had a grim and punitive side himself. His private nature, I thought, came to be very different from his image as the grinning public man. He had an immense appetite for power, and when he was thwarted, he became bitter. He wanted the presidency of the United States. He pursued it with an odd indirection, however—odd in a man of his ambition and his habit of having his way in the world. He kept finessing himself out of it. His staff in the later years found him a peremptory and even nasty man to work for. William Ronan and my father were the only ones who called him "Nelson." The others called him "Governor." Now, in private, he became "Fang." In the last few years of his life Rockefeller seemed hard, vindictive and even irrational. He certainly became rather strange.

I had a glimpse of that peculiarity once, in 1975. My father and I waited for Rockefeller one Monday morning beside a chain-link fence at the Westchester County Airport. We were to fly down to Washington in his private jet. He was commuting from Pocantico to his job as Vice President.

My father was briskly official now. He wore a black overcoat and a navy-blue three-piece suit and carried two briefcases. His eyes—he is far-sighted—searched the sky off to the northeast. At last, long before I could make them out, he spotted three specks in the distance. The helicopters grew quickly larger, boring in with a purpose. Rockefeller bustled off one of them and into the jet.

We sat side by side. My father, who as always had set up the interview, arranged himself watchfully in the back of the plane. The steward brought Rockefeller what seems (in view of the heart disease that killed him) an alarmingly rich breakfast of bacon and fried eggs and buttered toast. I asked political questions for an article I was writing for *Time*.

I watched Rockefeller's extraordinarily complicated face: his hooded eyes, the facial lines arranged in amazing contradictions, the whole mask of flesh tugged somewhat downward now by gravity and age. His head seemed 10,000 years old, a coelacanth fetched up from the depths off Madagascar. I thought to myself that Rockefeller had lived so long with so much stratagem and craft and power and desire—his deepest desire thwarted forever—that he had become entirely unknowable, impenetrable.

The interview soon began to turn into a Rockefeller monologue. He veered off suddenly into unexpected territory. He started to talk about the Communists who infested Capitol Hill like termites, who were eating away at the Republic. The accusations came across on a gust of awful breath. I sat up straight.

"Can you tell me exactly who these people are?" I asked. "Are they agents? Sympathizers? What?"

Rockefeller looked at me for a long moment, then said softly, "Come on, Lanny. You're a knowledgeable guy. You know the score." Then he worked his eyebrows up and down in semaphor—using his face, as he often did, as a subsidiary instrument of communication, all the features hinting vividly at meanings that the tongue was enjoined from uttering. Rockefeller's eloquent silence often expressed mirth and playful ridicule, meaning: Look, this is absurd, and you and I understand the joke. The stratagem of the silence was to draw one into a spirit of collaboration with Rockefeller, almost a conspiracy of sympathies without ever defining the terms of the conspiracy. Now, however, Rockefeller's face, gray and mottled, was mobile with darker meaning. But he would not say more.

Several months later, this fantasy of Communist infiltration came out publicly. Rockefeller suggested that a woman in Senator Henry

Jackson's office had Communist connections. Eventually, Rockefeller had to deliver an oblique apology for that.

I wondered if Rockefeller's mind was altogether sound. Some years later my father remarked to me enigmatically, "Thank God Squeaky Fromme couldn't shoot straight."

But the real reason I disliked Rockefeller, I came to understand, involved my father. I had grown up with a sort of wistful reverence for my father. He seemed to me ideal and heroic. He was wonderfully handsome; as a young man he looked like a somewhat more elegant version of Albert Camus, and he smoked Camel cigarettes with a squint, like Humphrey Bogart. What at last appalled me, profoundly, was my father's hireling deference in Rockefeller's presence. I cringed to see him for very long in Rockefeller's presence; I noticed then a diffidence I hated to associate with my idealized father. I saw an anxiousness, a watchfulness in my father's eyes, and I came to hate it. I felt shamed by the imperious control that Rockefeller exercised upon him. I was humiliated for him.

It was a strange configuration: I believe that Rockefeller was my father's father, in some sense—generous, irrationally demanding, punitive and beneficent. Perhaps, to me, my father somehow ceased to seem my father in precisely the degree to which he functioned as the seigneurial Rockefeller's page boy or, more closely, his Polonius. Children judge hard and sometimes stupidly: in my sight, Rockefeller cost my father something of his manhood.

Once, when Rockefeller was Vice President, *Time* invited him to address a luncheon meeting of its editors and correspondents at a Washington hotel. My father ushered Rockefeller in; my father hovered in the background. When Rockefeller told a mild joke, my father's laugh, a little too quick, too loud, rang out in the dining room, alone. I was thereupon ashamed of my father in the presence of my peers, and simultaneously ashamed of my shame.

Some years earlier I had flown to Miami with a group of *Time* writers and editors to cover the 1968 Republican convention. My father was on the same flight, on his way to join Rockefeller for yet another unconsummated moment of flirtation with Republican power. As I stood talking to my father at the luggage-claim carousel in Miami, Henry Grunwald, then the managing editor of *Time*, came by. I introduced him to my father. My father bowed. He called Grunwald "sir." He acted, I thought, with a certain press agent's deference. I was surprised and embarrassed again.

The last and worst of it came when Nelson Rockefeller died. My father was at home, in bed, when an ABC television reporter called him and asked about a tip he had that Rockefeller was in an ambulance, on his way to the hospital. My father called Rockefeller's security men. They said, "It's true. It looks bad."

My father dressed and drove to Lenox Hill Hospital on the East Side of Manhattan. Rockefeller was dead when my father arrived. My father went out to face the TV lights outside the emergency room, the minicams, the light cables, the reporters tiding in with notebooks and that hurried, feeding look on their faces. My father gravely announced that Rockefeller had died that evening of a heart attack while working late on an art book in his office at Rockefeller Center.

When I saw my father on the television news the next day, I felt rather proud of him: looking handsome, commanding, saddened, dignified, giving the word of the death. But presently came all of the squalid contradictions. Rockefeller, it came out, had not died in his office; he had died in a town house on West Fifty-fourth Street. He had not been alone. A woman had been there. The newspapers, feeling that they had been lied to, that my father had sleekly, blandly used them, investing his death with a virtuous dignity (working on an art book, indeed) that it manifestly did not possess, pursued the story as if it were some incipient Watergate. Jimmy Breslin, the columnist for the New York *Daily News*, roared into the telephone at my father: "It was murder, Hughie! It was murder!" The New York *Times* Metropolitan desk mobilized itself; the *Times* printed long, slightly sardonic accounts of the night of Rockefeller's death, recapitulating my father's original announcement in roughly the same spirit in which newspapers a few years before had quoted Nixon's "I am not a crook." The New York *Post* sent a reporter up to Bronxville to bang on the door and confront my half sister Carolyn and try to bully the truth out of her.

I watched it all in rising rage and bewilderment. When I saw television news clips of my father at Rockefeller's funeral, he looked ashen. His skin, so firm the night of Rockefeller's death, seemed to have gone slack around his jowls. He looked exhausted and demoralized. I was alarmed. I called him on the phone and asked if he was all right. I commiserated, and for a moment I found myself almost weeping.

I felt, in part, that the attacks on my father were attacks on me. Also, I half believed them. I was covertly ashamed—both to believe them and to have my father behave so. More than that, I thought that the obsequiousness exacted by Rockefeller during his life had now been exacted one last time, grotesquely, in death, that with his departing gust of imperious will, Rockefeller had forced my father to squirm, to do his squalid work, an intimate and dirty service, an orderly's task of seeing to the master's mess. The joke around the Rockefeller office in the weeks after the death was this: What were Nelson's last words? "Good luck, Hughie."

My rage cooked up. I became obsessed by what I thought was the unfairness of the press attacks, especially the comparisons, always implicit, to Watergate. Or worse. A reverse Chappaquiddick, in a sense: only here, the girl got away. But somehow the dead man was being blamed for his own death; or, since the dead man was not available, my father was being blamed—for the death and the cover-up. So my father became Nelson's posthumous surrogate: the stand-in of his ghost, scapegoat for the privileged departed.

I waited for my father to retaliate, to put his enemies to flight, to vindicate himself. Or I cherished small fantasies that it was up to me to vindicate him. I would ride to my father's rescue.

I imagined that I would publish an article on the Op-Ed page of the New York *Times*, all moral splendor and handsomely sliced distinctions. I elaborated these columns furiously as I rode to work on my bicycle: a cavalry charge. Colonel Albert rides again.

The comparison to Watergate was absurd. My father had not lied. There had been confusion at the hospital when he first arrived. A doctor said that Rockefeller died at the office, and my father thought it meant the Rockefeller Center office, not the town house (which also contained offices). Or, if he did shade the truth, he did so to protect Happy Rockefeller and her children. But where was the offense in seeking to protect a widow from the public's raillery at what is surely one of the oldest stories in the world—the great man's coronary in a cathouse?

I suspected that he knew that Megan Marshak, whom he detested, had been with Rockefeller at the time of death. He knew a great deal about the affair. Megan had been foisted upon him as part of his staff. He told me later, with a rueful hilarity, about some of the evenings he had spent at Rockefeller's house on Foxhall Road in Washington. The mansion was Rockefeller's weeknight residence during his time as Vice President. My father stayed there as well, in a guest room. One evening Megan was there for dinner. After coffee my father said to Megan and Rockefeller, "Well, I guess I'll leave you two kids alone and go get my beauty sleep." Several hours later there was a knock on his door. Nelson was there. He said, "Well, Hughie, I guess your friend wants to go home now." So my father got dressed and drove Megan Marshak home.

I later recalled another Marshak story. We were all on Martha's Vineyard. My stepmother had died in June. I had taken a large house on Lagoon Pond for the month of August. It was a five-bedroom place with a lawn that swept down to the water. My father brought my half brother Dave and half sister Carolyn up to stay with us for a few days. Patrick came, as well, and Hughie with several of his children. One day all of us drove out to South Beach for a swim, and one of the girls said she wanted to take a picture of the Morrow boys—my father and Hughie and Patrick and me and Davey. We all stood in our bathing suits on South Beach squinting in the afternoon sunlight, with the Atlantic behind us. Patrick, the only member of the family who is aggressively demonstrative, threw his large arm around my father's shoulders and gave him a squeeze. In the picture, you can see my father's recoil, his abrupt shying off from this display of affection.

That afternoon when we returned to the house, the phone was ringing. It was Megan Marshak. She had been left in control of things in the Rockefeller press office and some crisis had arisen. My father spoke to her for a long time. Then he wandered out onto the large porch of the house, rolling his eyes and shaking his head. "Megan," he said. "*Oy vay.*"

After Nelson's death, my father seemed overtaken by an immense and complicated hurt. Aside from his own sense of grief about Rockefeller, there was the pain of the aftermath, a wound of frustration, the powerlessness in which he found himself, unable to reply. He was being stifled, finally, by Nelson Rockefeller once again. Somehow he, not Marshak, not Rockefeller, was made to absorb all of the gossip and the moralizing in which the newspapers indulged themselves.

The morning after the funeral, I went to my office at *Time* and picked up the New York *Daily News*. I found that my father had written a piece about Nelson, a farewell, a eulogy. It appeared on page 34 on January 30, 1979.

The headline read: "Rocky: A vulnerable man who relished life." Then: "By HUGH MORROW."

I thought, Oh, God.

One could talk endlessly about vulnerabilities. The last man in the room—in the Republic—who needed the adjective "vulnerable" might have been Nelson Rockefeller, I thought. Vulnerable to what? To the cold?

My father began his eulogy: "Yesterday, they put the ashes of Nelson Aldrich Rockefeller into the fertile soil of the Hudson River country he loved so well.

"To Happy Rockefeller, and to many of us who also loved him, it was a symbol of ongoing life and renewal for a great human being—one whose like we shall never see again."

I cringed.

My father continued: "Let others appraise his fabulous career. Let me just say a few words about the man I knew."

I felt now the way that I had felt the day we went to Centre Hall and my father drove my Saab ridiculously badly, as if he had never handled a stick shift before.

He could write. He had the same instinct for the English language that he had for good automobile motors: he had perfect pitch. He knew the gears of the sentences, and how much pressure to put on the accelerator, up to what rhetorical rev, and when to shift, up or down, and when to brake. And yet here, in his first bylined article in years, he was capable only of awkward bombast.

My father went on: "No one was neutral about my friend, Nelson. He infuriated some—but he inspired some to a profound and lasting love. The reason was very simple—he was so much larger than life-size."

The article continued: "At 3 o'clock in the morning, on the night he died, I sat up with Happy Rockefeller and Nelson A. Rockefeller Jr. and we talked about what made him tick.

" 'I loved him,' Happy said. 'I loved him because he was a big man, big in hopes, big in ambition, big in his aspirations for people, and big in his accomplishments for the state and the nation. Nelson cared—he really cared.' "

It occurred to me that my father had done some editing of the conversation, to Happy Rockefeller's advantage. First grief is not usually so inspirational, especially not under those circumstances.

In the *Daily News* piece, my father recorded that he then turned to Nelson Junior. W. C. Fields asserted himself.

"I looked at Nelson Rockefeller Jr.

" 'We'll miss him,' he said.

"I felt moved to advise this boy as to the importance of the proud name he bears. He sat erect, and looked outward—at some far horizon—much in the style of his father."

Then my father played more personal chords: "You can't work almost 20 years with a man like Nelson Rockefeller without being touched. And in the end, I was touched most of all by his sensitivity.

"To people who did not really know him, he could seem arrogant, insensitive, ruthless on occasion.

"To Happy—and to those of us who had the privilege of understanding him—he was a very vulnerable human being: Blessed with opportunities beyond those of most mortals; but also a person who loved beauty, cherished creativity, and suffered hurts even as you and I.

"He had a way of turning a disadvantage to an advantage— witness his dyslexia problem . . ."

Certain lights and sirens had been flashing and wailing in my brain for several minutes. It occurred to me that my father was writing so clumsily because he did not believe a word of it, or at least not much of it, and that his own fulsome, hagiological prose, and his own necessity to write it, turned his stomach a little. I liked to think that he was doing it badly because he was trying too hard, in his anger and grief, to utter graceful feelings about a man for whom his feelings were infinitely more confused and ambivalent than he could admit in public. I hoped that that was so.

"Nelson had a full set of human faults—but he also had even more than the usual number of human virtues. He was wildly generous—and very Latin about it.

"I'll never forget a night years ago when we were working in his art gallery at Pocantico on his annual message to the state Legislature. As we walked past a large Brazilian painting, I gestured toward it and commented casually, 'That's nice.'

"In a moment, I realized Nelson had stopped. I turned around. Nelson was standing there with the painting in his hands.

" 'It's yours,' he said."

That painting—ghostly white horses rearing in a brownish murk, as I remember—was nice, as my father said. It hung for years in the morning room in Bronxville.

My father recorded an anecdote about the 1976 convention.

"He loved controversy. He created it, he relished it, he lived by it.

"During the Republican National Convention in 1976, I had walked off the convention floor to get a Coke when I heard a loud roaring sound—thousands of voices cheering, booing, yelling.

"I hurried back to the floor. There, in the middle of the New York delegation, stood Nelson Rockefeller, grinning like Christmas morning [good phrase, I thought, getting better now for a little while] and holding aloft part of a blue telephone with a torn wire hanging fom it.

"That was the famous occasion when Nelson got into an argument with a hostile delegate and pushed down the Reagan sign the delegate had been holding in Nelson's face, obstructing his view.

"Infuriated, the delegate had torn apart the telephone placed in front of Vice President Rockefeller—and Nelson was impudently making certain that everyone in America had a good view of what the delegate had done."

My father described Rockefeller giving the finger to a group of hecklers on an upstate New York campus once when he was Vice President: "I finally expressed myself in the only way that they would let me—using their own language."

"Some foolish people," my father went on, winding toward a conclusion, "tried to peck him to death recently with savage criticism of his art reproduction enterprises. Nobody really cared—and the controversy simply boomed Nelson's business.

"Like his foes in politics, the art world elitists failed to realize that only indifference could have defeated Nelson Rockefeller.

"And wherever his departed spirit may have gone, you can bet your boots no one is being indifferent about him.

"So long, Chief."

I put down the *Daily News*. Hail to the Chief. Nelson never went that far. That was never his music, no matter how badly he wanted it. Hail and Farewell.

I said out loud, addressing my empty office, "You son of a bitch!"

I played pool with my father a few Sundays when I drove out to Bronxville. We played on the Brunswick table that my stepmother had bought him three years earlier as a gift (after the Mercedes), again paid for by Nelson, to take his mind off the fact that she was dying upstairs. My father used the $100 cue that Hughie and I had bought him for Father's Day that year for exactly the same purpose—to help him pass the time while she died.

Billiard games with my father have always been an elaborate psychological transaction. When Hughie and I were young—around ten and eight—my father took us on Saturday afternoons to the National Press Club in Washington. We loved the Press Club, its hallway walls inlaid with the mats of great front pages (WAR OVER, HST SAYS), the old Southern black waiters like plantation house servants, with their first names and their fringes of white hair and their rich soft voices, the old leather of the couches, the AP and UP tickers chattering in from around the world, the racks of newspapers, the fuzz in the air of amiable alcoholism.

Upstairs from the lobby was the billiard room. My father taught us to play there. He would order a Scotch and soda from the waiter, meditatively chalk his cue, squint through his haze of Camel smoke and then address the table with his swift, svelte strokes. All of his life my father has shot too fast at pool; it is the defect of his game. He likes the drama of it, the deadly carelessness. He also shoots too hard, instead of calculating for position. He likes the decisive *smack-thonk* of cueball driving object ball into pocket. If his game is working, however, he can run ten or twelve balls at a time, moving with absorbed elegance around the table, never taking his eyes off the ever-changing molecular formations on the felt, always calculating the next shot.

I did not become much of a pool player until I went to Harvard; there I spent enough nights at the table in the basement of Dunster House to play a good amateur game. Now when I play my father, he likes to talk with an odd jocular snarl about the benefits of a Harvard education. In any case, I usually play more carefully than my father; I figure English and position. I can beat him.

One day when my stepmother was in the last stages of her illness, she somehow managed, with a nurse's help, to make her way downstairs. She said she wanted to watch us play pool on the table she had bought. She sat painfully on a high stool while my father and I ran off rack after rack of balls.

I never played better pool in my life. Obscure combinations and impossible bank shots fell in. I ran ten and fifteen balls at a time. I seemed to wish to deal my father a veiled, minute humiliation in front of my perishing stepmother. Why?

Now, after Nelson Rockefeller's death, I drove up to Bronxville on a Sunday with Jamie, who was four. I came to commiserate, to be close. My father and I went into the pool room, a large sun room off the main downstairs hall of the house. Late winter sun poured in. My half sister's Samoyed frisked in the yard outside. I racked the balls for straight pool.

My father was in a mood of vaguely nihilistic giddiness, several steps on the other side of depression and shame. He told Rockefeller-family anecdotes in a rush, stories about the maddening capacity of money to purchase immunities from the embarrassment, disgrace and inconvenience the rest of us endure for our transgressions.

It was an odd moment of communion with my father. He was being naughty, rebellious, telling more than he should have, and to a journalist. He spilled to me some things that he could not give to the importunate rewrite men from the New York *Times* and the *Daily News*. But I sensed that it was more than rebellion. The absurdity of Rockefeller's departure had professionally shadowed my father, or so he had become convinced. His father (of a sort), Nelson Rockefeller, had suddenly deserted him, and in that abandonment, had humiliated him as well. Incredibly, he left my father behind to explain the foolish squalor of his leaving. It was, my father observed, "a no-win situation."

As my father talked, I ran off pool balls. Pool is almost entirely mental. It almost perfectly reproduces on the table the state of the mind. My calculation of the angles began to fray. I was not throwing the game. I was too authentically distraught by my father's giddy woe to shoot straight.

And I noticed that his sardonic recklessness was beginning to pay off for him. So he started to win. He was trying anything now—kisses and caroms, double banks. They all went in. He finished with a run of thirteen balls.

At last he racked up his cue. He sighed, and said softly, "Well, poor Nelson. He went out on a banana peel."

15·More Boys

My wife's labor started sometime before Johnny Carson's monologue. I saw the labor on her face before she told me, before she
made any noise about it. She was ready. She had been waiting
many days for it. When it came, Brooke virtually clapped her hands.
She wanted to get on with it.

I started to time the contractions. I was giddily efficient. Against
back labor, we discovered the rocking chair. We watched a co-
median on the Carson show, and we laughed at him hysterically,
very high and reckless, as if we were invulnerable. Nothing could
go wrong. Everything was in sweet process.

The baby was heaving hard in the belly. We laughed and laughed,
as if it had nothing to do with us.

We would not take the elevator. We walked down ten flights,
lest we be stuck. I did not want to deliver my child.

The Dialcab was waiting. We rode down Second Avenue to New
York Hospital in a weird slow motion. The cab driver had the
perversity to think that a maternity run, the mother groaning and
ripe and ready, demanded a dreamlike no-bumps slide downtown.
He barely breathed on his accelerator. We moved along like a
funeral, or a truck full of nitroglycerine. The driver did not say a
word to us. He was superstititous. He did not want to deliver the
baby either.

Brooke was in labor for fifteen hours, and the giddiness passed.
We tried to go by Lamaze. We had taken the classes: young couples
huffing and puffing on Wednesday nights, the women seven months

along, rolling on the floor with that touching clumsiness and weariness and mild, rueful self-disgust that pregnant women have in the last stages. We all paid such earnest attention. We would go into the presence of the mystery with technique and grave, clear eyes. We would be wholesome and cheerful. There would be no violence or blood or terror. We could carry tennis balls to press against back labor, and a Freezit, everything packed in a "goody bag." But we all looked slightly apprehensive somewhere down beneath the self-satisfaction and even bravado.

But now, nothing seemed to work as predicted. Brooke lay in a labor room with a fetal monitor strapped across her belly. It registered the contractions and the supply of oxygen that was getting to the baby. I sat by her bed in a hospital gown and used my watch to time the pains. But it was pointless. I began to think that the entire natural childbirth discipline had been a deception, a smug fantasy that bore no relationship to the real world in which these agonies were now occurring.

The contractions became erratic and wild and severe. But they were not forcing the baby out. He stayed high in the belly. The contractions registered on the graph paper in shapes that looked like savage mesas. Brooke endured them with remarkable fortitude and control, holding on, silent.

It was after dawn now. Down the hall a mother screamed for drugs, for something to relieve the pain. The white-lit maternity floor, after many hours, began to seem to throb with groans and wails, like the basement of a police station in an extremely neat totalitarianism.

The labor went on for hours. And still the baby would not descend. Then, abruptly, the monitor showed that the baby was losing oxygen. They chased me down the hall and whisked Brooke off on a gurney and knocked her out.

As I stood by the nurses' station outside the operating room, a new father, bitterly dry-eyed, filled out the forms involved in disposing of his son, who had just been still-born. The nurse seemed to want to know what they should do with the body of the baby, and the father kept saying he did not care, it did not matter. I pictured the baby somewhere in a plastic bag that would look like the amniotic sac that he came in. They could not simply dispose of him in the garbage. There was surely, fleetingly, a soul involved, something. What were the ceremonies to be done with him? Would they really need a tiny casket, and a funeral service, and a little rectangular hole in the gound? Could they really dig it six feet deep but only one-by-two? Like a pet's grave, but so steep and deep, as deep as any other human's?

Brooke's doctor touched my arm and steered me toward the elevator. "And tell me," he said, "is your little wife a devotee of the bikini?"

I wheeled on him, puzzled. "What?"

He ignored me. "Well, I should think she would be. So I shall make a bikini cut, you know, and that way it won't show atall."

He pushed me into the elevator and told me to wait in the lobby downstairs. He would call.

He performed a Caesarian section just after one in the afternoon. He called me in the lobby. "You have a perfect baby boy," he said.

When I first saw Jamie, he lay naked under a heat lamp in one of those aquarium windows. Having emerged by special arrangement instead of the customary route, his face was unmarked. His skull was perfectly rounded, not elongated by the long struggle through the pelvic straits. His expression was wondering and serene and alert. At first I did not recognize him. Then I did.

He looked like a Morrow. He had my father's brow. In fact, I saw an entire procession of Morrows in him, aunts and uncles. The architecture of his face belonged so distinctly to the tribe that I marveled at it. Such replication seemed funny, almost, like one of those cartoons in which everyone on the street of a town has the same large nose and the same glasses.

A few years later at a cocktail party I met a man whose wife was soon to have a baby, their first. The man was a drama critic, overweight and dreamily smug. He looked like a baby himself. Making conversation, I told him, "Becoming a father is like falling in love ten times, all at once." The critic looked exasperated. He turned without speaking and plunged off in the direction of the bar.

In any case, I was right. The force of the paternal instinct in me seemed as powerful as any I had felt, as strong as any drive, I would guess, that prompts a woman toward mothering. I was unprepared for the impact of it. I loved Jamie, as I later loved a second son, Justin, with an emotion that was fierce and elemental.

That night I telephoned my father to tell him about the baby. I was alone in the apartment, trying to fix myself dinner, filled with an exhausted exhilaration. I telephoned everyone.

My father made official noises of congratulation, but he was abstractedly rueful. And the undertone of his words was that no good can probably come from this. I hung up angry.

A year later I took Brooke and Jamie up to Bronxville one day to spend an afternoon. We would swim in another one of my father's above-ground pools. We would make hamburgers on his outdoor grill.

It was a bright June day. We found my father padding around the yard in his Sunday Bermuda shorts. I took Jamie out of his stroller and held him up, and he squinted in the sun, half turning his face. At the same time he made smacking noises with his mouth, as if he were hungry.

My father watched Jamie's face for an instant, and I saw that he was now drawn toward him. He stretched out his arms as he moved toward Jamie, and his face wore an expression of melting, dreamy love that I had never seen before.

My father gathered Jamie into his arms and held him close, cooing and nuzzling. My father was time-traveling for that instant, and the voyage took him back to Philadelphia thirty-five years before.

My father, there in Bronxville, with his eyes closed, squeezed Jamie gently to his chest. He repeated, in his low, loving moan, "Ohhhhh, Snuffy! Ohhhhhhh, Snuffy!"

Justin arrived a few years later. This time Brooke was awake during the Caesarean at New York Hospital, and I stood a few feet away as Justin was lifted out, like a rabbit from a hat—Justin departing his nonentity, his prehistory, his mother's blood, and bursting into the bright upper air. His face wore an expression of astonishing serenity.

Justin is three years old now. He is gregarious, social, very nearly political. He walks the neighborhood like a politician, greeting the doormen and the passers-by. He is beautiful and—something I have never seen in a child—charismatic. He tours upper Madison Avenue as if he were running for mayor. I think that I should teach him to say, "Hiya, fella—hiya, fella!" and wink.

These fantasies of supercession: another generation marches on-stage, blue eyes wondrously alive, bright as a dime. Fang is extinct. Mike, too, of course—Mike, too.

Now Justin and I arrive at the corner of Madison Avenue and Ninety-third Street on a sunny winter morning.

I say to him, conversationally: "Hey, Justin. What's new?"

And he grins and replies, with perfect accuracy, for him, "Everything!"

About the Author

LANCE MORROW is the son of Hugh Morrow, who was for twenty years Nelson Rockefeller's speech writer, press secretary and confidant. He grew up in Washington, D.C., and was graduated from Harvard. He has written for *Time* for eighteen years and in 1981 won a National Magazine Award for his essays and criticism. He lives in New York City and has two sons. This is his first book.